TERMITES
THEIR RECOGNITION AND CONTROL

TROPICAL AGRICULTURAL SERIES

The Tropical Agriculture Series, of which this volume forms part, is published under the editorship of D. Rhind, C.M.G., O.B.E., B.Sc., F.L.S., F.I.Biol.

ALREADY PUBLISHED

B. C. Akehurst
Tobacco

R. Child
Coconuts

D. G. Coursey
Yams

H. Doggett
Sorghum

T. Eden
Tea

D. H. Grist
Rice

C. W. S. Hartley
The Oil Palm

G. W. Lock
Sisal

W. J. A. Payne
Cattle Production in the Tropics Volume I

N. W. Simmonds
Bananas

D. H. Urquhart
Cocoa

C. C. Webster and P. N. Wilson
Agriculture in the Tropics

G. Williamson and W. J. A. Payne
An Introduction to Animal Husbandry
in the Tropics

TERMITES
THEIR RECOGNITION AND CONTROL

SECOND EDITION

William

W. VICTOR HARRIS
O.B.E., D.Sc., F.I.Biol.

LONGMAN

LONGMAN GROUP LIMITED
LONDON

*Associated companies, branches and representatives
throughout the world*

© *Longman Group Ltd, 1961, 1971*

First published 1961
Second Edition 1971

ISBN 0 582 46656 3

PRINTED IN GREAT BRITAIN BY
WESTERN PRINTING SERVICES LTD, BRISTOL

CONTENTS

PLATES

IN COLOUR

facing page 18

facing page 19

facing page 34

facing page 35

PLATES

IN BLACK AND WHITE

Introduction to the First Edition

Termites are an integral part of the extensive fauna of all the warmer countries of the world. They are neither conspicuous as individuals, nor do they attract attention by any violent fluctuations in numbers: their very ubiquity helps them to pass unnoticed. Since, however their food is mainly wood and the woody tissues of plants, they do in fact come into competition with man, causing a steady loss of property and amenity. Within their geographical boundaries, termites are a threat to structural timbers, to manufactured goods of wood, paper and cloth—and for reasons not yet fully understood, to certain plastics—to plantations of trees of particular kinds and to a number of growing crops.

The purpose of this book is to assist the diagnosis of termite damage and to suggest measures for its prevention and control. The economic entomologist will appreciate the value of knowing the kind of termite concerned out of the two thousand different species at present described, though the task of providing a key to all of them is not attempted here. Effective control of injurious insects usually depends on knowledge of the life history and habits of each one individually. Since prevention is both better and cheaper than control, especially where termite damage to buildings is concerned, it is hoped to interest the architect and the builder in measures which would prevent, or at least delay, such attack. The farmer and the forester might weigh up the economics of measures to prevent termites from feeding on their crops, as well as giving consideration to the ecological effects of termites in soil and, by their mounds, on the vegetation of an area.

There are many things about termites that are of interest to a wide variety of biologists, to entomologists, to protozoologists and to students of animal behaviour, to which no more than passing reference can be made here. Further details will be found in publications listed in the bibliography on these and similar topics.

In an endeavour to make each section of this book self-contained, some duplication has been unavoidable. The first three chapters are intended as an outline of the biology and classification of termites and to serve as an introduction to the chapters which follow.

The scope of this book and its form are derived from the experience of the author as officer-in-charge of a termite research unit under the Colonial Advisory Committee for Agricultural and Forestry Research.

The functions of the unit have been the study of the taxonomy of termites at the British Museum (Natural History), and of their biology in the field in various parts of the tropics. To these has been added the pleasant task of attempting to answer a large number of questions on termite control, for which purpose much of the information given here has been accumulated.

I wish to thank the following for so kindly providing me with illustrations, as indicated, and permitting their reproduction here: Dr W. G. H. Coaton; Dr Peter Hesse; Mr P. C. Joubert; Dr Hans Schmidt; the Director, D.S.I.R. Building Research Station, Watford; the Director, Commonwealth Experimental Building Station, New South Wales; The Iranian Oil Operating Companies; the Trustees, British Museum (Nat. Hist.).

In addition I have to acknowledge the assistance in photographic matters given me by Messrs M. E. Bacchus, P. N. Lawrence, W. A. Sands and W. Wilkinson.

For assistance in proof-reading I am indebted to my wife and Mr W. A. Sands.

W.V.H.

Termite Research Unit,
Commonwealth Institute of Entomology,
c/o British Museum (Nat. Hist.),
London, S.W.7

Introduction to Second Edition

In preparing a revised edition I have been concerned mainly with developments in the economic aspects of termite study during the past ten years, and accordingly chapters 5, 6 and 8 have been rewritten. Note has been taken of recent changes in termite nomenclature, especially in the genus *Macrotermes* and the family Kalotermitidae, and in consequence the names of a number of economic species have, regrettably, had to be altered. The bibliography has been brought up to date and enlarged, but it remains highly selective. The considerable advances in our knowledge of termite biology in recent years have been dealt with fully elsewhere, and the introductory nature of Chapters 1 and 2 remains unchanged apart from minor corrections.

W.V.H.

CHAPTER 1

Termite Biology—The Individual

The adult winged termite, the imago or alate, is a dull creature which rarely catches the attention of the field entomologist or insect collector; and more rarely still that of the specialist in those other groups of insects whose colours, size or elegance of flight are so much more in evidence. Again, termites spend only a little time in flight; from the moment when they emerge from the nest to their disappearance again, having found their mates, no more than a few minutes will have passed, since the hordes of enemies attracted to every swarming site will account for the laggards. Swarming termites may have their active lives prolonged by being carried into the upper reaches of the air by ascending currents, but then their chances of meeting with the opposite sex will be greatly diminished. The mass emergence of imagos from the nest may be quite conspicuous for a brief time if it takes place during daylight hours, or at night if it is in the vicinity of lights which will attract the flyers. More often one comes across little heaps of discarded wings on the ground, marking the places where the pairs had alighted and encountered one another, by which time the now wingless insects have returned to obscurity.

The mayfly, the periodical cicada and the dragonfly are insects well known for adult lives so brief in comparison with the long developmental periods that have preceded them, and after which they die. The adult termite has an even shorter time in which to enjoy its freedom, but is compensated with a life span of many years, confined but fruitful.

Termites are better known as the workers, soldiers and nymphs which make up the bulk of a community exposed to view when a mound is broken open, or when a piece of timber is found to be newly attacked (Plate 1). These are wingless creatures, all but a few of which have been arrested in their development and side-tracked as food gatherers, nest builders, nurses or guards, to suit the needs of the community. The soldiers are the more conspicuous because of the great development of their heads and jaws for defensive purposes, which has led to a great diversity of size and form and made the different species more readily recognizable in this caste than they are in the adult stage (Fig. 1).

1

strongly chitinised. Cross-veins are a character of the primitive families. A distinctive feature unique in the Isoptera is the presence of a humeral suture near the base of the wing, a line of weakness that permits the termite to shed its wings at will, leaving behind a triangular stump or scale attached to the thorax (Fig. 2).

The abdomen consists of ten segments, each with a tergum, a chitinised plate, on the dorsal surface. Below, there is a ventral plate or sternite on each segment except the first, the terminal segments differing in the two sexes. The female has a large sternite on the seventh segment which obscures the rest. In the male all are visible, with the ninth divided longitudinally in some higher termites, and the tenth always consisting of two small sclerites. A pair of cerci is to be found on the sides of the tenth segment; in the primitive families these are composed of from three to eight joints, while in the Termitidae they are reduced to one or at most two joints. In addition, male termites have a pair of small, unsegmented anal styles on the posterior border of the ninth sternite (Fig. 3).

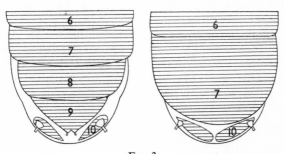

FIG. 3

Ventral view of the terminal abdominal segments of
Cryptotermes: left, male; right, female

Male and female show little external difference apart from that of the terminal sternites. There are no external genitalia. In some species there are slight differences in size between the sexes, and minor differences in the position of the ocelli relative to the eyes.

THE REPRODUCTIVES

The winged adults, having left the nest and succeeded in finding a mate, shed their wings and become reproductives. They are commonly known as kings and queens. The males pass the rest of their lives relatively unaltered, but the females develop large abdomens over a number of years as their egg-laying capacity increases to meet the growing needs of the family. This expansion, known as *physogastry*, is found in other insects, but to a less spectacular extent. The intersegmental membrane of the female abdomen continues to grow until the sclerites become widely separated and appear as brown spots on a cream-coloured cylinder (Plate 2). In the primitive family Kalotermitidae where the numbers in each colony are small, the queen is only a little larger than her mate. In the other families the growth of the female abdomen is more noticeable, and in the genus *Macrotermes* queens are found five inches (127 mm) in length. *Odontotermes badius* queens, only a trifle smaller, have an egg-laying capacity of one every two seconds.

THE WORKER

The derivation of the worker caste is discussed more fully below, but briefly they are young stages whose development has been arrested some time after the second moult. They have strongly chitinised mandibles of the adult pattern, and more lightly chitinised heads, but otherwise keep close to the nymphal pattern. Their potential sex can be determined from the terminal sternites as in the adults. In some of the Termitidae there are two distinct sizes of workers.

It is a matter of some doubt just where the true worker caste appears in the primitive termites. There seems to be no clear division between the ageing of nymphs arrested in the course of their development towards the imago and the results of a single moult, in what might be termed an oblique direction, in adding specific worker characters such as enlargement of the head and pigmentation of the head and thorax.

THE SOLDIER

Soldier termites are characterised by the great development of the head and mandibles. The rest of the body is changed little from the nymphal form, apart from increased chitinisation and the resulting deepening in colour. The head capsule is elongated to accommodate the muscles necessary for the large mandibles. The mouthparts, other than the mandibles, vary little from the basic pattern already described in the imago. Compound eyes are present in *Mastotermes*, *Hodotermes* and *Anacanthotermes*, progressively reduced in the Termopsidae, and absent in the rest. Traces of the ocelli are present only in the most primitive species. The antennae are filiform, and the number of segments is liable to greater variation than in adult forms (Fig. 4).

The Rhinotermitidae and Termitidae possess frontal glands which occupy a variable proportion of the head and in extreme cases spread into the abdominal cavity. This gland has its external opening as a pore on the frontal area of the head, usually just behind a line joining the bases of the antennae, and known as the fontanelle. In *Coptotermes* and

Rhinotermes the fontanelle is large and conspicuous, and is used for the ejection of quantities of viscous white fluid when the termite is disturbed. In *Rhinotermes* the clypeus is greatly lengthened with a median groove to carry this fluid beyond the tips of the mandibles. It again appears large in several of the small Termitinae such as *Proboscitermes*, accompanied by a forward projection of the head capsule. This is carried to its limit in the subfamily Nasutitermitinae, where the less primitive genera have developed pear-shaped heads with the fontanelle at the apex as their sole defence, and the mandibles have become reduced to mere rudiments (Fig. 18).

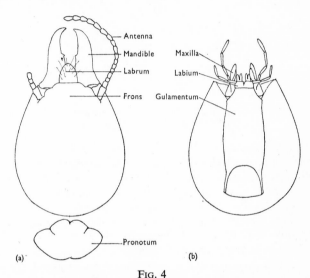

FIG. 4

The soldier head, showing the principal parts. a, above; b, below

Development

The development of termites is essentially similar to such insects as locusts and plant bugs, being hemi-metabolous or an incomplete metamorphosis. The young termite on hatching from the egg already possesses many characters found in the adult insect—legs, mouthparts, etc. —the most obvious differences being the absence of wings and the softness of the integument. The nymph, as it is called, increases in size in a series of moults, at the same time moving towards its adult form in stages, without a quiescent pupal stage as in the Lepidoptera and other holometabola. The life cycle has three well-defined phases: egg—nymph —imago.

Termite eggs are small and cylindrical, with a slight curve. Those of *Macrotermes bellicosus* measure 1·0 by 0·4 mm and of *Mastotermes darwiniensis* 1·5 by 0·5 mm. They are laid singly by the queen, though sometimes in quick succession, as in the case of *Macrotermes* with an average of one every two seconds over quite long periods. An exception is found in *Mastotermes*, where the eggs are laid in batches of from 16 to 24, cemented together in two rows after the manner of the oothecae of some cockroaches and grasshoppers, though without an envelope (Fig. 5).

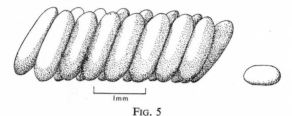

1mm

Fig. 5

Eggs of *Mastotermes darwiniensis*, with a single egg of *Macrotermes bellicosus* (right) for comparison

The nymphal phase consists of a series of instars separated by moults, which may be recognised by the size of the nymph, by the number of segments in its antennae, and after the second instar by the development of the wing pads. Normally the internal development keeps in step with the external, and the reproductive organs become functional after the final or imaginal moult. Termites differ from most other insects in having a potential adult life of many years, during which, in the case of the female, further external changes take place through the growth of the abdomen to accommodate the ever-enlarging reproductive organs. Wings are needed for only a brief period of the adult life to achieve dispersal from the home, and they are discarded as soon as the opposite sexes have met, leaving them to all intents and purposes as wingless insects (Fig. 6).

The incomplete metamorphosis of the termites divides them from the other social insects—the ants, bees and wasps—which proceed by way of egg, larva and pupa to the adult stage. A further striking difference lies in the presence of a male parent through the life of the termite community, whereas in the others the female returns alone from the nuptial flight to produce a family for just so long as her single act of mating permits.

Apart from the social insects named, the development of insects is under the influence of the environment in which the female deposits her eggs, and in which the young must remain until they are able to leave on their own volition. Their development is, in consequence, influenced to a great degree by the climate, and tends to be governed by the seasons, both directly by reaction to temperature and indirectly by fluctuations in the availability of food. This holds true for plant-feeding insects and carnivores, as well as many parasitic forms. It is thus possible to define in fairly precise terms their life cycle as being so many generations per annum, each generation having a reasonably predictable period in the egg, in each of a definite number of nymphal or larval stages, and even the probable life of the imago.

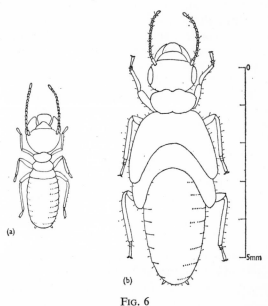

FIG. 6

Nymphal stages of *Odontotermes latericius*. a, undifferentiated second-stage nymph; b, fifth-stage nymph with developing wing pads

Termites develop in environments which are largely under the control of their community, and insulated from outside influences. They tend to be less seasonal than most other insects. In addition, the community is able to influence the development of each nymph in accordance with the requirements of community, even to diverting it into a developmental cul-de-sac and producing a sterile worker or soldier. As we shall see later, this subjugation of the individual to the community continues even to the winged adults which are awaiting the arrival of suitable conditions for swarming, for these may have their wings removed and be retained in the nest as extra workers while their newly developed reproductive organs atrophy.

The internal development of a termite nymph may also be influenced by the needs of the community. Sexual maturity can be accelerated without corresponding external changes to enable nymphs of the fourth and later instars to become substitute reproductives should the need arise. The most noticeable feature in this case is the lack of wings in what is otherwise an adult. Regressive moults are possible should the community decide that there are too many nymphs approaching maturity, or where there is a shortage of workers or soldiers.

As a result of this influence which the community exercises on the development of nymphs, it is not possible to do more than indicate the general lines of termite development. It is only with the more primitive families, Kalotermitidae, Termopsidae and Rhinotermitidae, that laboratory cultures proceed in an apparently normal manner and so permit detailed observations on life history to be made.

The first and second nymphal instars are feeble creatures without signs of wing buds or other indications of the line along which they will develop. They are not infrequently referred to as larvae. Those which are destined to become workers may do so after the next moult, or at most after one further stage. Those becoming soldiers appear as 'white soldiers' at the third or later instars, and moult once more into the tough mature form. Workers are immature forms stabilised with one particular adult feature, the shape and hardness of the mandibles.

LIFE CYCLE OF THE IMAGO

The following developmental periods were obtained with colonies maintained at a uniform temperature of 25° C by Harvey (1934) for *Kalotermes minor* and by Buchli (1958) for *Reticulitermes lucifugus santonensis*.

	K. minor	*R.l. santonensis*
Egg	77 days	20–25 days
Nymphal instar I..............	21–35 ,,	7– 8 ,,
II..............	30–42 ,,	10–11 ,,
III–VII..........	137–338 ,,	
III–VIII		average 147 day
Total time from oviposition to emergence of imago	9–16 months	6–7 months

Since there is no worker caste in *Kalotermes*, the development of nymphs is arrested at any time after the third instar when they have become able to gnaw wood and to digest it with the aid of intestinal protozoa. Then they are able to produce saliva and regurgitated food for the younger nymphs and the royal pair. These individuals may never become adult during their life, unless some pressing need arises. In young colonies of *Kalotermes* winged adults do not appear during the first two or three years; in some other families they may appear after only eighteen months, but generally the same time elapses as in *Kalotermes*.

1. Colony of the dry-wood termite *Cryptotermes havilandi* in inner lamina of plywood

2. *Pseudacanthotermes militaris* queen and soldiers

3. *Pseudacanthotermes militaris* winged adults

4. Worker *Macrotermes subhyalinus* collecting eggs as they leave the queen

(Dr P. R. Hesse)

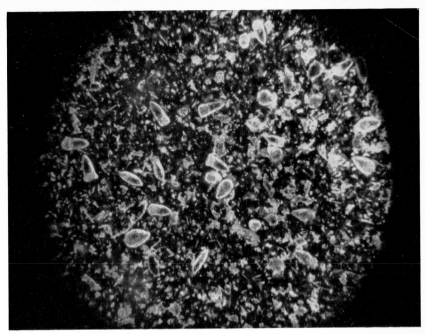

5. Living protozoa, mainly *Trichonympha spp.* from the gut of *Zootermopsis angusticollis* (2/3 inch (16 mm) objective, phase contrast illumination)

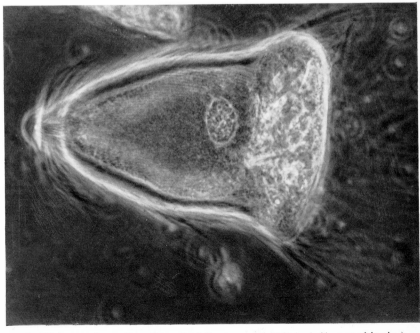

6. *Trichonympha sp.* from the gut of *Zootermopsis* (1/6 inch (4 mm) objective)

7. Site of *Kalotermes* colony in dead branch of *Acacia*, Kenya

8. Nest of *Coptotermes amanii* exposed when tree is blown over by storm, Tanzania

LIFE CYCLE OF THE WORKER

With *Reticulitermes lucifugus*, Buchli observed that workers developed their final form on moulting after the second instar in young colonies, and after a third instar in larger colonies. No doubt this is due to the urgency with which workers are required in new communities. However, they continue to moult to a total of ten instars over a period of five months, and live for a period of from 19 to 24 months under favourable conditions, or even longer. The period from oviposition to active work in this species is from 6 to 7 months.

Tenuirostritermes tenuirostris, an American nasute termite, is stated by Weesner (1953) to develop workers after two 'larval instars' each of 14 to 15 days, a total of 60 days after the egg was laid.

Cubitermes ugandensis, according to Williams (1959), produces workers in four months; average egg stage, 68 days; instar I, 22 days; instar II, 28 days; the range met during the experiments being 114 to 140 days.

LIFE CYCLE OF THE SOLDIER

The development of the soldier of *Kalotermes flavicollis*, according to Grassé and Noirot (1958), is as follows:

Egg	50–60	days
Nymphal instar I	11–13	„
II	13–18	„
III	16–32	„
IV	30–50	„
(white soldier) V	14	„
Total	4–6	months

The first soldier to appear in a young colony, usually from the first batch of eggs laid, may reach the 'white soldier' stage in the fourth, or even the third, instar so reducing the time to as little as three months. In this case its size is not so great as those which will follow at a more leisurely pace.

In *Reticulitermes lucifugus*, according to Buchli, 'white soldiers' develop from workers which are in any instar from the third to the eighth. These, presumably, have remained in active growth, and this gives rise to some doubt whether or not the worker caste in the Rhinotermitidae is as well established as an entity as it is in the Termitidae. No narrow limits of time can be given for the development of soldiers in *R. lucifugus*, since they appear to be produced as needed from individuals that would otherwise remain as workers.

Soldiers of *Tenuirostritermes tenuirostris* are produced after four instars, each of which is of shorter duration than is the case with workers, on average seven days, enabling them to appear in about the same total time, 58 days after oviposition.

Foods and Feeding

THE ALIMENTARY CANAL

The collection and digestion of food have an important influence on termite behaviour, and a knowledge of the workings of the alimentary canal, especially that of the worker, provides a basis for understanding some of the striking differences between the various families.

The ailmentary canal is a simple tube consisting of three main parts, the fore-gut, mid-gut and hind-gut. The fore-gut is made up of a straight, narrow oesophagus, flanked by well-developed salivary glands, which leads to a wider section, the crop. At the base of the crop is a muscular organ, the proventriculus, with chitinous plates fitted to the inner wall for extra grinding power in those termites which need them. The proventriculus is contracted below to a narrow passage which controls the movement of the food onwards to the mid-gut. This is a more or less short, uniform tube. In the more primitive termites there are a number of blind tubes or caeca at the junction with the proventriculus, and in all cases a number of Malpighian tubes mark the other end. Digestion continues throughout the passage of the food down the mid-gut, and it is believed that absorption begins in the lower part. Most of the absorption takes place in the first part of the hind-gut, in the capacious thin-walled sac known as the large intestine. The narrow colon leads from the large intestine to the rectum, and varies greatly in length according to the family, being short or absent in the dry-wood termites and lengthy in the more highly developed Termitidae. The rectum also varies in size, being proportionately largest in the Kalotermitidae, where muscular force is required to produce the hard dry faecal pellets. It is not much smaller, however, though less muscular, in some of the soil-feeding Termitinae.

In so far as there is precise information available, three types of ali-mentary canal may be related to the known feeding habits of the termites as follows:

1. Primitive wood-eating termites (*Archotermopsis, Zootermopsis*) living in their feeding galleries and possessing an intestinal fauna of protozoa which assist in digesting cellulose—crop long and cylindrical, only slightly dilated; proventriculus small, annular and with internal grinding plates; caeca present at junction with mid-gut; hind-gut greatly dilated to form a rectal pouch, with abbreviated colon, and large muscular rectum. The protozoa congregate in the large intestine (Fig. 7).

2. Soil-feeding Termitinae (*Cubitermes, Termes, Capritermes*) ingesting large quantities of soil containing broken down vegetable debris, plant roots, etc., and using the voluminous excreta for nest construction; no protozoa—crop asymmetrically dilated, proventriculus small and with-

out heavy chitinous lining; mid-gut short, without caeca; hind-gut long, the large intestine divided into two compartments by a valve, the colon long and the rectum capacious.

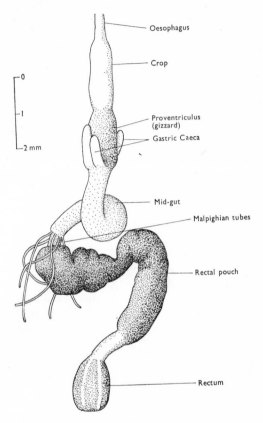

Oesophagus

Crop

Proventriculus (gizzard)

Gastric Caeca

Mid-gut

Malpighian tubes

Rectal pouch

Rectum

FIG. 7
Alimentary canal of *Zootermopsis* worker, a damp-wood termite with cellulose-digesting protozoa

3. Fungus-growing Macrotermitinae (*Macrotermes, Odontotermes, Microtermes*), feeding on wood and vegetable debris, some at least of which has been subject to fungus action while in the form of 'fungus comb' or stored as fragments within the warm, humid nest; in addition to providing suitable ground food for the brood, the proventriculus and crop are used by workers on building construction to transport large amounts of a clay and saliva mortar—crop small, proventriculus muscular with internal chitinous grinding plates; mid-gut short, narrow and

without caeca; hind-gut dilated to form a spherical rectal pouch, with medium-length colon leading to small rectum (Fig. 8).

Further details of the alimentary canal will be found in Holmgren (1909), and in Imms (1913) for *Archotermopsis wroughtoni*, Child (1934) for *Zootermopsis nevadensis*, Mukerji and Raychaudhuri (1943) for *Odontotermes redemanni*, Noirot and Kovoor (1958) for the subfamily Termitinae, and Schmidt (1959) for *Macrotermes natalensis*.

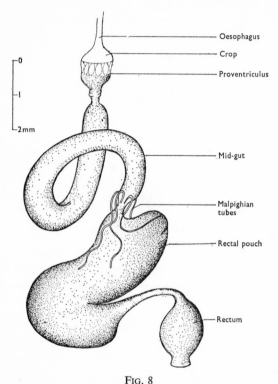

Oesophagus

Crop

Proventriculus

Mid-gut

Malpighian tubes

Rectal pouch

Rectum

0

1

2mm

Fig. 8

Alimentary canal of *Macrotermes* worker, a ground-dwelling termite without cellulose-digesting protozoa (H. Schmidt, 1959)

UTILISATION OF FOODSTUFFS

The diet of termites consists entirely of plant material of a woody nature, principally cellulose. Young nymphs, reproductives, many soldiers, and winged adults awaiting their mass exodus from the nest, these all require to be fed by the workers, or, where these do not occur, by the older nymphs. As a result, the proventriculus and rectum of these various forms are not so well developed as in the worker or older nymph. The grinding of the food is not the only contribution made by the workers, since they may be observed to offer clear fluid, presumably saliva, on occasion. It has been recorded that dry-wood termites will respond to the demands of others in the nest and excrete quantities of a semi-fluid matter containing particles of wood and large numbers of protozoa, instead of the customary hard dry pellets. This will undoubtedly have food value to the recipient. Information is lacking on the part played by this proctodeal feeding in other families.

Trophallaxis, the exchange of food by mouth between termites, is probably one of the main factors in maintaining the social structure. It provides, together with the associated grooming actions, a means whereby stimuli in one form or another are transmitted to regulate the organisation of the community. This is discussed further in the section on the community. The food material exchanged varies from the semi-solid regurgitated contents of the crop to a clear fluid, presumably saliva.

The primitive wood-boring termites tear away small fragments with their toothed mandibles and swallow them, to be ground up in the muscular proventriculus. As these termites do not themselves secrete cellulase, the enzyme which breaks down cellulose, they have to rely on the protozoa which live in the hind-gut to do this for them. These protozoa were observed by Lespès over a hundred years ago, but their function was demonstrated by Cleveland in 1923. Unfortunately the interest which was aroused by Cleveland's work has tended to obscure the fact that most termites do not possess protozoa and employ other methods to this end. There is a close relationship between the species of protozoa present and their particular host termite. Even under low magnification the gut contents of dry-wood and damp-wood termites gives an interesting picture of protozoal life. With a two-third-inch (16 mm) objective, for example, *Zootermopsis angusticollis* will show *Trichonympha campanula* and *T. collaris* (Plates 5 and 6), while more species come into view with higher powers. Without their protozoa these termites slowly starve. Loss of protozoa is usually the cause of unthrifty laboratory colonies. Certain wood preservatives are more effective against dry-wood termites than they are against the subterranean species because they destroy the protozoa at concentrations too low to affect the termites themselves. Boron is an example of this type of action.

Harvester termites of the genus *Hodotermes* forage unprotected in the open air for grass, which they cut into short lengths and carry back to the openings of the shafts which lead down to their subterranean nests. There appears to be some system of inspection here by the workers who carry the grass down to be stored in chambers, under conditions of uniform temperature and high humidity. The related *Anacanthotermes* was found collecting camel dung around wells in southern Arabia at a time when there was no grass available. A similar habit of foraging in the open and storing grass in the nest is met with again in the Nasutitermitinae, one of the more highly developed subfamilies of the Termitidae, some species of which are important pests of grazing land.

Reference has already been made to the presence of fungus comb in the nests of all members of the subfamily Macrotermitinae. They are ovoid or near-spherical sponge-like masses constructed of chewed wood, built up to fit the chambers of the nest, and in a design which is peculiar to each species of termite (Colour Plate I). They become coated with a fine white fungus mycelium, and spotted with small white spherical masses of conidia. There has been much speculation as to the function of this fungus comb. From observations carried out over a number of years on *Odontotermes badius* in East Africa, there appears to be little doubt that it forms an essential part of the food supply of the community. Sands (1956) showed that small quantities of fresh fungus comb added to a diet of filter paper or wood chips increased the life of *O. badius* workers in the laboratory from an average of eleven days to one of fifty-five days. There is a continual breaking-down and renewal of fungus comb in the nest. Old combs are removed from below until only the outer shell remains and, when this too has gone, new comb is built. At a suitable season early in the rains, it is the custom of several species of African *Odontotermes* to shave away the outer layers of some fungus combs and spread this crumb-like material in a thin layer on the surface of the ground above their subterranean nests. After a day or two there is a carpet of small, edible mushrooms of the genus *Termitomyces*, which lasts only a day before the mushrooms wither and allow their spores to be blown over the ground. Then there is intense activity on the part of the workers, who come to the surface and collect vegetable debris, presumably contaminated with these fungus spores, and this they take below and set about replacing the surface of the fungus combs (Colour Plate II). The fructifications of the species of fungi living in the nests of *Macrotermes* appear as much larger mushrooms forcing their way to the surface of the ground above a subterranean nest, or around the base of a mound, usually after such a nest has been abandoned in part or altogether. In chambers near the top of the hive in *Macrotermes* and *Pseudacanthotermes*, stores of wood and other vegetable matter are found, moist and fermenting in the high humidity. They attract large numbers of Collembola and mites. It is a common occurrence in Africa and has been described by Kalshoven (1956) for *Macrotermes javanicus* in Java. It is not known if such stores are used direct for food, or if they are made into fungus comb.

There are still a number of termites which possess no intestinal protozoa, have no food stores, do not construct fungus combs, nor eat large quantities of soil rich in vegetable matter. They feed on wood and dried vegetation, but it is not known how they manage to digest the cellulose.

CHAPTER 2

Termite Biology—The Society

In the beginning the termite community consists of a pair of adults, or imagos, that have discarded their wings, constructed a cell in a situation of their choice and, in due course, mated. With the onset of oviposition they show parental care, first for the eggs and then for the feeble white first-stage nymphs which hatch out from them. The problem of providing food for the brood must be great as the parent termites do not leave their cell, and particularly so in the case of the Macrotermitinae which depend on fungus combs in their nests once these are fully organised. Full use appears to be made of the parents' internal reserves. In laboratory colonies it is observed that eggs and young brood may disappear at intervals, presumably when the feeding capacity of the parents is overstrained. Oviposition is discontinuous at first, and after laying an initial batch of eggs the female rests. The first brood usually turns into rather undersized workers, though in dry-wood termites there is generally one soldier in this first batch. No more soldiers are produced until the number of mature workers has reached twenty or thirty, unless, of course, the first one dies.

Once there are a number of workers available to feed the young brood and enlarge the accommodation, the female tends to increase the rate of her egg production. This is less evident in the Kalotermitidae, where egg-laying remains intermittent and the population small. In no case does there appear to be any spectacular increase, as happens with many other insects when they become established in favourable conditions. After one year numbers are similar in both *Kalotermes* and *Reticulitermes* in laboratory cultures, being of the order of thirty or forty. While communities of *Kalotermes flavicollis* in the field rarely number more than 1 000, with 500 as a probable mean, *Reticulitermes lucifugus* reaches very much larger figures, while tropical genera such as *Macrotermes* and *Coptotermes* ultimately reach the hundreds of thousands. Such large populations take many years to develop.

In the second stage of the termite society we find the adult pair exclusively concerned with egg production, while the care of the brood, the collection of food and the provision of accommodation are all done by the worker caste, or in its absence by worker-nymphs. Soldiers are usual in all but two tropical genera, *Anoplotermes* and *Speculitermes*, though they do not form more than about 5 per cent of the population.

17

And finally there will be the brood, consisting of first- and second-stage 'larvae', newly moulted workers, and perhaps one or two 'white soldiers'. In the case of the Kalotermitidae, there will be no workers, but nymphs of various stages, newly moulted or arrested in their development, acting as workers. This stage continues until the community is well established, and then third-instar nymphs begin to appear with minute wing rudiments or pads. These nymphs grow in stages, at each of which the wing pads get larger, until they moult for the last time and appear as adult winged termites. Such development occupies several months, and in temperate climates usually involves a period of over-wintering which further increases the time taken. With the mass flight or swarming from the nest of these imagos, in conjunction with all the others of the same species in that locality, the cycle of development is complete, but the society still remains to produce more adults and to continue indefinitely as an entity.

As time passes the original parents will reach the end of their reproductive capacity, or they will prove inadequate to the demands of the community, and be liquidated by the workers. Additionally, one or both of them may be killed by accident or by a predator. To replace them, nymphs of the appropriate sex are stimulated to maturity without further moulting and, in consequence, without further change in outward appearance. The younger the nymphs that have to be developed in this way, the greater the number that are required to provide the desired egg-potential. If winged imagos are present, awaiting the swarming season, they will have their untried wings removed by chewing, leaving the stumps irregular and not cleanly broken off along the suture as is the case after flight. These last are known as first-form substitute reproductives, and the female may approach the degree of physogastry of the original queen. Second-form substitute reproductives are derived from nymphs of various ages and are recognised by the presence of wing rudiments, indicative of the stage they had reached before they were chosen for their new role. As these substitute forms are limited in their egg-laying powers, they are developed in numbers. Coaton has recorded fifty functioning second-form substitute queens in a nest of *Hodotermes* in South Africa. It appears to be a practice among African *Cubitermes* to remove the primary queen at a given stage in the development of a community and replace her with something of the order of twenty second-form substitute females, each of limited egg-potential, but collectively more prolific. In the Macrotermitinae, on the other hand, the original queen appears to be able to keep pace with the needs of her enormous community, and is replaced only when she becomes too old (Fig. 9).

Among the more primitive families, particularly the Rhinotermitidae which nest in damp dead wood, there is evidence of the regular forma-

I. Fungus comb from a nest of *Odontotermes badius*, with white spheres of conidia developing on the mycelium, and young termites

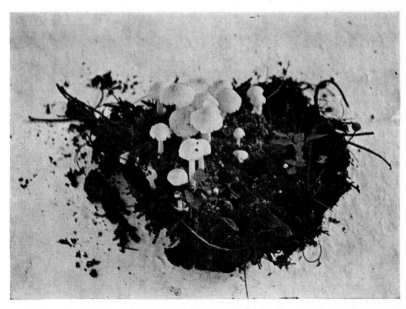

II. Mushrooms of the genus *Termitomyces* developing on fragments of fungus comb scattered on the soil above a nest of *Odontotermes badius*

III

III and IV. Mounds of
*Macrotermes subhya-
linus*

III. On diatomaceous soil
at Olorgasaile, Kenya

IV. On lateritic soil at
Nachingwea, Tanzani

IV

tion of new colonies by a process of fission, and the development of substitute reproductives in the portion of the community which has become isolated from the main body. Such a new colony increases in size much faster than one started by a pair of imagos, because the parents are at no time concerned with feeding the brood, since workers are already present. There is no great difficulty in developing colonies this way in the laboratory with such genera as *Kalotermes, Neotermes, Reticulitermes* and *Zootermopsis*. Grassi and Sandias (1893) examined thousands of colonies of *Reticulitermes lucifugus* in Italy without finding a single one with primary reproductives. In every case there were substitute reproductives, numbering from 10 to 200 per nest. In East Africa,

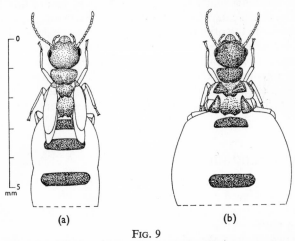

(a)   (b)

FIG. 9

Queens of *Microcerotermes subtilis* from the Seychelles. a, substitution or second form queen with nymphal wing pads; b, primary queen. The greater part of the distended abdomen has been omitted in each case

Schedorhinotermes lamanianus, also a member of the Rhinotermitidae, commonly builds its primary nest at ground level, attached to the trunk of a tree in the angle formed by a buttress root. Covered runways lead up the trunk to wounds and dead snags of branches which provide food. If in addition these provide suitable cavities which can be divided up into floors with a carton material such as the termites construct in their nest below, they then come into use as secondary nurseries where eggs are brought up from below, incubated and the brood tended by workers. In time, presumably when they have a sufficiently representative cross-section of the community present including nymphs of the later instars, these develop into self-supporting communities, losing contact with the parent body. Invariably such daughter colonies are headed by second-form supplementary kings and queens.

Grassé has proposed the name 'pseudergate', or false worker, for the large aged nymphs found in colonies of the Kalotermitidae, whose development has ceased but who keep on with the domestic duties of the nest. He proposes the name 'achrestogonime' for a second type found in such communities, which are imagos whose wings have been removed before they could leave the nest and who then appear to have been put to work after the manner of the pseudergate. In course of time their reproductive organs atrophy.

Because of this plasticity in the development of the young termite, the relatively long period passed in the various nymphal instars during which the demands of the community may change, and the opportunities for minor accidents which arise in a biological system of this degree of complexity, intermediate castes are not particularly rare. They are more often met with in the primitive Kalotermitidae and Hodotermitidae, and in the Rhinotermitidae. Not only are substitute reproductives found with a variety of nymphal characters, but soldiers may occur with wing pads of various lengths, either because they have developed from nymphs in advanced stages, or because they have proceeded on the road to sexual maturity after the more noticeable soldier characters have been laid down.

Colony Foundation

There are three different ways in which new communities are formed:
1. by pairs of winged adults, or flying termites;
2. by the isolation of part of an existing colony, and the development of substitute reproductives;
3. by the migration of part of a colony, including the reproductives, to a new site, leaving the residue to develop substitute reproductives.

SWARMING, AND COLONY FOUNDATION BY WINGED TERMITES

The departure of winged termites from the nest is a social event which causes considerable activity among individuals of the other castes present. By way of preparation for the event the working nymphs of the Kalotermitidae bore holes from their galleries within timber to the outside. As this is also done when they wish to discard an accumulation of faecal pellets in the galleries, holes must not necessarily be regarded as indicating swarming. These holes are plugged up immediately after the swarm has emerged, to be reopened on another occasion. The Rhinotermitidae construct covered ways and tunnels from their subterranean nests to the outer world, conducting the swarm to situations as favourable as possible for the take-off. For example, the exits tend to be more numerous on the sides of buildings where night temperatures are highest. Among the more highly organised Termitidae more elaborate preparations are to be found, particularly among the Macrotermitinae, including the construction of wide shafts from subterranean nests to the surface of the ground with the openings ringed in walls formed in gentle curves, serving as launching platforms for the flyers. Common to all is a temporary reversal of that dislike of light which most termites, workers, soldiers and imagos alike, show so strongly at other times, and a temporary relaxation of that preoccupation with repairs to any gaps in the walls which isolate the nest from the outside world. Once the flight is over, the soldiers guarding the exit holes return inside, the openings are sealed, and only the constructional work remains as evidence of the event.

The primitive pattern of swarming may be summed up as 'little and often'. Kalshoven records the appearance of imagos of the teak termite, *Neotermes tectonae*, in Java on many nights over a period of three months. In Florida, Miller found that five of the nine species of *Kalotermes* there swarmed during five or more months in the year, and that only during July were there no flights at all. Laboratory colonies of *Reticulitermes lucifugus* in Germany are recorded by Herfs as producing winged forms during every month over a period of ten years, though he adds that 75 per cent of emergences took place within the period March to May.

Turning to the Termitidae it is seen that swarming becomes increasingly restricted, not only to certain periods of the year but also to limited times of the day, with the result that much larger numbers of imagos emerge together than is to be seen among the more primitive families. Skaife (1955) records that colonies of *Amitermes atlanticus* in South Africa have one main swarming flight each year, with a small secondary swarm some two months later. Records of swarms kept by the author at one locality in Tanzania during 1934–5 and 1935–6 showed a season of emergence covering December to April in the first instance and November to May in the second, corresponding to a variation in the pattern of rainfall. In both cases swarms occurred during periods when the rain fell in other than scattered showers. In Uganda, where the rainfall is more evenly distributed, the emergence of Termitidae occurs during the longer period of March to October. As an example of the precise conditions which some, at least, of the higher termites require for swarming may be instanced the results of observations carried out over three years on *Odontotermes badius* near Nairobi, Kenya. Swarming commenced one hour after sunset, providing there had been good damping rain in progress half an hour previously. No rain, or only a light drizzle at about 6.30 p.m., meant that there would be no flight at about 7 p.m., even though there had been enough rain earlier in the day to stimulate the workers in their subterranean nest to excavate emergence shafts and start their excited patrolling of the surface of the ground above.

The behaviour pattern of the sexes during swarming is at its simplest and most plastic among the Kalotermitidae. They are, in the main, crepuscular flyers. Males and females alight after flight and await the arrival of the opposite sex. Wings may be shed as soon as the pair have met, but frequently they are retained during the subsequent parade and later dislodged by rubbing against wood or even chewed off by the partner. They parade in pairs, either sex taking the lead, breaking off and regrouping if others are met on the way until the site for digging in is finally chosen.

In the higher termites the female usually lands first and adopts an attractive attitude, generally elevating the abdomen. It has been suggested that scent signals are made by the female to attract the male, but this appears to be unsupported by any evidence. When a male approaches near enough both insects shed their wings with a simple muscular action of the thorax, and the wingless pair proceed to parade, with the female in the lead. In Africa the day-flying *Pseudacanthotermes militaris* imagos have the habit of swarming around the tops of tall trees, particularly one with a pointed canopy as in many eucalypts. Where suitable trees are absent they will congregate round some isolated shrub. Males have been observed to clasp the females of their choice around the abdomen and shed their wings while still airborne, leaving the female to provide the motive power for a successful landing on the ground below. Even in night-flying *Macrotermes* there is evidence in the concentration of wings around the base of tobacco plants and similar vegetation that some form of assembly develops around pointed objects (Plate 21).

Having chosen their mates, the imagos of all families, whether they are day or night flyers, quickly reverse their attitude to light and seek darkness and shelter. Their only interest at this time is to excavate a chamber in which they can live in some degree of security. Copulation follows afterwards. Grassé and Noirot (1958) record mating ten to fifteen days after flight in the case of the dry-wood termite, *Kalotermes flavicollis*. Soil-dwelling *Macrotermes* have been found to produce eggs one week after swarming. The small mound-building *Cubitermes ugandensis*, according to Williams (1959), copulates after the third day, by which time the excavation of the cell is complete, and with eggs on the fifth day.

Lüscher (1951) sums up his observations on colony foundation as follows: 'One may conclude that the behaviour of the Kalotermitidae during the period of swarming and colony foundation is very unstable; among the higher termites the behaviour pattern is more rigid and interruption of the chain of reactions at any point is fatal.' The practical difficulties in the way of establishing colonies of the higher termites in the laboratory bear this out. Buchli produced colonies of *Reticulitermes lucifugus* from newly pigmented imagos placed in pairs in breeding tubes without opportunity for flight or any other of the normal preliminaries to colony foundation. Among the Termitidae, flight appears to be one of a number of essential steps.

COLONY FOUNDATION BY PART OF AN EXISTING COLONY

The foundation of a new community by the isolation of part of an existing one depends on the successful development of substitute reproductives, and on the original nest system being of a sufficiently diffuse nature to allow of portions being isolated. Substitute reproductives are more commonly met with among the more primitive families than among the Termitidae, especially those derived from nymphs in early instars with only short wing pads. The nests of the Kalotermitidae are unorganised, there being no queen cells to act as hubs for the community. In the Rhinotermitidae the nest is organised to a certain degree, but subsidiary nests are common since the root or buried tree trunk used does not always permit of unlimited expansion. Development is generally towards a compact nest system in the Termitidae. It would appear, however, that when seasonal increases of population cannot be accommodated by increasing the size of the mound for constructional reasons, duplicate mounds may be built, which by isolation and the development of substitute queens become 'budded off' into separate communities.

Examples of 'budded' colonies are frequently found in two of the Rhinotermitidae common in eastern Africa, *Schedorhinotermes lamanianus* and *Coptotermes amanii*; reference to the first of these has already been made. In temperate regions *Reticulitermes* appears to use this method in preference to swarming, if one can judge by the scarcity of winged adults in laboratory colonies of *R. flavipes* in Germany, and to the prevalence of substitute queens in nests of *R. lucifugus* in Italy.

It is usual in all termites that have been studied to find that the eggs are removed by workers or worker-nymphs from the vicinity of the queen as they are laid, and carried away to nursery chambers for incubation (Plate 4). As the nest grows in size the eggs tend to be taken further away from the queen. In the case of the dry-wood termites they go into newly excavated side galleries, and in the moist-wood termites to new sites in rotten wood, and as the lines of communication lengthen, the chances of accidental isolation increase.

Although the very primitive *Mastotermes darwiniensis* in Australia has large populations which suggest that social organisation has far outstripped any anatomical change since the Miocene epoch, numerous substitute queens are usually found in the larger nests, while the prevalence of small nests with substitute queens suggests that budding is a common occurrence.

There would appear to be advantages in the formation of new colonies by fission, since the presence of a full complement of the various castes in a new community avoids that very vulnerable stage when the parents are existing on their internal food reserves, awaiting the development of the first workers. On the other hand the ability of the queens of the higher termites to lay eggs at a much higher rate may be of greater use in the end in building up a large population.

COLONY FOUNDATION BY MIGRATION

A hitherto unsuspected method of colony foundation was described by Grassé and Noirot (1951) in West Africa. They observed a species of *Anoplotermes* emerging from the ground in a regular column, made up of a physogastric queen, her consort, workers, nymphs and some termitophiles—this genus does not possess a soldier caste. This column moved some distance and then dug itself in. From the original emergence hole, small bands were later observed to emerge without reproductives, march awhile and then return below ground by the same hole from which they had emerged. Similar columns in movement have been observed in East Africa, involving two species of *Anoplotermes*, but in these instances the emergence from the original nests was not seen and there were thus no indications that a part of the community had been left behind.

Migrations of other termites have been noted which may belong to this type of colony formation. They include *Syntermes* in Guyana, and *Trinervitermes* in both West and East Africa. A radical change in behaviour is involved in that for the time being strong light is not avoided by the termites, comparable with a similar action when preparations are being made for swarming.

Such social fragmentation depends on the ability of the residue of the community to develop substitute reproductives and no doubt would be conditioned by the presence of nymphs in an advanced stage of development, since the phenomenon has so far been observed only among the higher termites.

Caste Determination

There has been considerable speculation on the mechanism of caste determination since 1893, when Grassi announced that he had obtained a colony with all the normal castes by keeping a number of nymphs of *Kalotermes flavicollis* in the laboratory, suitably moist and provided with food. He found that in course of time some nymphs became soldiers, while others developed into substitute reproductives. The removal of the soldiers led to the formation of new ones. On the other hand, if soldiers were added from another colony they were killed off until a proper proportion only remained. Such a balancing of the population, Grassi suggested, was a result of continual contacts between all members arising from reciprocal grooming, stroking of antennae and exchange of food.

Later it was held by Thompson, Imms and others that the development of each nymph was already determined in the egg by its genetic pattern, or was conditioned while yet in embryo. This has now been replaced by the concept of inhibitory substances circulating in the community, as suggested by Pickens (1932), and for which confirmatory evidence has been produced in experiments with *Zootermopsis* and *Kalotermes*. Using *Kalotermes flavicollis*, Lüscher (1952) showed that with two colonies separated by wire gauze that allowed a certain amount of physical contact, the presence of reproductives in one colony made the other colony destroy any nymphs which had developed into reproductives. When the colonies were separated by two layers of gauze with a gap between them sufficient to prevent actual physical contact between their members, then the colony without reproductives allowed its nymphs to complete their development. It had already been recorded that with *Zootermopsis angusticollis*, the removal of the single soldier in a young colony always led to the production of another soldier, while the removal of either parent in a colony with well-developed nymphs led to the production of a substitute reproductive of the same sex.

The term 'pheromone' has recently been proposed by Lüscher and Karlson for substances which are secreted to the outside by an individual and received by a second individual of the same species, in which is then released a specific action. Earlier, use had been made of the term 'social hormone' for the same principle. The idea of the circulation of an inhibitory substance to regulate the production of castes has also been developed by experimental work on the honey bee leading to Butler's 'queen substance', produced by the queen and actively circulated by the workers, which prevents the development of further queens. The pheromones have a short life and require to be produced more or less continuously to be effective.

There is a practical bearing in this topic. The removal of queens from the larger mounds and subterranean nests is a well-known method of destroying colonies of *Macrotermes* and *Odontotermes* in parts of Africa and Asia. The large physogastric females—the queens—are easy to distinguish from the rest of the community, providing, of course, that they can be located in their thick-walled cells. Owners of termite-infested buildings, and those about to build, frequently employ a local 'termite expert' to destroy the queens in order to remove the source of danger, at a price. Apart from the fact that the larger and more obvious species of termites are less frequently the cause of damage to buildings than are their less conspicuous relatives, queen removal is no guarantee of the death of the community. Unless ants and other enemies gain access to the nest through the breaches made in its outer defences, or insecticides are used further to reduce the population or to poison the fungus combs and induce starvation, there is always the possibility that the colony will produce substitute reproductives. After a period of quiescence, during which the termite nest is recovering from the loss in egg production, the trouble would then start all over again.

The Nest

As there are no solitary termites, all members of the Isoptera live in communities, large or small, within the limits of a nest system. The amount of communication between the nest and the outside world depends on the particular feeding habits of the species. The nest system is a controlled environment in which the young are brought up. The complexity of the method employed to maintain this isolation depends on the situation of the nest, and this, in turn, is related to competition for the more favourable niches. It is this ability in the termite to control the micro-climate within its nest which contributes largely to their success in surviving in the intense competition of the tropics beside other insects which appear so much more aggressive and strong.

Two families of the more primitive termites, Kalotermitidae and Termopsidae, continue to live in what may be the ancestral style by burrowing in wood; the first in dry wood, the second in damp wood (Plate 7). They are surrounded by their food, and live within a microclimate of their choice, making openings to the exterior only on special occasions. New excavations are made in the most favourable direction, as may be seen in the case of *Epicalotermes aethiopicus* which lives in the dead branches of thorn trees under very dry conditions on the shores of the Arabian and Red Seas. New tunnels are made as near as possible to the living wound tissues with which the tree endeavours to isolate the dead branch, presumably to assist in maintaining a reasonable degree of humidity in the nest. Kalotermitidae in less rigorous climates appear generally less interested in the living tissues, though they limit the volume of the nest system by sealing off the older galleries with dumps of excreta pellets (Plate 1).

The Hodotermitidae, or harvester termites, are also a primitive family but they have become adapted to life in dry grassland areas where trees are few. They make their nests below ground in a series of large chambers with intercommunicating galleries. *Hodotermes mossambicus* has been studied in detail by Coaton (1958) in South Africa, and a diagrammatic representation of one of the nests is shown in Fig. 10. A new principle is introduced by the harvester termites in having well-defined, fixed nest sites from which the workers set out to forage for food for the community. The nests are situated deep enough in the ground to avoid extreme temperatures, those of the desert-dwelling *Anacanthotermes* going to considerable depths.

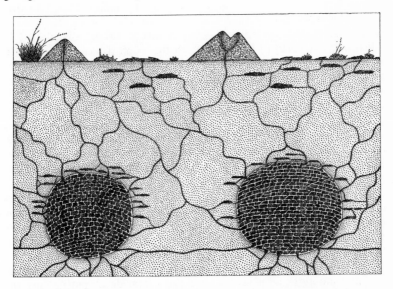

FIG. 10

The nest system of *Hodotermes mossambicus* showing the interrelationship of hives, soil dumps, and foraging holes with their storage cavities
(W. G. H. Coaton, 1958)

The Rhinotermitidae, moist-wood termites, show further developments in the organisation of their nests. *Reticulitermes* and *Heterotermes* have fixed nest sites in old tree roots, buried logs, or timber that is kept from becoming too dry by a high soil water-table or a leaking water pipe. There may be a series of small chambers connected by galleries, and by tunnels through the soil if they are in separate pieces of wood. Covered runways of carton are built over obstacles to lead the termites to sources of food. When the dimensions of the root permit, a single large chamber may be developed to house the brood, with a sponge-like mass of carton forming small cells and horizontal floors and so increasing greatly the effective area. In the tropical genera *Coptotermes* and *Schedorhinotermes* a preference is seen for dead tree roots or wounds near the collar of standing trees, and these are excavated and filled with thin laminae of carton (Plate 8). Such nests may bulge outwards into the soil and have a protective outer layer of hard ligneous carton. There is a distinct thick-walled queen cell in the nest to house the reproductives, the female becoming less mobile as increased egg-laying extends the abdomen. The dampness which may be found under certain circumstances in timber far removed from contact with the soil, as in dug-out canoes and junks, and in timber buildings, with air-conditioning units allowed to drip down the walls, also provides suitable nest sites for *Coptotermes* in south-east Asia. *Coptotermes acinaciformis* is widely distributed in Australia, but north of latitude 20°, in the tropical heat, it changes its style and produces mounds with an interior nest of honeycomb cells built of carton, and a thick exterior protective covering of soil cemented with carton.

The many diverse subfamilies which make up the Termitidae show a wide variety of detail in their nest construction, depending on the materials available, on adaptations to restricted ecological niches, and on the need for protection from the climate (Plates 16 and 17). The ele-mentary form is represented by a simple chamber, or cluster of cham-bers, excavated in the soil or in part of a large mound occupied by a different kind of termite. The next stage is to enlarge the chamber and partition it into floors or cells with clay, or carton excreted by the workers. The provision of an outer protective envelope of carton or clay enables the nest to be sited on the surface of the ground as a mound, or be attached to the trunk or limbs of a tree. It is believed that all new communities of Termitidae start their existence in cavities below ground, and that mounds and arboreal nests are a later development once the population is adequate for the move.

Amitermes, *Microcerotermes* and associated genera feed on wood and dried vegetation. Their excreta is largely of lignin, cellulose and other vegetable residues and dried to form a carton material with which a cellular nest structure is constructed. Soil is added to this carton to make the outer layer when the nest is sited in a mound. The queen cell is thick-walled, and made of the same carton material as the rest of the nest (Plate 14).

The subfamily Termitinae, with *Cubitermes*, *Termes*, *Capritermes* and many smaller genera, is made up of soil-feeding termites, which derive some, if not all, of their nourishment from the digestion of topsoil con-taining much humus. Their excreta is a more or less homogeneous mix-ture of fine clay and a little vegetable matter, in a plastic condition suit-able for moulding into thin-walled cells or shallow floors supported on pillars. The outer walls of mounds, both freestanding and attached to tree trunks, are strengthened by the addition of sand. Individual colonies in this subfamily are not among the most populous and their construc-tions generally can be classed as 'small mounds' (Plates 9, 10 and 11).

Nasutitermes and allied genera have a nest similar to *Amitermes* in its cellular structure. While it is usually made of carton, in some cases considerable amounts of clay may be used and the superficial appearance is like that of *Cubitermes*. The Far-Eastern species and those of the American tropics are predominantly tree-nesting, while in Africa and Australia they mostly live in mounds, the outer walls of which are of earth (Colour Plates V and VI).

Finally there are the Macrotermitinae, which differ from other termites in building with sand and clay mixed with saliva. Their possession of fungus combs, essential as a link in the utilization of wood as food and used too as nurseries, entails the construction of large chambers. These are grouped round a substantial queen cell (Plate 18). In addition to a maze of passages leading to the fungus gardens, there are wide vertical chimneys whose precise function is not fully established but which certainly serve in emergencies, or during periods of intense building activities, to facilitate the rapid deployment of large numbers of soil-carrying workers to the outer walls. *Microtermes* and other small species have a somewhat diffuse pattern of chambers below ground. *Odontotermes* has a more compact layout around the queen cell, and several vertical shafts linked with the communicating passages and leading to, or just short of, the surface of the ground. These shafts are opened at swarming time, usually after building them into short turrets. In a number of species these turrets get washed down during the rains and gradually accumulate to form a hummock of soil over the site of the subterranean nest (Plate 19). In *Macrotermes* the nest or hive is most compact, and in most cases situated above the level of the ground in a distinctive mound. Below the hive is a complex pattern of corridors leading away into the surrounding country, and through which the workers travel in search of wood for food and soil for building material. *Macrotermes bellicosus* develops a cellar-like space below the entire hive, the base of which is supported on wide columns (Plate 26). *M. subhyalinus* on the other hand builds the hive around one or more vertical shafts, according to circumstances (Fig. 11). The thick outer walls of the hive are pierced with a number of galleries of moderate diameter.

The nest of a healthy termite community is not static, but constantly being renewed, enlarged or even being moved to suit the season. The interior is maintained at a high relative humidity, over 90 per cent as a rule, and the walls are in consequence fairly plastic and workable; not hard as in museum specimens. The thick-walled queen cell can be enlarged without difficulty, or opened up rapidly should it become necessary to move the queen. When climatic conditions are too extreme for the termites to maintain the desired temperature and humidity in the mounds they would normally inhabit, they may remain permanently in subterranean nests, as does *Macrotermes natalensis* in the high plateau of South Africa, where the winters are cold. In the western part of South Arabia where *Macrotermes subhyalinus* mounds occur in certain flood plains, it was found that these mounds are vacated by the termites during periods of extreme heat and drought; presumably the colonies move down into the depths of the soil since foraging workers were observed to come to the surface of the ground in the vicinity to collect vegetable debris under cover of their earthen tubes. A similar behaviour is found among some of the small mound termites of the African savannas, including species of *Trinervitermes*, which move down into underground galleries during the dry season, and in so doing avoid the risk of being burnt during the grass fires which precede the arrival of the rains.

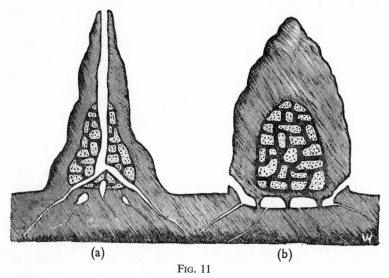

(a)   (b)

Fig. 11

Macrotermes mounds in cross-section, diagrammatic, to show the basic pattern followed by a, *Macrotermes subhyalinus* and b, *M. bellicosus*. The fungus gardens are indicated by stippling

Some termites appear to prefer to make their nests in close association with those of other species. It cannot be said with any degree of certainty that they never build on their own, as the records were all obtained while examining the mounds of other species, while independent nests may well have escaped notice underground, with no indication on the surface of their presence. In Africa the genus *Anoplotermes* is commonly found in association with *Cubitermes*. Since *Anoplotermes* has no soldiers it is easy to fail to recognize the workers in the confusion following the breaking open of a *Cubitermes* mound. As a result the winged adults of *Anoplotermes* have been mistaken for those of *Cubitermes* by more than one author. The walls of the larger mounds offer accommodation for numerous subterranean-nesting Termitinae and Amitermitinae. In one case the large *Pseudacanthotermes spiniger* was found occupying the walls of a still-active mound of *Macrotermes bellicosus*, and had caused the latter to seal off the hive in an unusual way (Plate 27). Abandoned mounds are not infrequently taken over by various ground-dwelling species, which sometimes are credited with architectural powers far beyond their true capabilities. It is not always wise to assume that the species in residence was the original builder of a mound.

Termite Architecture

The term architecture is used here for the outward and visible form of nest structure. It is an advanced expression of social activity which is found, with one exception, only in the more highly developed family Termitidae. Mounds and arboreal nests of diverse forms are conspicuous in many localities, becoming essential parts of some types of landscape. By their influence on the soil some mounds may be said to be a controlling factor in the development of certain types of vegetation, though this is secondary to any plans which the termites themselves may have.

Termite mounds vary in size and shape according to the species of their builders, but their uniformity throughout a stable environment, even though this may continue for several hundred miles, is striking. Such constancy suggests an equilibrium between two main factors: (1) the design potential of each species; (2) the influence of the environment. When a species is restricted in its distribution to a limited ecological zone there is no variation in the influence of the environment and the ultimate appearance of the mounds is typical of that species. When, however, a species has a wide range over several different ecological zones then differences in mound architecture will be apparent when one zone is compared with another, and such differences may serve as convenient pointers to ecological changes.

The design of a mound, or a nest on a tree, is governed by the basic feeding habits of the species, which, as has been discussed in a previous section, fall into three main groups in influencing the structure of the nest. There are the *wood-feeders* which make their nests in the form of a honeycomb of small cells, whose walls are of carton material derived from partly digested wood, and rich in lignin. When such nests are contained in mounds they are given a protective layer of earth, or earth mixed with carton, shaped to a particular design. When attached to the trunk or branches of a tree these nests are enclosed in an envelope of the same carton material as is used for the cells. Next there are the *soil-feeding termites* which use their copious excreta, composed mainly of fine clay with comminuted vegetable residues, as building material. The nest itself may be a honeycomb of small cells, or a series of horizontal floors supported by pillars, while the outer layer is a more or less solid mass of clay, with the addition of varying amounts of sand on the surface. This highly plastic building material lends itself to a wide range of architectural styles, usually of modest dimensions though not necessarily so. The third group is made up of the *fungus-growing termites* which build with particles of sand cemented with a mortar of fine clay and saliva, and do not use their excreta for this purpose. This last group is found only in Africa and Asia, and their method of construction produces the largest of all termite structures. Mounds almost as large, however, are built by one or two representatives of the other two groups in Australia, *Amitermes* and *Nasutitermes*, and—as the exception already mentioned to the rule that all mounds are built by Termitidae—by *Coptotermes*. In South America the largest mounds to be found there are built either by *Syntermes*, one of the primitive Nasutitermitinae, or by *Anoplotermes*, a somewhat doubtful member of the Amitermitinae.

The effect of the environment can be striking. Lack of trees to support a normally arboreal nesting termite may drive it to building mounds, as happens to *Nasutitermes ephratae*, a Caribbean termite, on the savannas in Trinidad. Cold weather suppresses the normal mound building of *Macrotermes natalensis* on the high plateau of the Transvaal. When a mound-building termite has a wide range, as for example *Macrotermes bellicosus* and *M. subhyalinus* in Africa and *M. gilvus* in south-east Asia, the outward appearance of the mound varies through the interplay of environmental factors, such as the seasonal intensity of rainfall and the proportion of clay in the finer fractions of the subsoil. The internal arrangement of the nest remains fairly constant, and the actual method of building with particles of sand cemented by clay mortar does not change. Given an adequate supply of clay and a low rainfall *Macrotermes subhyalinus* produces a tall, steeple-shaped mound with a narrow base, built round a single central chimney, and reaching a height of 30 feet (9 m) in parts of northern Kenya and the Horn of Africa. With the increased rainfall that produces a dry woodland vegetation, mounds are eroded and there is an accumulation of soil around the base. If shortage of clay leads to the mounds having a more friable texture, the result is the common domed mound of six or seven feet (around 2 m) high, with several pinnacles forming during the period of intense building activity at the beginning of the wet season, only to be washed away before the end of the rains. Broad-based dome mounds usually have more than one vertical shaft or chimney. Some of the different architectural styles of *M. subhyalinus* are shown in Colour Plates III and IV and Plate 17.

Architectural ability of a quite different nature is shown in the African genus *Apicotermes*. Those species occurring in Malawi and Mozambique live as lodgers in the mounds of *Cubitermes*, usually below the active part of the nest, where they construct a thick-walled queen cell of clay surrounded by a number of thin-walled chambers also of clay. Though the *Apicotermes* nest can be distinguished from the work of *Cubitermes* by differences in colour and texture, there does not appear to be any well-defined partition wall between them. In Angola, however, the several species of *Apicotermes* found there live independent lives in nests buried in the soil, each of which is enclosed in a wall of clay ornamented with the most regular pattern of pores and bosses, according to the species, like the pottery of some early culture. The nests are divided inside into a series of horizontal floors, communicating with ramps leading from one to the other. They are described in detail by Desneux (1952). Two types are illustrated in Plates 12 and 13. The problem, already mentioned, of how such uniformity in appearance is achieved by separate colonies of the same species, presents itself with even greater force here, since not only are the worker *Apicotermes* blind like all the other mound builders, but their task is carried out underground. Their skill can only be transmitted by the imagos, who take no part in the building work, and can never have a clear view of what has been achieved.

Covered runways, which are used by practically all but the more primitive termites for reaching food supplies not accessible by tunnels in the ground, are an extension of nest and mound construction. These runways vary in size and material according to the genus of the termites constructing them. There may be some variation within the subfamily as, for example, is shown on Plate 20 where *Odontotermes* and *Allodon-termes* runways occur on the same tree trunk. *Coptotermes* and *Nasutitermes* employ mostly carton material for their runways, while *Macrotermes* and *Odontotermes* build with sand particles and clay moistened with saliva in the same manner as they build their mounds. The function of these runways is protection for the workers from predatory animals, especially ants, but more especially from the desiccating effect of dry warm air on bodies used to the high moisture content of the air in the nest. Covered ways become expanded to form large sheets of earth when *Odontotermes* in particular are scavenging on tree trunks, or any of the Macrotermitinae are feeding on fallen logs, dried leaves and similar debris.

Termitophiles

Within the nest of many kinds of termites there are other insects which appear to be tolerated by their hosts, and which are known collectively as termitophiles. Some are active predators feeding on the termite brood, others are given food in return for secretions, while there are those which act as scavengers. Adaptations to this mode of life take various forms, and such modified insects are not found in other situations. Some pass the whole of their lives within the nest, while others are there either as larvae or as adults. Termitophiles appear to be more common and more varied in tropical rain forest areas than in drier climates.

Beetles of the family Staphylinidae are both numerous and widely distributed as termitophiles. In particular they are associated with the Nasutitermitinae of the New World. The swelling of the abdomen is characteristic, though there is some doubt about its precise function. Some Carabid beetles are termitophiles, showing physogastry in either larval or adult stages, while some larvae are densely covered in hairs, apparently as a protection.

Some Diptera of the family Phoridae occur as termitophiles, while the closely related Termitoxenidae are exclusively so. The adult flies are wingless, and in some cases the swollen abdomen is carried arched over the thorax as in some of the Staphylinid beetles. They are associated in particular with the Macrotermitinae of Africa and Asia (Fig. 12b).

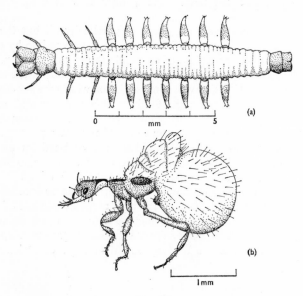

FIG. 12

Termitophiles. a, larva of a moth *Passalactis tentatrix* Meyrick (Tineidae) found with *Schedorhinotermes lamanianus* in eastern Africa. b, a fly, *Termitoxenia hemicyclia* Schmitz from Java (after Schmitz)

V. Nest of *Nasutitermes nigriceps* on a fence, British Honduras

VI. Nest of *Bulbitermes sp.* on a gatepost, Sabah

VII. Woody vegetation developing on *Macrotermes* mounds in grassland, Rwanda, with bare new mound in foreground

VIII. *Macrotermes* mounds selected as sites for tobacco gardens in Malawi

The caterpillars of a small Tineid moth, *Passalactis tentatrix*, are found only in association with *Schedorhinotermes lamanianus* in eastern Africa. They even accompany the workers along the covered runways built up tree trunks to sources of food, and are most active. They have developed large lateral tubercles on the abdominal segments (Fig. 12a).

Also worthy of mention are the Colembola, which are particularly numerous in food-storage chambers. *Calobatinus grassei* rides on the heads of soldiers of *Macrotermes bellicosus* in West Africa and snatches food from the jaws of workers attempting to feed its host. A similar habit is reported from Java in the case of a small Staphylinid beetle.

Some Enemies of Termites

Flying termites are much sought after as food by a wide variety of animals. A swarm emerging is the signal for birds of many kinds, from hawks to swallows and smaller birds, wheeling around the ascending cloud or perching on convenient branches overlooking the emergence holes. Many birds not generally insectivorous join in. On the ground collecting the slow starters, or the parading couples after they have shed their wings, are frogs, toads, lizards and spiders. Flying termites approaching too close to the surface of lakes and rivers are snapped up by crocodiles and fish, as examination of stomach contents shows. In Rhodesia, fishing-tackle makers include among their trout lures an effective representation of *Odontotermes*. Monkeys too enjoy the larger termites, and so does man.

The large populations of termite nests provide food for many animals. The small mounds of *Cubitermes* and *Amitermes* and the tree nests of *Nasutitermes* and *Microcerotermes* are collected by the inhabitants of many countries and given to their domestic fowls. Guinea-fowl, starlings and other birds of the African bush feed on the foraging Harvester Termites, and break open the covered runways of subterranean termites to catch the workers. The long-nosed mammals known as 'ant bears' and 'anteaters' appear to prefer termites as a diet, if not feeding exclusively on them as is the case with the Australian *Echidna* and the African *Orycteropus*. Pangolins, however, seem to prefer ants, but will eat termites if necessary. These larger mammals overturn the smaller mounds, or dig into the earth or the base of a large mound to reach a nest, and even if they fail to devour the whole community they leave the survivors with little or no protection against marauding ants, which finish off the work of destruction.

The continuous conflict between ants and termites is well known. In some cases it appears to be a dispute over territory, but in others, as for example the African driver ant *Dorylus*, raids are carried out and the nest may be occupied as their home by the raiders. The ant does not have it all his own way, since termite soldiers, with their large jaws, are capable of cutting them up. Some of the weak-looking Termitinae are able to snap their slender mandibles with sufficient force to disembowel an ant, while workers can cut off limbs if given an opportunity. Nasute soldier termites have an effective defence against ants in the sticky fluid ejected from their pear-shaped heads.

Termites as Food for Man

In practically all countries where the termites reach an adequate size, the indigenous inhabitants capture the flying forms for food. In places where meat is scarce, termites form a useful source of animal protein. The yield from a single colony of *Macrotermes* is not inconsiderable, one owner of a *M. natalensis* mound in Uganda estimating his annual crop as four sackfuls. Some species are preferred to others. For example, in Uganda *Pseudacanthotermes spiniger*, which emerges during the afternoon, is more popular than *P. militaris* coming out near to sunset. *Macrotermes bellicosus* and *M. natalensis*, both of which fly at night, are collected by attracting them to torches and are offered for sale in marketplaces over much of tropical Africa, as are related species in south-east Asia. Traps for collecting flying termites are varied and ingenious (Plate 24). Some people are able to induce swarming, providing of course that the winged termites are already present in the nest, by means of sprinkling water, playing drums, beating logs to imitate rain, and much singing of suitable songs; one or all of which measures has the desired effect.

An analysis of flying termites, lightly roasted, offered for sale in Leopoldville market in the Congo is given by Tihon (1946) as follows:

Ash	6·42	per cent
Fat	44·40	
Protein	36·00	
Chitin	5·09	
Total dry matter		93·97
Moisture		6·03
		100·00

Calorific value: 560 per hundred grammes

Queen termites, especially the large physogastric types, are eaten as a delicacy, raw and roasted, all over the tropics. They are not common enough to form a regular item of diet, and appear to be prized for supposed attributes other than their food value.

CHAPTER 3

The Classification of Termites

There appear to be few references to termites in classical literature, apart from that of India. The Latin *Tarmes* and *Termes* were used for timber-boring larvae, most probably of beetles. With the rapid development of exploration in the tropics during the seventeenth century, references to termites, their mounds and their destructive potentialities became more frequent. Linnaeus in 1767 used *Termes* as the genus for three wingless insects, two of which proved to be Embiids, while two winged forms which he included in *Hemerobius* (the brown lace-wings) were in fact termites. So far as is known Linnaeus saw no specimens of *Termes*, but relied on Rolander's illustrations of insects seen during a visit to Surinam. The identity of Forskal's *Termes arda destructor* described in 1775 from Egypt and Arabia can only be surmised from his illustration, and De Geer, in 1778, appears to have been the first to produce recognisable descriptions of termites from actual specimens.

Hagen (1858) provided a foundation for our present classification of termites, which he regarded as a family Termitina of the Corrodentia, to which also belong the Embidina. The sixty species known to him were included in four genera, *Calotermes*, *Termopsis*, *Hodotermes* and *Termes*, the first three of which are good 'natural' genera while the last includes the balance.

Desneux (1904), with over 300 species, develops the classification of what had by now come to be recognised as an Order—Isoptera—with a single family, Termitidae, divided into three subfamilies, Mastotermitinae, Calotermitinae and Termitinae. Mastotermitinae were erected on a then recent Australian discovery, *Mastotermes darwiniensis*. Calotermitinae were divided into three 'tribes', Termopsis, Hodotermitini and Calotermitini, while the Termitinae remained an assemblage of six widely divergent subgenera.

At the present time, some 1800 species of termites have been described, and while the adult winged reproductives—the alates—are not known in all cases, it seems desirable that a general classification should be based on these forms alone. So far as the taxa above generic rank are concerned no characters are considered to be of real value which cannot be determined by examination of the types. Six families are here suggested, based on Hagen's four genera, with *Mastotermes* already mentioned, and *Rhinotermes* split off from his *Termes*. But it must be admitted

37

that even thus the family Termitidae remains, as Desneux terms it, an assemblage of divergent forms. In ascribing the names of these higher taxa to a particular author, it must be pointed out that rarely is the original citation accompanied by a diagnosis, which must in consequence be inferred from the genera which that author includes within his group.

Classification

Order		ISOPTERA	Brullé	1832
Family 1		MASTOTERMITIDAE	Silvestri	1908
2		KALOTERMITIDAE	Enderlein	1909
3		TERMOPSIDAE	Karny	1930
	subfamily	Termopsinae	Holmgren	1911
		Porotermitinae	Emerson	1942
		Stolotermitinae	Holmgren	1911
4		HODOTERMITIDAE	Sjöstedt	1925
5		RHINOTERMITIDAE	Light	1921
	subfamily	Psammotermitinae	Holmgren	1911
		Heterotermitinae	Froggatt	1896
		Stylotermitinae	Holmgren	1917
		Coptotermitinae	Holmgren	1909
		Termitogetoninae	Holmgren	1909
		Rhinotermitinae	Froggatt	1891
6		TERMITIDAE	Westwood	1840
	subfamily	Amitermitinae	Kemner	1934
		Termitinae	Sjöstedt	1926
		Macrotermitinae	Kemner	1934
		Nasutitermitinae	Hare	1937

(The South American termite *Serritermes serrifer*, forming the subfamily Serritermitinae, has been variously placed in the Kalotermitidae, Rhinotermitidae and Termitidae, and is not included in the above list.)

Order Isoptera

Insects with mouthparts of the typical biting type, and filiform antennae; with two pairs of membraneous wings which are superposed flat over the back when at rest. Anterior and posterior wings longer than the body, superficially similar with strongly sclerotized anterior veins and no true cross-veins, the venation progressively reduced in the higher forms; in the most primitive family the hindwing has a well-developed anal lobe, in others this lobe is absent but there are differences in the relative position of the anal veins; wings with a humeral suture near the base which permits of shedding; tarsi 4- or, in a few cases, 5-segmented; abdomen with one pair of cerci, usually very short, and with either rudimentary or no external genitalia in both sexes; without metamorphosis, but conspicuously polymorphic, both sexes represented in the several castes. All known species existing only in social units.

Family 1. MASTOTERMITIDAE

This family is represented by a single living species, *Mastotermes darwiniensis* Froggatt from Australia. It occurs only in the tropical north of that continent, in parts of Western Australia, the Northern Territory and Queensland. Fossil termites belonging to this genus are found in Oligocene, Eocene and Miocene formations and include *M. anglicus* and *M. batheri* from the Isle of Wight and *M. bournemouthensis* also from England, several species from Croatia, and one from the U.S.A. Related fossil genera have been recorded from Siberia, Germany and Croatia (Fig. 20.1).

Mastotermes darwiniensis alates are unique among living termites in possessing anal lobes on their hind-wings. Not only does this make them a striking exception to the rule that fore- and hind-wings of the Isoptera are virtually alike, but it provides a link with the cockroach-like common ancestor of termites, cockroaches and mantids, which together form the super-order Blattopteridea. Other primitive features are the possession of five distinct tarsal segments in all the castes, reticulate wing membranes, many-segmented antennae (alates 29–32 segments, soldiers 20–26). The head is broadly rounded, with large protruding eyes, and with large ocelli adjacent to the eyes. The pronotum of the alate is very large, and wider than the head, while in the soldier it is about as wide as the head. Unlike all other termites, the eggs are laid in pods of about twenty, in two regular rows cemented together, similar to those of some cockroaches (Fig. 5).

Despite its many primitive anatomical characters, the social organisation of *M. darwiniensis* is quite highly developed. Communities are estimated to number over one million individuals when fully developed. There is some doubt about the precise status of the 'workers'; by analogy with the Kalotermitidae, which has no worker caste, it has been suggested that *Mastotermes* also has none and that the numerous immature forms are nymphs. Grassé suggests that they are 'pseudergates', i.e. aged nymphs no longer capable of moulting into winged adults and stablised in their condition. Australian writers, however, prefer to regard them as true workers. No mounds are built, the nests being near ground level in hollowed-out old tree stumps, poles or posts. From these nests, the termites journey forth in search of food, if necessary building covered runways of soil to protect themselves when forced out into the open. They are voracious feeders on growing plants and constructional timber, and, less frequently, on a wide variety of materials from billard balls to electric cables and asbestos packing.

Family 2. KALOTERMITIDAE

The Kalotermitidae are dry-wood termites. They are divided into two subfamilies, one of which consists of fossil species, the other of those living today.

The alates have oval heads, with more or less flattened sides, eyes comparatively small, and small ocelli close to the eyes. The mandibles show affinities with those of *Mastotermes* and some cockroaches, though not so pronounced as in the Termopsidae. The left mandible has the apical and two marginal teeth all fairly equal in size, while the right one has the apical and one marginal equally prominent. The wings have a reticulate membrane and the hind-wing differs from the fore-wing in having distinct veins in the anal area. The anterior wing stumps are large and cover those of the hind-wings. The subcostal vein is weak, the radius short and generally unbranched, the radius sector is well developed, and the medius varies in form and position relative to the other veins according to the genus (Figs. 20.2 and 21.1).

The pronotum is broader than the head, flat, somewhat rectangular, with the anterior margin variously concave. The anal cerci, with two segments, appear quite short.

Soldiers all have large heads with strongly developed mandibles. In most genera the head is longer than broad, from flat to moderately deep, but in others the phragmotic type is developed, almost cylindrical and with a sculptured frontal area. Antennae consist of 10 to 19 segments. Functional eyes are not present, though there are frequently relic spots just behind the antennal pits (Figs. 20.1 and 2).

Workers are absent in this family. The communities are small in number and work is done by the nymphs. All species live inside galleries excavated in wood for feeding purposes. Intestinal flagellate protozoa are present.

The classification of the Kalotermitidae was revised by Krishna (1961), dividing the existing species into twenty-one genera, eight of which were new. The main effect has been the breaking up of the large genus *Kalotermes* into a number of smaller genera, with the consequent change of name of a number of economically important dry-wood termites.

The *Kalotermes* group have the medius of the fore-wing midway between radius sector and cubitus, and antennae with 16–19 segments. Soldiers have relatively large, somewhat swollen heads, flattened towards the front, and antennae with 13–18 segments. *Kalotermes*, as now defined, is widely distributed with *K. flavicollis* in southern Europe, *K. approximatus* in U.S.A., and *K. insularis* in Australia and New Zealand (Fig. 13). *Incisitermes* is present in all continents except Africa; *Bifiditermes* is absent from the Americas; *Postelectrotermes* is confined to Africa and the Indo-Malayan Region.

Neotermes with medius of fore-wing parallel to and near the radius sector, and equally well chitinised. Soldiers much as in *Kalotermes*. Widely distributed in all tropical areas and part of the subtropics, with dead branches of trees as the main habitat.

Rugitermes with medius of fore-wing united with radius sector almost immediately after the basal suture. Antennae 16–19 segments. Soldiers as in the previous genera. Antennae 13–18 segments. Restricted to Central and South America.

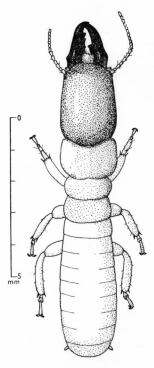

FIG. 13

Soldier of *Kalotermes flavicollis*,
the European dry-wood termite

Cryptotermes, in which the union of medius and radius sector is in the distal half of the wing. Wings iridescent. Antennae 14–16 segments. Soldiers with phragmotic heads. Occurs throughout the tropics, a number of species having been spread through the agency of men. Included are some of the most serious pests of building timbers such as *C. brevis*, the West Indian dry-wood termite, *C. domesticus* in Asia and the Pacific, and *C. dudleyi* in Central America, south-east Asia and East Africa (Fig. 14).

Glyptotermes with the medius parallel and near the radius sector, both being without branches; antennae 13 segments. Soldiers with long, narrow heads, flattened; mandibles relatively short; antennae 10–12 segments. Occurs throughout the tropics, and in subtropical parts of Australia, occasionally as pests of trees of economic importance.

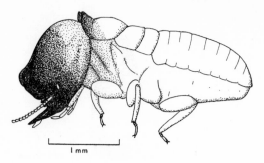

FIG. 14

Cryptotermes havilandi, side view of soldier

Family 3. TERMOPSIDAE

The Termopsidae are damp-wood termites. They are a primitive family; anatomically they show characters more primitive than the preceding Kalotermitidae, while their social organisation is in some cases further advanced. The alates have neither ocelli nor a fontanelle, but like the Rhinotermitidae have a small subsidiary tooth on the distal edge of the first marginal tooth of the right mandible (Fig. 21.3). The pronotum is flat and not so broad as the head, again as in the Rhinotermitidae. On the other hand, the colonies are small in size and there is no worker caste. Intestinal flagellate protozoa are present.

There are three subfamilies recognised at present, the first of which, Termopsinae, differs in a number of ways from the other two—Porotermitinae and Stolotermitinae. All consist of relatively few living genera and species, each with limited and well-defined areas either just inside or well outside the tropics.

Subfamily: Termopsinae

Tarsi appear incompletely 5-segmented when viewed from below, with pulvilli; wing scales all small; cerci long, 4–8 segmented. Soldiers large, robust, with rectangular head and mandibles with distinctive triangular marginal teeth.

Archotermopsis wroughtoni from the Himalayas and Kashmir, where it lives in old stumps of *Pinus*.

Hodotermopsis japonicus from the Ryuku Islands, between Formosa and Japan; *H. sjostedti* from Tonkin is known only from the alates.

Zootermopsis, with three species—*angusticollis*, *laticeps* and *neva-*

densis, occurring in the Rocky Mountains and western coast areas from British Columbia south to Lower California. They live in old stumps, rotting logs and wounds in Douglas fir, Californian redwood, etc. *Z. angusticollis* is transported long distances in low-grade Douglas fir timber (Fig. 15).

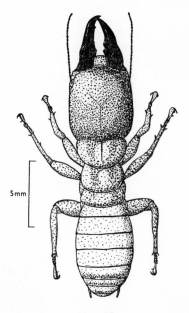

FIG. 15

Soldier of the damp-wood termite,
Zootermopsis angusticollis

Subfamily: Stolotermitinae

Tarsi 4-segmented; scales of fore-wings larger than those of hind-wings; cerci rather long, 4-segmented; abdominal styli present only in the males. Soldiers with longer heads, well rounded behind and markedly flattened; mandibles half the length of the head or more, with well-developed teeth; pronotum approximately square.

The single genus *Stolotermes* is represented by five species from eastern Australia, Tasmania and New Zealand, and one from Cape Province in South Africa. None is of economic importance. They occur in tree stumps and logs, damp and rotting under shade. With the single genus *Porotermes* in the next subfamily, they form an interesting group of relict species now restricted to the more distant parts of the continents of the Southern Hemisphere.

Subfamily: Porotermitinae

Tarsi 4-segmented; cerci 5-segmented; fore-wing scales longer than those of hind-wing; males with well-developed abdominal styli. Soldiers have long rectangular heads, with lightly curved sides; mandibles very stout, about one-third the length of the head.

There is a single genus *Porotermes* with three species, *adamsoni* in south-east Australia and Tasmania, *planiceps* in Cape Province, South Africa, and *quadricollis* in Chile, all of which live in tree stumps and fallen logs, under conditions of high humidity.

P. adamsoni is an important forest pest in New South Wales and Victoria, eating out the heartwood of growing trees, mainly eucalyptus. In South Africa *P. planiceps* has adapted itself to exotic pine stumps and logs. Nothing is recorded of the biology of *P. quadricollis*.

Family 4. HODOTERMITIDAE

The Hodotermitidae are known as Harvester Termites. All castes, including workers, have functional compound eyes, while only rudimentary ocelli are present, if at all. Alates have short conical cerci of 2–5

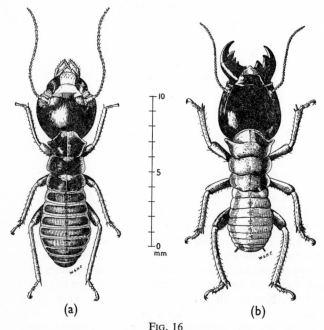

(a)   (b)

FIG. 16

Hodotermes mossambicus, a harvester termite with functional eyes

(a), worker; (b), soldier.   (W.G.H. Coaton, 1946)

segments and minute styli in both sexes. Wings are long and narrow, with the anterior scales never completely overlapping the posterior scales. Pronotum saddle-shaped. Left mandible with apical and first marginal teeth close together, the second marginal absent or much reduced (Fig. 21.2). Soldiers present in two distinct forms, both, like the workers, with large legs. The antennae are long and filamentous, composed of 23–31 segments. Mandibles robust, with large pointed marginal teeth. The soldier pronotum is saddle-shaped with distinct lateral elongations.

There are three genera: *Hodotermes* and *Microhodotermes*, whose alates have lateral tibial spines, and *Anacanthotermes* with none. *Microhodotermes* has definite abdominal styli, which in *Hodotermes* are minute or absent. The soldiers of *Hodotermes* are dark coloured, while those of *Anacanthotermes* are more sand coloured.

Hodotermes mossambicus covers a wide area of arid country from Ethiopia to the Republic of South Africa. *H. erithreensis* has a more limited distribution in Somalia and Eritrea, to the north (Figs. 16 and 22.3).

Microhodotermes viator occurs over most of the Union of South Africa, in areas of moderate to low rainfall. *M. maroccanus* occurs in Morocco and *M. wasmanni* in Tunis.

Anacanthotermes is found throughout a more or less continuous area of arid country stretching from Algeria through Egypt and Arabia to Iraq, Persia, Transcaspia and north-east India, with an additional species in South India. *A. ochraceus* occurs in Africa and Arabia, and penetrates far into the desert. *A. vagans* occurs in Iraq and Persia.

Family 5. RHINOTERMITIDAE

In this family the fontanelle, or opening of the frontal gland, is apparent for the first time, and in the soldier caste becomes highly developed as a defensive organ. The anterior wing scales are small in the subfamily Psammotermitinae and large in the other five subfamilies. Antennae consist of from 14 to 22 segments, and cerci are reduced to 2 segments. Mandibles are of a more primitive type, resembling the Termopsidae in having, on the left, a group of one apical and two marginal teeth, and on the right a small subsidiary tooth at the base of the first marginal. The pronotum is flat. They are all small wood-eating termites, subterranean in habit, characterised by the habit of the soldiers when alarmed of exuding a drop of sticky fluid from the frontal gland; the 'subterranean termites' of American authors.

Subfamily: Psammotermitinae

In the single genus *Psammotermes* there are two distinct castes of soldiers, both with characteristic filiform antennae and mandibles with many marginal teeth. The alates, as mentioned above, have small wing scales, head is broadly oval. Distribution is restricted to Africa and Madagascar (Figs. 20.3–21.4).

Psammotermes hybostoma occurs right around the edges of the Sahara Desert and on either coast of the Red Sea, and *P. allocerus* in South Africa, mainly in the arid western costal area and along the Orange River, where it has been found to damage constructional timbers. *P. voeltzkowi* is recorded from Madacasgar as feeding on dried vegetation and constructional timbers.

Subfamily: Heterotermitinae

Anterior wing scales larger than the posterior; head long oval with flattened sides; antennae in all castes moniliform. Soldiers small in size with long rectangular heads, long labrum with hyaline tip, mandibles sabre-like without marginal teeth, or at most three or four low protuberances, pronotum flat, small with anterior and posterior margins concave. No abdominal cerci.

There are two genera, *Reticulitermes* and *Heterotermes*, both subterranean in habit. *Reticulitermes* is restricted to the northern temperate zone—Europe, North America and Asia. Among the more destructive species, *R. lucifugus* occurs in the Mediterranean area, coming as far north as La Rochelle on the Atlantic coast of France, *R. flavipes* is an important pest of buildings in the United States and *R. speratus* is found in Japan and Korea. *Heterotermes* is found in warmer climates, in North and South America, India, Malaya and Australia and a single species from Ethiopia. Four species in Australia are minor pests of timber. *H. philippensis* from the Philippine Islands has been introduced into Mauritius and Madagascar. Some species are pests of sugar-cane and other crops in the West Indies and Central America (Fig. 22.6).

Subfamily: Stylotermitinae

Alate with circular head, clypeus small and wing scales large. Soldier large and robust, resembling *Kalotermes*. The precise systematic position of this insect is doubtful, the single species, *Stylotermes fletcheri*, coming from South India, where it was burrowing in both rotten and sound wood of a mango tree.

Subfamily: Coptotermitinae

Alate with circular head, small clypeus, and relatively broad pronotum. Soldier with more or less pear-shaped head, narrower towards the front, with large fontanelle, and pointed labrum; mandibles slender, sharp-pointed without marginal teeth (Fig. 17).

One genus, *Coptotermes*, is present throughout the tropics, with forty-five species at present described. It is particularly well represented in the

Australian and Malayan regions. A number of species have been distributed by man, including *C. formosanus* into Hawaii, U.S.A. and South Africa, *C. havilandi* from Malaya into the West Indies and Madagascar. *Coptotermes acinaciformis* is well known in Australia, *C. testaceus* in Central America, and *C. heimi* in India, as serious pests of constructional timber, and in some places, of growing trees.

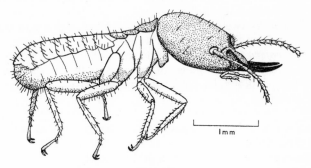

FIG. 17
Soldier of *Coptotermes niger*

Subfamily: Termitogetoninae

Alate with head strongly contracted towards the front; pronotum only half the width of the head, with anterior margin prolonged into a median spine; anterior wing scales large. Soldiers with large head, narrowed in front, labrum long and narrow, mandibles long, smooth with incurved tips.

A single little-known genus with two species *Termitogeton umbilicatus* from Ceylon and *T. planus* from Borneo.

Subfamily: Rhinotermitinae

Alate with circular head and well-developed clypeus, inflated, often elongated, with median groove leading from fontanelle to labrum; pronotum flat; wings distinctly reticulated. Soldiers have elongated labrum with median groove, conspicuous fontanelle, mandibles usually robust, with large marginal teeth. In most genera there are two distinct classes of soldier.

Prorhinotermes: alate with head broadly ovate to circular, inflated, clypeus relatively large or swollen; pronotum a little broader than the head. Soldier with head contricted in front, compound eyes visible, distinct groove from fontanelle forwards, large frontal gland stretching back into the abdomen, mandibles without definite marginal teeth.

There are thirteen species known from islands in the Indian and Pacific

Oceans, and from Formosa, Panama and Florida on continental mainlands. They are usually found in the dead wood of trees.

Parrhinotermes: alate with head almost circular, relatively flat, well-defined frontal groove leading from the fontanelle, labrum short, clypeus short; pronotum narrower than head, flat. Soldiers of one size only, with broad flat head, narrowed towards the front, with long broad labrum, bluntly rounded, and mandibles each with a large leaf-shaped marginal tooth.

Represented by two species from the Malayan region and one from North Queensland, living in rotten wood.

Schedorhinotermes: alate with head circular, clypeus slightly drawn out or markedly arched. Soldiers of two sizes, both with sharp marginal teeth on the mandibles, labrum comparatively broad, with bifurcate tip (Fig. 22.8 and 9).

Thirty-five species from Australia, the Malayan region, Solomon Islands, and tropical Africa. They do much damage to structural timbers, though normally they live in tree stumps and rotting logs.

Rhinotermes: alate with circular head, the clypeus drawn out into distinct 'nose' over the labrum. Soldiers of two sizes, the smaller with smooth mandibles reduced in size, and conspicuous long-drawn-out labrum.

Eight species from Central and South America (including the closely related genera *Dolichorhinotermes* and *Acorhinotermes*).

Family 6. TERMITIDAE

This family includes about four-fifths of all the known species of termites. It is divided into four subfamilies on the customary morphological grounds. The soldiers are diverse in form and offer the easiest characters for identification.

A subfamily Serritermitinae, containing a single species from Brazil, is placed by some authors in this family, while others prefer the Rhinotermitidae.

They are all wood-eating, mainly subterranean or mound builders, but a few make arboreal nests. Fungus combs are found in the nests of the Macrotermitinae.

Subfamily: Amitermitinae

Adult insect head broadly oval, labrum broader than long or equally broad as long, usually without chitinous band, clypeus no longer than half its breadth. Antennae with 11–15 segments. Wings dark, with minute spots or hairs (Figs. 20.4 and 21.5).

Soldiers with oval or rectangular heads, mandibles sabre-shaped, more rarely rod-like, either hook-like with a marginal tooth on each mandible (*Amitermes*, etc.) or more or less serrated (*Microcerotermes*).

Among the twenty genera which make up this subfamily are:

Microcerotermes: A widely distributed genus represented in all parts of the tropics; the soldiers have long rectangular heads generally dark brown in colour, long mandibles with incurved tips, frequently with the inner margins serrated; antennae with 12–15 segments. *M. arboreus* builds dark brown carton nests on tree trunks in South America and the West Indies. *M. edentatus* builds similar tree nests in the tropical African forest zone. *M. parvus* is a small mound-builder in the dry woodlands of Africa from the Sudan and Ghana to Natal. *M. biroi* is common on a large number of islands in Melanesia and Central Polynesia (Fig. 23.2). *M. diversus* occurs in Arabia and Iraq.

Amitermes: A large genus of over sixty species found in most parts of the tropics and subtropics, with a special ability to exist in arid areas. The soldiers have rounded or pear-shaped heads with well-curved mandibles, on each of which is a sharp-pointed median tooth; antennae with 13–17 segments. This is a mound-building genus. *A. meridionalis* constructs the so-called compass mounds in North Australia; wedge-shaped, they reach a height of 12 feet (3·5 m) and have their long axis always running north–south. *A. desertorum* is found in Algeria, *A. wheeleri* in the south-western U.S.A., and Mexico, *A. vilis* in Arabia and Persia. *A. messinae* has a wide range from Aden south to the Limpopo River, in deciduous woodland and acacia scrub (Fig. 23.1).

Globitermes: A small genus similar to *Amitermes*, but differing in the rounder shape of the soldiers' heads. It occurs in Burma and south-east Asia. *G. sulphureus* is commonly found feeding on dead or dying trees in Malaya.

Eremotermes: Another small genus near to *Amitermes*, but the soldiers have a more rectangular head and straighter mandibles. *E. indicatus* occurs in Tunis and Tripoli, *E. sabaeus* in southern Arabia.

Anoplotermes: Adult insect with broad head, usually hairy, with small prominent eyes, and small ocelli some distance away; clypeus swollen; antennae with 15 segments. Meso- and metanota with hind margins more or less deeply notched.

Knowledge of this genus is far from complete, since it has no soldiers, and for this reason is difficult to recognise in the field. It had previously been thought to be mainly South American in distribution, but current work indicates that there are a large number of undescribed species present in Africa south of the Sahara. *Speculitermes* is a closely related genus from South America, with one species present in India, Burma and Ceylon.

Subfamily: Termitinae

This subfamily has been divided into a large number of genera mainly on the great differences to be found in the soldiers. The winged adults are a more homogeneous group and in fact a great number were originally described under the old generic name of *Mirotermes*. The mandibles are characteristic in having apical teeth much larger than the first marginals and separated from them by an unusually long gap. The soldiers fall into two main groups, those with biting mandibles, and those with asymmetrical mandibles used for snapping. They have been divided into thirty-two genera, some of which are monospecific. The Termitinae are humus feeders, many of them consume large quantities of soil which after extracting the humus is excreted and used for building mounds.

Cubitermes: A purely African genus containing many species; the soldiers have relatively large rectangular heads much inflated, and long slender mandibles, straight with incurved tips. The labrum is forked (Fig. 23.4).

Termes: A tropicopolitan genus of small termites whose soldiers have rounded-rectangular heads, inflated, and long fine mandibles with incurved tips; labrum with the front margin cut off straight, or at most lightly rounded, and with projecting corners.

Capritermes: Soldiers with long rectangular heads and conspicuously asymmetrical mandibles. Thirty-two species have been described from India, Malayan region and China.

Pericapritermes: Similar to *Capritermes* with twelve species from Africa (Fig. 23.5).

Neocapritermes: Similar to *Capritermes* with nine species from Central and South America.

Subfamily: Macrotermitinae

Adult forms with the labrum longer than broad, and a chitinous transverse band; mandibles of a fairly uniform pattern, the left with apical and first marginal teeth about equal in size, and second marginal reduced to long blade-like area (Fig. 21.7). Soldiers with sabre-like mandibles, smooth or with a single marginal tooth; pronotum saddle-shaped. So far as is known, all species have fungus combs in their nests, which may be subterranean, or in mounds of great size. Occurs in Africa, India, China and Malayan region. Many are of economic importance.

Acanthotermes is a monospecific genus from the Congo and West African rain forests, with soldiers distinguished by the presence of lateral spines on the meso- and metathorax.

Pseudacanthotermes has two species widely distributed in the woodlands of Africa south of the Sahara down to Rhodesia. In these the prothorax of the soldier has two spines on the anterior margin, but no lateral spines on the meso- and metathorax. Alates are widely sought for food.

Macrotermes includes some of the largest termites. The soldier mandibles are without teeth. The mounds are generally large, conspicuous and of ecological significance. Destruction of timber and dead vegetation may be spectacular if the enormous populations of individual communities are directed towards limited supplies. The darker, more triangular-headed species are confined to African rain forests, while the orange-brown, oval-headed species are more widespread over Africa, south and south-east Asia.

Odontotermes has soldiers with a marginal tooth on the left mandible, and sometimes on the right also. Somewhat smaller than *Macrotermes*, and with little or no mound-building, it has a slightly greater range into southern Africa and China; this genus includes a number of species whose feeding in wood and dead vegetation is of economic importance (Fig. 23.7).

Microtermes soldiers are very small, with smooth mandibles. Most numerous in Africa, it also occurs in India and Malaysia. In Africa it is one of the most widely distributed soil-dwelling termites. Several species damage economic crops (Fig. 23.6).

Ancistrotermes, Allodontermes, Synacanthotermes, Sphaerotermes and *Protermes* are all African in distribution. They resemble *Microtermes* apart from the soldier mandibles, which are more robust and toothed. As individual species they are more restricted than most *Microtermes*, but they form a significant part of the soil fauna of tropical Africa.

Subfamily: Nasutitermitinae

Imago with long narrow labrum, without a transverse chitinous band, mandibles similar to those of the Macrotermitinae (Figs. 20.6 and 21.8). Soldiers with pear-shaped heads and greatly reduced mandibles, apart from some primitive American genera with rectangular heads and sabre-shaped mandibles, but having the fontanelle opening at the end of a distinct frontal tube. Many species construct spherical nests on tree trunks, others build small dome-shaped mounds.

Syntermes and *Cornitermes* are among the five primitive genera in Central and South America, without nasute soldiers (Fig. 23.8).

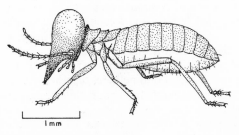

1 mm

FIG. 18

Nasutitermes infuscatus, side view of soldier

Nasutitermes has numerous species in all parts of the tropics, only one size of soldier as a rule, with pear-shaped head straight above in profile, and without distinct constriction when seen from above. The soldier antennae are of normal length (Figs. 18, 23.9).

Bulbitermes is distinguished from *Nasutitermes* by the soldier head being constricted behind the antennae. This genus occurs in the Malayan Region.

Trinervitermes is found in Africa and to a lesser extent in India. There are two sizes of soldier.

Grallatotermes and *Lacessititermes* are Indian and Malayan genera with two sizes of dark-headed soldiers. The dark colouration, long legs and long antennae of these insects give them a very ant-like appearance.

Geographical Distribution

Generally speaking the number of different kinds of termites present in any locality is greatest in tropical rain forests, but the general level of their activity appears to be highest in deciduous woodlands and the so-called 'cultivation steppes' where man has farmed. Both the number of species and of individual termites present fall rapidly outside the tropics, or where the elevation of the land leads to low minimum temperatures. Some primitive forms, however, live on as relics in what are now cold situations, such as *Archotermopsis wroughtoni* high up in the Himalayas, *Zootermopsis angusticollis* and *Z. nevadensis* in the American Rockies as far north as Vancouver, and the genus *Porotermes* with three species in the tips of continents in the Southern Hemisphere, in Chile, in Cape Province, and in Tasmania and south-eastern Australia. In the northern temperate zone generally, the genus *Reticulitermes* has adapted itself to cold winters alternating with hot summers, and where these conditions prevail is noticeable as a pest (Fig. 19).

The part that water has played as a barrier to the spread of termites through the ages is obscured by the rise and fall of land bridges, by the increasing immobility of communities as the higher termites developed more complex social systems and forsook rotting logs as a habitat, and finally by man's recent appearance as a factor in insect distribution. The spread of termites by man is discussed below.

The general composition of the termite fauna of the main geographical areas is given in broad outline here, together with a list of publications which may be consulted for such details of particular localities as are available.

EUROPE. There are two inconspicuous termites native to southern Europe: *Kalotermes flavicollis*, the yellow-necked, dry-wood termite, and *Reticulitermes lucifugus*, a small moist-wood species. The latter has

53

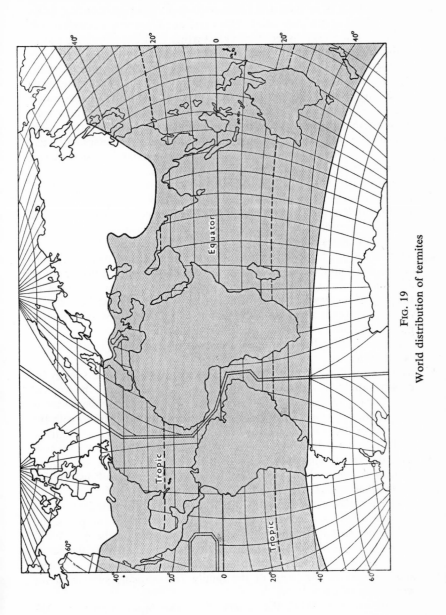

Fig. 19

World distribution of termites

a more northerly distribution, reaching La Rochelle on the warm Atlantic coast of France, and Dnepropetrovsk, some one hundred miles north of the Black Sea coast. However, an American *Reticulitermes, R. flavipes*, has established itself even further north in Hamburg and in Hallein, near Salzburg.

NORTH AFRICA and THE MIDDLE EAST. In the Mediterranean basin, *K. flavicollis* and *R. flavipes* are found from Tunis to Turkey, but with increasingly arid conditions away from the coast there appear specialised sand-dwelling termites, notably *Anacanthotermes ochraceus* and *Psammotermes hybostoma*. East of the Red Sea and the Dead Sea rift valley, *Anacanthotermes vagans* appears, while *Amitermes vilis* replaces *Reticulitermes lucifugus*. Species of *Microcerotermes* appear in the northern Saharan oases, in Saudi Arabia, Iraq and Persia.

TEMPERATE ASIA. Northern China and Japan share three species of *Reticulitermes*. A dry-wood termite *Glyptotermes satsumensis* occurs in Japan. *Coptotermes formosanus* spreads further north into China than one would expect from the distribution of this genus in other parts of the world. It reaches the provinces of Fukien, Chekiang and Kiangsu.

NORTH AMERICA. Two species of *Reticulitermes* and two of *Zootermopsis* are found as far north as the Canadian border. Further south additional species of *Reticulitermes* appear with dry-wood termites of the genus *Kalotermes*, and in the desert lands *Amitermes* and *Gnathamitermes*. In Texas there are representatives of more typically tropical genera in *Tenuirostritermes*. Apart from the damage they cause, there are few visible indications of the presence of termites in most parts of North America.

AFRICA SOUTH OF THE SAHARA. The number of termite species increases rapidly as one moves from the arid Sahara towards the tropical rain forest. The peak of visible termite activity is reached in the savannas and deciduous woodlands which cover a large part of Africa, with the mounds of *Macrotermes*, *Cubitermes*, *Nasutitermes* and their relatives. In 1926 Sjöstedt listed 416 species of African termites, but many have been described since then. Some of them, as *Macrotermes subhyalinus* and *Odontotermes badius* for example, have a wide range of distribution while others are restricted to localised habitats.

The temperate southern tip of the continent has a limited fauna. *Microhodotermes*, a harvester termite, occurs in the more arid parts, and *Amitermes hastatus* builds small stone-like mounds on the grasslands. There is no equivalent to *Reticulitermes* of the northern temperate countries. Two primitive damp-wood termites, *Stolotermes africanus* and *Porotermes planiceps*, of the family *Termopsidae*, survive in the woodlands of Cape Province.

TROPICAL ASIA. While the variety of termites is much greater in the southern part of the Indian subcontinent, the general distribution of the fungus-growing species, *Macrotermes, Odontotermes* and *Microtermes*, gives the order an economic significance over the whole area. *Archotermopsis wroughtoni* survives as a relic in the upper slopes of the Himalayas. In southern India and Ceylon dry-wood termites are in great variety, as is the genus *Coptotermes*. Among the Termitinae, the genus *Capritermes* is represented by fourteen species. The subfamily Nasutitermitinae is also well represented.

MALAYA and THE EAST INDIES are rich in termites. *Coptotermes* and *Schedorhinotermes* are numerous on trees and on building timber. Mound-building *Macrotermes* and *Odontotermes* are found as far east as the Celebes. The Nasutitermitinae are probably the dominant group both in numbers and variety. In Malaya, for instance, they provide thirty out of the eighty species of termites listed (Harris, 1957).

INDO-CHINA, SOUTHERN CHINA and FORMOSA show a steady reduction in the number of species as one proceeds northwards. However, *Odontotermes* spreads as far as the Chinese province of Kiangsi, and *Macrotermes* as far as Hong Kong. *Coptotermes formosanus* accompanies these and actually overlaps with the temperate genus *Reticulitermes*.

AUSTRALIA. The tropical north of Australia contains a wide variety of termites, while south in Tasmania the number is reduced to three. Typical of the north is the most primitive in form of all living termites, *Mastotermes darwiniensis*; also *Amitermes meridionalis* which builds the well-known compass or magnetic mounds. In the north too is a great variety of *Nasutitermes, Microcerotermes* and *Amitermes*. The dry-wood *Kalotermes* and *Cryptotermes* are almost as widely distributed as the trees of the genus *Eucalyptus*, which form their principal hosts. *Coptotermes* builds mounds over much of the continent, and like *Nasutitermes*, which is also widely distributed, builds them far larger than related species do in other parts of the world.

Australian termites are remarkable for their unusual behaviour, in comparison with their close relatives elsewhere. In the absence of the fungus-growing genera *Macrotermes* and *Odontotermes*, which are the dominant mound-builders in Africa and Asia, *Amitermes* and *Coptotermes* become large mound-builders to fill that particular ecological niche.

NEW ZEALAND had only two species of termites, belonging to the primitive genera *Kalotermes* and *Stolotermes*, until further *Kalotermes* and three *Coptotermes* were introduced from Australia in commercial timber.

TROPICAL AMERICA. In a varied termite fauna in tropical America the subfamily Nasutitermitinae, with nasute soldiers, appears to be dominant. Of the eighty-one species recorded from Guyana, thirty-six belong to this group. Not only are they conspicuous for their arboreal nests, or 'nigger heads', but four genera in South America—*Cornitermes, Syntermes, Armitermes* and *Nasutitermes*—build mounds from one to six feet (0·3 to 1·8 m) high on the grassy savannas. *Anoplotermes*, a genus without soldiers also occurring in Africa, builds cylindrical mounds to a height of nine feet (3 m) in the Matto Grosso area of Brazil.

Though *Heterotermes* and *Coptotermes* have few species here they are numerous as individuals and economically important. A variety of dry-wood termites also occurs, mainly in coastal areas.

In the southern part of the continent beyond the Tropic of Capricorn survives the primitive *Porotermes quadricollis*, a genus already noted in the southern parts of Australia and South Africa.

THE SPREAD OF TERMITES BY MAN

There is abundant evidence that certain species of termites have been, and continue to be, distributed unwittingly by man. They are transported in lumber, in timber crates and cases for merchandise, in manufacturered articles such as furniture, in ships' dunnage and in the actual timbers of small boats. Fortunately the variety of termites which it is possible to spread in this way is limited to two of the six families, the dry-wood Kalotermitidae and the moist-wood Rhinotermitidae, with odd exceptions from other families. The Kalotermitidae are natural travellers, in view of their small communities able to exist within seasoned timber and no external sources of moisture. The Rhinotermitidae need moist surroundings for their nest, and prefer some degree of moisture in the wood they attack, so they are to be found in ship's timbers near the waterline, in dug-out canoes, lighters, barges and naval patrol boats in the tropics. As a rule it is one or other of the species of *Coptotermes* that is so involved. Other potential vehicles are wooden tubs holding plants in soil, and packing-cases which have stood on damp ground prior to shipment. *Zootermopsis angusticollis*, a damp-wood termite of the family Termopsidae, arrives in England occasionally in Douglas fir from the west coast of North America. It should not do so since the wound tissues necessary for its survival ought to be spotted on inspection and the timber rejected prior to export.

It is not easy, as a rule, to decide where were the original homes of some of the now widely distributed termites. The locality from which they were first described is no guide, since they are usually noticed when they cause economic losses, and this is more likely to be in buildings in a new country than in the dead branches of trees in their native habitat. For instance, *Reticulitermes flavipes* was described by Kollar in 1837 from specimens collected in the greenhouses of the Imperial Palace of Schönbrunn, near Vienna. Seven years later it was described under another name in the eastern United States and was ultimately found 'in the wild' all the way from the Canadian border to the Gulf of Mexico. In recent years, *R. flavipes* has again been found in Europe, this time established in old buildings and fences in certain parts of Hamburg. In 1957 *R. flavipes* was found in a factory building at Hallein, in the Salzburg district of Austria. It would be a reasonable assumption that in its native country a termite will be readily found in natural habitats, if not exclusively so, while in its country of adoption it will occur in buildings, bridges, plantations of exotic trees and similar man-made habitats. Seaports on the main shipping routes are likely places for introduced termites to gain a footing.

The following are some of the injurious termites which are believed to have been spread in recent times through man's agency:

Cryptotermes brevis: widely distributed in buildings throughout the Caribbean and tropical South America. In recent times it has been found in Madeira and the Canary Islands, in Gambia, Sierra Leone and Ghana, in the Lower Congo, on Ascension and St. Helena Islands, and on the south-east coast of South Africa (Durban, Port Elizabeth and East London). In the opposite direction, *C. brevis* has been collected on the Hawaiian and Marquesas Islands in the Pacific Ocean.

Cryptotermes domesticus: occurs around the South China Sea, in Formosa, Thailand, Malaya, Indonesia and then in the Solomon Islands, Fiji and Samoa. It has also been recorded in buildings in Panama and Ceylon.

Cryptotermes dudleyi: found in Central America from Panama to Colombia, and in Trinidad. In south-east Asia it is present in the Philippines, in Malaya, Indonesia, New Guinea and also in Northern Australia. More recently it has been recorded from Ceylon, and along the East African coast as a serious pest in buildings from Mogadishu to the Rovuma River.

Cryptotermes havilandi: in eastern Africa from Kenya to Zululand, in dead trees and only rarely in houses. It occurs also in Madagascar. In West Africa it infests buildings from Senegal to the Cameroons. Further afield it is known from Bengal, Trinidad, Guyana and Brazil.

Reticulitermes flavipes: native to the eastern seaboard of North America. Once occurred in greenhouses near Vienna, and in recent times found in Hamburg and the Austrian town of Hallein.

Coptotermes formosanus: widely distributed in China, Formosa and Japan, and now present in Hawaii, South Africa (Simonstown) and a number of the southern states of U.S.A.

Coptotermes havilandi: native to south-east Asia, from Thailand to Java, and introduced into Mauritius, Madagascar, Barbados and Jamaica.

The wide distribution of several species of *Coptotermes* around the shores and islands of the Pacific Ocean is probably due to their ability to survive in floating logs. *Coptotermes truncatus* of Madagascar was found in the damp timbers of a lighter in the harbour of Port Victoria in the Seychelles. Reference has already been made to other species in ship's timbers.

THE IDENTIFICATION OF TERMITES

The identification of termites becomes less difficult as the knowledge of the fauna of a particular area increases, and one knows what to look out for. Characters are present in the alate and soldier castes which facilitate identification to the genus, but specific determination is generally less straightforward and may even be possible in only one of these castes. Workers have few specific characters and, while they may become recognisable on acquaintance, it is difficult to be precise beyond the subfamily level, using the form of the mandibles. Ideally, species of termites are described from all three castes, but this is not always possible.

In a work of this nature space does not permit of keys to genera and species. The following keys are intended to lead to the appropriate families of each of the three castes, and a list is given of some of the faunal lists and keys which have been published and to which reference may be made for further identification. As the key to the workers is based on mandible characters, and as mandibles are similar in workers and alates, the key may be used for reproductives and fifth-stage nymphs in addition to workers.

KEY TO FAMILIES OF ALATE TERMITES

1. Tarsi distinctly 5-segmented, with pulvillus; antennae
   with about 30 segments; hind-wing with anal lobe   MASTOTERMITIDAE
   Tarsi 4-segmented, viewed from above; antennae rarely
   with more than 27 segments; hind-wing without anal
   lobe   2
2. Anterior wing scales large enough to cover the posterior
   scales; wings reticulate   3
   Anterior wing scales short, not reaching to base of pos-
   sterior scales; wings not wholly reticulate   TERMITIDAE
3. Ocelli present   4
   Ocelli absent   5
4. Fontanelle present   RHINOTERMITIDAE
   Fontanelle absent   KALOTERMITIDAE
5. Pronotum saddle-shaped; tarsi definitely 4-segmented   HODOTERMITIDAE
   Pronotum flat; tarsi viewed from below seen to possess
   a rudimentary fifth segment   TERMOPSIDAE

KEY TO FAMILIES OF WORKER TERMITES

1. Right mandible with a subsidiary tooth at base of first
   marginal tooth   2
   Right mandible without subsidiary tooth   3
2. Relatively large insect usually pigmented   TERMOPSIDAE
   Relatively small and white   RHINOTERMITIDAE
3. Eyes present   HODOTERMITIDAE
   Eyes absent   TERMITIDAE

Note. A true worker caste is considered absent in the Mastotermitidae and Kalo-termitidae; the older nymphs can be determined from the key to alate characters (Fig. 21).

KEY TO FAMILIES OF SOLDIER TERMITES

1. Tarsi 5-segmented   MASTOTERMITIDAE
   Tarsi 4-segmented, rarely with a rudimentary fifth segment   2
2. Pigmented eyes and large abdominal cerci   3
   Pigmented eyes and rudimentary abdominal cerci   4
3. Head rounded, generally sub-conical   HODOTERMITIDAE
   Head flattened, more angular   TERMOPSIDAE
4. Fontanelle present   5
   Fontanelle absent   KALOTERMITIDAE
5. Pronotum flat without anterior lobes   RHINOTERMITIDAE
   Pronotum saddle-shaped with anterior lobes   TERMITIDAE

Note. The soldier caste is absent in the genera *Anoplotermes* and *Speculitermes* (Figs. 22 and 23).

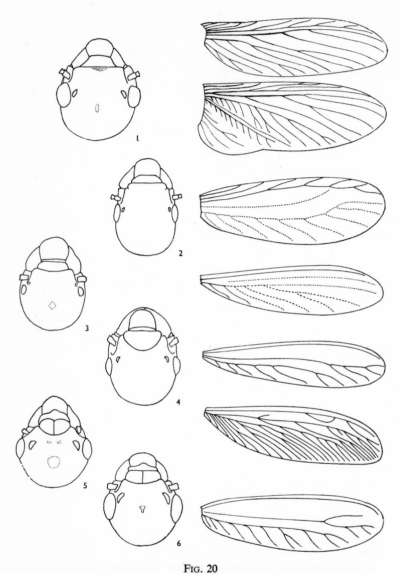

Fig. 20

Imago heads and wings: 1. *Mastotermes darwiniensis*, head, fore- and hind-wing; 2. *Procryptotermes dioscureae*, head and fore-wing; 3. *Psammotermes hybostoma*; 4. *Microcerotermes massaiaticus*; 5. *Odontotermes lacustris* 6. *Grallatotermes africanus*

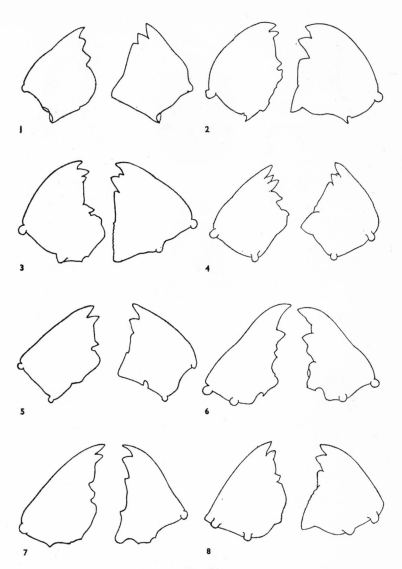

FIG. 21

The mandibles of imago and worker termites: 1. *Kalotermes angulatus*;
2. *Hodotermes erithreensis*; 3. *Zootermopsis angusticollis*; 4. *Psammotermes
hybostoma*; 5. *Microcerotermes nemoralis*; 6. *Cubitermes minitabundus*;
7. *Odontotermes badius*; 8. *Grallatotermes africanus*

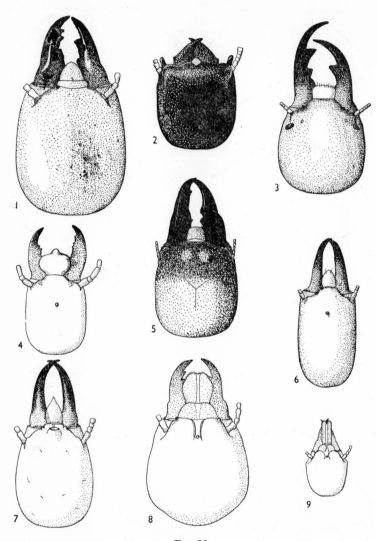

FIG. 22

Soldier heads: 1. *Neotermes sanctae-crucis*; 2. *Cryptotermes domesticus*; 3. *Hodotermes erithreensis*; 4. *Psammotermes hybostoma*; 5. *Zootermopsis angusticollis*; 6. *Reticulitermes lucifugus*; 7. *Coptotermes grandiceps*; 8. *Schedorhinotermes marjoriae* (major); 9. *S. marjoriae* (minor)

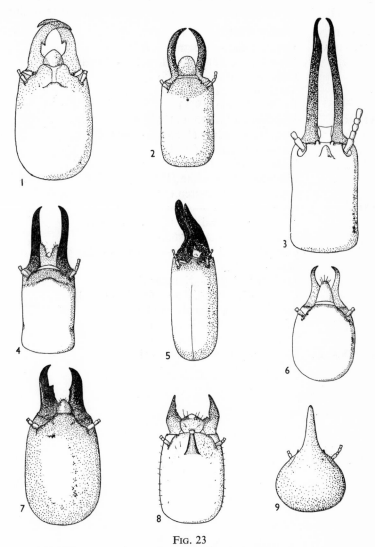

FIG. 23

Soldier heads: 1. *Amitermes messinae*; 2. *Microcerotermes biroi*; 3. *Termes odontomachus*; 4. *Cubitermes minitabundus*; 5. *Pericapritermes dumicola*; 6. *Microtermes luteus*; 7. *Odontotermes montanus*; 8. *Cornitermes silvestri*; 9. *Nasutitermes novarum-hebridarum*

The following are among the faunal lists and keys which may be consulted for details of the species of termites present in particular localities:

WORLD   Snyder (1949)

AMERICA   United States—Weesner (1965)
            West Indies, Bahamas, Bermuda—Snyder (1956)
            Guyana—Emerson (1925)
            South America—Silvestri (1903)
            Brazil—Araujo (1958)

AFRICA   Bouillon and Mathot (1965–66)
            Angola—Weidner (1955 and 1961)
            Congo—Emerson (1928)
            Sudan—Harris (1968b)
            Madagascar—Cachan (1949)
            Seychelles—Holmgren (1910)

ASIA   India and Burma—Ahmad (1958)
            Assam—Roonwal and Chhotani (1962)
            Thailand—Ahmad (1965)
            Cambodia and Vietnam—Harris (1968b)
            Malaya—Harris (1957)
            Java and Celebes—Kemner (1934)
            China—Wu (1935), Tsai and Chen (1964)
            Asiatic Russia—Jacobson (1904)
            Afghanistan—Harris (1967)
            Southern Arabia—Harris (1957)

AUSTRALIA   Ratcliffe, Gay and Greaves (1952).

CHAPTER 4

Termites and the Soil

A great many termites live in the soil in all the warmer parts of the world, some in chambers hidden from view below the surface with little or no indication of their presence, while others build conspicuous mounds rising above the surface, some mounds being only a few centimetres high while others attain a height of 30 feet (9 m). This chapter deals with two questions often asked by agriculturists and ecologists—what do termites do with soil, and what are the results of this activity.

The primitive harvester termites of Africa and the Middle East excavate elaborate nest systems of chambers and communicating galleries without, so far as is known, ingesting any of the soil so removed. They carry it to the surface and form conical dumps of friable earth which are spread around by the weather without forming more than slight humps on the ground to indicate the site of a nest. The smaller genera of the fungus-growing termites—*Microtermes*, *Ancistrotermes* and some *Odontotermes* for example—live underground in diffuse nest systems with little or no indication on the surface apart from the construction, at swarming time, of small funnel-like structures around the emergence holes to serve as launching platforms for the flying adults. Usually these funnels get washed away very quickly, as they are built during the rainy season. The larger fungus-growers—*Macrotermes*, *Pseudacanthotermes*, and some of the larger *Odontotermes*—tend to construct mounds of particular forms as soon as the community is sufficiently large, and according to the suitability of soil and climate. No doubt this habit arose from the necessity of disposing of the soil in the construction of their large, compact nest systems. As the fungus-growing termites do not ingest a noticeable amount of soil during feeding, their constructional work is done with sandy particles carried to the site in the jaws and cemented with a mixture of fine clay and saliva regurgitated from the crop of worker termites.

A second group of termites, principally of the subfamily Termitinae, feed on vegetable residues in the soil, and in the process large quantities of earth pass through their alimentary canal, leaving them with much excretory matter to be disposed of. This they do by constructing small mounds, as in the case of *Cubitermes* and its allies, or by enclosing their subterranean nests in hard envelopes of distinctive pattern, as is found with *Apicotermes*. These mounds are small in comparison with those of

65

the fungus-growers, but, as an exception, the genus *Anoplotermes* builds cylindrical mounds on the savannas of South America which reach a height of 10 feet (3 m). The mounds of the Termitinae indicate the nature of their construction, being typically of a uniform hardness throughout, and with a 'brain case' type of surface suggesting a plastic material squeezed out, in contrast with the flatter, friable surface produced by the sand-and-mortar type of building. Within the mounds are character- istic honeycomblike masses of thin-walled cells, which are enclosed in a thin, hard outer crust of the same material.

A third group of termites feed on woody material with a high propor- tion of ligneous matter, and as only a proportion of the cellulose is digested, these too have available a large quantity of excreta for building purposes. Two subfamilies of the Termitidae belong to this group, the Amitermitinae (*Amitermes*, *Microcerotermes*, etc.) and the Nasutiter- mitinae (*Nasutitermes*, *Syntermes*, etc.) and in Australia the genus *Coptotermes* of the family Rhinotermitidae. The nests are compact masses of small cells constructed of carton—mainly excreted cellulose and lignin with a little soil. When these are above ground they are enclosed in a thick layer of predominantly earthy matter cemented with excreted lignin, and built to distinctive designs. Nests in trees are en- closed in a thin envelope of ligneous matter as are the subterranean ones. It is interesting to note that some species may have nests in all three situations: subterranean, mound and arboreal in one general locality.

With the absence of fungus-growing termites in Australia, large mounds are built there by genera which elsewhere are typical small mound termites, such as *Coptotermes*, *Amitermes* and *Nasutitermes*. For example, *Amitermes meridionalis* builds wedge-shaped mounds up to 12 feet (4 m) high in the Darwin areas of the Northern Territory, with the peculiar characteristic of having the long axis of the wedge always in a north–south direction. (Plates 14 and 15)

It is not known what proportion of the soil used in the outer walls of this third group of mounds is brought up in the jaws of the workers, as in the case of the fungus-growers, or whether it is all excreted on the spot after passing through the alimentary canal. In Australia it has been shown that the organic content of the outer layers is low, while that of the cellular 'hive' is very high. Comparison with the outward appearance of mounds built by the soil-feeding Termitinae suggests that here too the earth used in the outer layers has passed through the alimen- tary canal.

To sum up then, there are three types of termite mounds, on the basis of their effects on soil:

1. Mounds that are built entirely of selected particles of subsoil carried direct to the site and cemented with a mixture of clay and saliva.

2. Mounds constructed entirely of digested soil from which most of the organic matter has been extracted.
3. Mounds of which only the outer layer is mainly of soil, probably digested, and the inner part is of digested woody material.

The Large Mounds of Fungus-growing Termites

Termite mounds which are constructed of earth collected for the purpose, and not in the process of obtaining food, are a feature of the African and Asian tropics, including the islands of the Indian Ocean and the East Indies. In certain well-defined areas these mounds reach a great size, remain for long periods of time after their original builders have gone, and influence greatly the landscape as a whole by providing habitats for vegetation different from that on the surrounding ground. Even the comparatively small mounds of this group may, by their numbers, prove serious obstacles to agricultural and civil engineering projects by impeding the progress of machines for cultivating or grading the soil, for road-building, or for preliminary site clearance before building. The very large domes built by *Macrotermes goliath* are found in a wide belt across tropical Africa south of the Congo rain forest, and the highlands of East Africa, and under optimum conditions reach a diameter of 40 feet (12 m) and a height of 12 feet (4 m) (Plates 24 and 25). The related *Macrotermes subhyalinus*, common from the southern border of the Sahara down to the Orange River, builds smaller mounds in a variety of shapes which, in the semi-arid plains of northern East Africa, rise as steeples as much as 30 feet (9 m) above the ground. Smaller mounds are built by the genus *Odontotermes* in Africa, and these become larger in Ceylon and India where they are principally the work of *O. redemanni* and *O. obesus* respectively. *Macrotermes* mounds appear again in Burma and thence throughout tropical south-east Asia including Indonesia and the Philippines. Referring to *Macrotermes gilvus*, Bathellier writes 'par le nombre, le volume de ses constructions, le roi des termites de la Cochinchine'.

The precise form taken by the large termite mounds in Africa and Asia appears to be determined by three forces—the behaviour of the particular species of termite, the nature of the soil, and the climate. As a result of variations in any of these forces, it follows that the same species of termite may construct mounds of widely differing external form, and also it is not inconceivable that two different species may construct mounds similar in appearance under particularly strong combinations of these forces. So far as the behaviour of the termites is concerned, there must be an urge to construct a mound along particular lines, and not as a fortuitous heap of earth derived from the dumping of soil from the excavations in the ground below. The soil with which these mounds are built is all subsoil, consequently the subsoil and not the surface soil of an area governs the colour and configuration of the prevailing termite mounds. An adequate supply of fine clay particles is necessary for building tall steeples resistant to rain, while sand has to be readily available if construction is to go on quickly during the building season. The climate has pronounced effects on the finished mound. If the weather is so cold as to be near the lower limits of tolerance of the termite concerned, then it is likely that there will be no mound at all above ground level. If, on the other hand, there is a prolonged dry season with high temperatures as in the Aden hinterland, then the termites do not build very tall mounds as they have to maintain subterranean 'summer quarters' into which the whole community may migrate when there is any danger of becoming too dry. Torrential rains tend to wash down the newly constructed turrets and so produce a rounded mound, or a broad-based cone with numerous small pinnacles, unless the earthworks are such that they harden quickly into a waterproof mass. The tallest mounds of all are found in the arid areas of northern Kenya, Somalia and the plains of eastern Ethiopia. The largest domes are found in northern Angola, the Katanga area of the Congo, and parts of Zambia and Malawi. Despite the variations found over the whole range of each widely distributed termite, within any particular area, and for so long as soil and climate remain uniform, the similarity in pattern of the larger mounds is striking (Colour Plates III and IV; Plates 16, 17, 18, 24, 25, 26).

The large earth mounds are built by worker termites which first proceed down into the subsoil and there gather a mouthful of fine clay particles and then a grain of sand which is held in the mandibles. The clay becomes moistened with saliva on the way back to the construction work so that, when the worker termite has placed the sand grain in position, it has ready a blob of mortar with which to fix it. A quick movement with the mandibles, as a bricklayer uses his trowel, and the mortar is smoothed over. Except in the dense mass of clay which is used to form the queen cell, the sand to clay ratio of the mound material is that of the subsoil and does not reflect any selection by the termites. Hesse found this to be so in East Africa, where the sand to clay ratio of tall thin mounds fell between 1 : 1 and 3 : 1, while that of the larger dome-shaped mounds was from 2 : 1 to 18 : 1; in all cases similar to that of the surrounding subsoil.

The essential parts of an earth mound are a thick outer layer of dense soil and an inner 'hive' of chambers and communicating passages arranged around the queen cell. Most of the chambers are filled with the so-called fungus gardens, spongelike masses of chewed wood carpeted with soft fungus mycelium and often spotted with white spheres of fungus conidiophores. According to the species of termite concerned, and to some extent the final shape of the mound, there will be found a system of shafts running vertically through the mound (Fig. 11a).

An earth mound does not develop from small beginnings, in step with the growth of a young termite community. It is not begun until the community is several years old and has built up a considerable population under conditions below ground not unlike those it will occupy when it moves up into a mound. The commencement of a mound is rather the expression of a stage in the maturity of the community. As a result, a new mound will reach from one-third to one-half its final height in the first year, under circumstances favourable to the growth of a more conical type of mound and not subject to much erosion during seasonal heavy rains. Thereafter the increase in size is slower. It would appear that in some species of termites there is a tendency to extend the inner hive to one side and in time to vacate the original site of this inner nest, thus causing the mound to increase its diameter greatly, and so lead to large low dome-shaped mounds. Earth mounds may be abandoned, for one reason or another, by their original builders and later taken over by a quite different species.

In parts of Africa where the land is covered with a thick and featureless blanket of red lateritic earths, prospecting for minerals is difficult owing to the scarcity of outcrops. Geochemical prospecting has been developed in recent years, and analyses of the surface soil for such metals as tungsten, molybdenum and nickel indicate the probability of their being present in the rocks below. The soils of the larger termite mounds, with their high proportion of unweathered subsoil, have been found to be especially suitable for this purpose.

The Question of Lime Accumulation

In 1936 G. Milne, soil chemist at the Amani Research Station in Tanzania, observed the highly calcareous nature of the earth in large termite mounds in Tabora district—where the soil is acidic in nature. Workers in adjacent territories reported similar occurrences, and in 1941 Pendleton described the same thing in Thailand. It had been recognized for some years by builders and road-makers in parts of southern and southwestern Tanzania that some termite mounds contained sufficient nodular limestone to make it worth while extracting this for road surfacing or for lime burning. On the other hand the examination of numbers of mounds over wide areas of East Africa failed to produce indications of lime accumulation in them. It was reported from several parts of the tropics that certain crops grew better on old termite mounds than on the surrounding land, and den-Doop (1938) working with sisal in Java and

Sumatra found that the levelling of mounds and their incorporation with the surrounding soil produced good effects. In parts of Malaya a similar practice of spreading mound soil has a place in local agriculture. Chemical analysis of mound soils in a number of countries has produced conflicting opinions as to their value in increasing available nutrients. In view of the shortage of lime in so many tropical countries, and to the great expense of practically all forms of fertilisers, the desire to exploit the ubiquitous termite mound can well be appreciated. This is the more so where the introduction of mechanical cultivation is impeded by the presence of mounds. In several recent books on geography and tropical soils it has been suggested that all large termite mounds are calcareous, or that they invariably provide soil which is more fertile than that of the surrounding land.

A detailed study of the chemical and physical properties of the soil of mounds built by termites of the genus *Macrotermes* in East Africa was made by Hesse (1955). He studied both inhabited and abandoned mounds of the species *goliath*, *subhyalinus* and *natalensis* as and when they occurred in ten different kinds of soil, with particular attention to the question of lime accumulation. He concludes that such mounds are built of subsoil which is not affected or altered directly in its chemical properties by the termites. The possibilities of alterations in base exchange capacities expressed in this paper have since been negatived by the author. Physical measurements confirm that the mounds are no more than heaps of subsoil with an altered soil structure resulting from the method of mound-building, uninfluenced by the species of termite concerned. Thus in cases where termite mounds are more fertile than the surrounding soil it is because the subsoil is more fertile than the topsoil. When the subsoil is less fertile than the topsoil, then termite mounds are in turn less fertile. With regard to the presence of lime in mounds, Hesse found that in one district this was directly related to the calcareous nature of the subsoil. In six other districts in which he found highly calcarous mounds, no such mounds were in occupation by their original builders, and in sixteen out of twenty instances these calcareous mounds were on or adjacent to seasonally waterlogged ground. In the remaining four cases they were associated with soil of poor drainage. In all areas where these particular conditions did not occur, there was no indication of lime accumulation in mounds. Hesse also shows that the fungus comb found in the inner nest of all these *Macrotermes* cannot be regarded as a potential source of lime even when the long life of a termite community is considered. He suggests as a likely reason for lime accumulation the periodical inundation of the mound with calcium-charged ground water; the tunnels and passages and general elevation of the mound providing a site for greatly increased evaporative capacity compared with the surrounding land, particularly if this surrounding land is apt to become waterlogged, all of which goes to show that the presence of lime-rich termite mounds is, at least in East Africa where the question has been much discussed, a purely local and inconsiderable phenomenon.

LATERITE FORMATION

Over large areas of Africa and southern Asia beds of hard ferruginous concretionary rock occur, either exposed on the surface or as a horizon below laterite soils and murram. It has been suggested that in parts of West Africa and the Congo the occurrence of this formation is the result of termite activity and Erhart (1951) proposes the term 'cuirasses termitiques'. The vacuolar structure of this 'bog ironstone', as it is sometimes called, resembles to some extent the interior of small mounds constructed by *Cubitermes, Nasutitermes* and their related genera. Erhart suggests that during more or less remote periods of the Quaternary epoch considerable changes took place on the earth's surface, during which the thin covering of decomposed rock with very large numbers of termite mounds was displaced into ancient valleys and peneplains. Subsequent fossilisation changed the termite mounds into the laterite blocks we now know.

Observations made in Trinidad by Griffith (1953) on soil horizons containing 'ironstone' fragments similar to those seen in Uganda suggest a progressive development of more or less continuous vesicular pavements without any termite activity. More recently, Sillans (1959) has given a detailed account of laterite crusts in Oubangi-Chari and, after discussing various theories regarding their formation, concludes that man and his domestic animals are a likely predisposing cause through the soil erosion they set in train.

The Fertility of Termite Soils

It is the general practice of fungus-growing termites, whether or not they build mounds, to bring up large quantities of subsoil for the purpose of constructing their covered ways through which they may travel in safety between nest and food supply and for making earth sheets over wood that is being attacked, so that they may work protected from the hot sun and desiccating air currents. They also use a lot of earth to replace wood removed from inside logs or building timber and so preserve some little strength in the structure until they have completed their task.

The large amount of soil brought to the surface in this way has attracted the attention of many observers since Drummond wrote in 1888: 'Some idea of the extent to which the underlying earth of the tropical forests is thus being brought to the surface will have been gathered from the facts already described; but no one who has not seen it with his own eyes can appreciate the gigantic magnitude of the process. Occasionally one sees a whole trunk or branch, and sometimes almost an entire tree, so swathed in red mud that the bark is almost completely concealed, the tree looking as if it had been taken bodily and dipped in some crystallising solution.'

Drummond suggested that in the tropics the termite plays a part in preserving soil fertility equal to that of the earthworm, as described by Darwin, in temperate countries. Since that time there has been much speculation on this point among agriculturists. Robinson (1958) gives an account of work carried out in coffee-growing areas in Kenya on the chemical characteristics of soil brought to the surface during the feeding operations of the subterranean-nesting *Odontotermes badius*. The growing practice of mulching perennial crops such as coffee, tea and bananas with grass and the apparent increase in termite activity which results therefrom have intensified discussion of the role played by these insects in soil fertility. The activities of *O. badius* in a coffee field are summarised as:

1. Beneficial effect of soil burrows which serve to increase the rate of rainfall infiltration and aeration of both topsoil and subsoil; the larger burrows in the subsoil, after infilling with washed down topsoil, providing favourable routes for axial root growth.

2. Stripping the dead bark of the entire coffee tree without apparent harmful results.

3. Destruction of organic mulch material laid over the soil, with emphasis on Napier grass (*Pennisetum purpureum*) grown specially for this purpose, and whose stalks are hollowed out by the termites and then filled with the remains of their covered ways.

However, analysis failed to show any significant differences between this 'termite soil' and the topsoil in the area, though the differences from the subsoil suggested that 'termite soil' originates in the topsoil and not from lower down. The conclusion arrived at is that this soil, brought up in great quantity during destruction of the mulch, is not a point to be considered against *O. badius* when assessing the pros and cons of its presence in mulched coffee. Since in coffee plantations generally the topsoil may be assumed to be fertile, the fact that termites do not appear to bring up subsoil in quantity is an advantage.

The Influence of Termite Mounds on Vegetation

'Termite savanna' is the term coined by Troll (1936) for vegetation formations in Africa and South America consisting of grasslands and sharply limited islands of woodland based on large termite mounds. In some of his examples from South America, as he points out, the mounds were those of the leaf-cutting ants of the genus *Atta*. These islands of woodland are not concentrations of those trees and shrubs otherwise sparsely distributed over the grasslands, but specialised types comparable with those forming gallery forest along the borders of watercourses. Three of the main factors which contribute to the stability of grassland formations are disturbed by the development of large termite mounds, viz. periodic flooding, fire and nutrient deficiency in the topsoil. The protection which mounds provide to vegetation from waterlogging and grass fires is a matter for direct observation. Soil analyses already discussed above provide the evidence on soil nutrients (Colour Plate VII).

Since *Macrotermes goliath, M. bellicosus, M. natalensis* and *M. subhyalinus*, the main large mound-builders in Africa, do not occur in primary tropical rain forest, the presence of mounds under a closed canopy would indicate its secondary nature on the supposition that more open savanna woodland conditions would be necessary for the mounds to be built. The species of *Macrotermes* which do occur in the tropical rain forests of West Africa and the Congo basin are not given to constructing large mounds. Jones (1956) considers that the numerous uninhabited mounds to be found in forests in Southern Nigeria were formed under climatic conditions quite different from those now prevailing, while Eggeling (1947) has shown how the Budongo Forest in western Uganda is actively spreading over grasslands containing *Macrotermes* mounds.

In the regeneration of vegetation after the passage of man, with his forest clearance, fire, overgrazing and soil exhaustion, the spread of termite mounds with their subsequent development as islands of thicket and woodland plays a useful part. When a mound has become stabilised, either because the original colony has died out or because the mound has grown so large that only a relatively small part is occupied at any one time, a grass cover develops. The wetter the climate, the sooner this initial colonisation appears to take place, due in part to the erosion of the mound by rain into more gentle slopes. Sillans (1959) describes the pure stands of *Pennisetum purpureum* on large mounds in high-rainfall savanna in Oubangi-Chari.

The sequence of vegetation on termite mounds on the Sese Islands in Lake Victoria, Uganda, has been described by Thomas (1941), who found that there the colonising grasses are *Eragrostis blepharoglumis* and *Hyparrhenia diplandra*. These are followed in succession by such shrubs as *Volkensia duemmeri* and *Harungana madagascarensis* with, in time, an undergrowth of *Renealmia* sp. and *Afromomum* sp., and finally tall trees, mainly *Maesopsis eminii* with *Sapium ellipticum* and *Vitex keniensis*. Where favourable conditions permit, these islands of woodland increase in size until they merge with each other and produce a closed canopy forest. Elsewhere in Africa, the spread of woodland, of which 'miombo' is a widespread type dominated by species of *Brachystegia* and *Isoberlinia*, into areas where man has obliterated the original cover is preceded by the development of large termite mounds and their colonisation in a manner parallel to that already described. In these drier areas, however, there is little or no spread outwards from the immediate vicinity of the mounds of this specialised vegetation, which remains in discrete islands in the final woodland formation. Details of the vegetation of termite mounds in 'miombo' and related formations in East Africa are given by Burtt (1942).

One practical outcome of this alteration of the environment by mounds of *Macrotermes* throughout tropical Africa and Asia is to be seen in their utilisation for peasant agriculture. Crops grown on a large scale, such as sisal, cotton and tobacco, indicate by increased growth and intensified green colour the presence of termite mounds even when these have been more or less obliterated by mechanical cultivation. Their difference from the surrounding flat land is emphasised most by the peasant who cultivates only the top and sides of a mound and leaves the surrounding grass untouched. Pendleton (1941) describes in detail the agricultural significance of termite mounds in Thailand. Examples from Africa are numerous as is the variety of both food and cash crops grown under these conditions. Peasant tobacco growing on *Macrotermes* mounds in Malawi is illustrated here (Colour Plate VIII).

Mounds of Non-fungus-growing Termites

To have called this group 'small-mound termites', as distinct from the large mounds of the fungus-growing Macrotermitinae, would have been to ignore the impressive mounds in tropical Australia built by *Amitermes meridionalis*, and the quite sizeable constructions of *Coptotermes*, *Amitermes* and *Nasutitermes* in many parts of that continent. On the whole, however, the term would not have been inappropriate over the remainder of the tropics.

The mounds of *Cubitermes* and other members of the Termitinae do not differ greatly from the surrounding soil on analysis. In the process of digestion only vegetable matter is removed. As the coarser particles of soil will be avoided by the worker termite when feeding, the clay fraction of the mound material is higher than in the soil generally.

The mounds of the Amitermitinae and Nasutitermitinae consist of an earthy outer wall with the inner living-quarters constructed of a brittle carton material, the residues of digested plant matter. Analytical data are few and the following are derived from the work of Holdaway (1933) on the mounds of *Nasutitermes exitiosus* in Australia. The mounds

9. Mound of *Cubitermes testaceus*, Uganda

10. Mounds of *Cubitermes sp.* in grassland, eastern Nigeria

11. *Cubitermes* mounds in mountain grassland, in the Kenya Highlands at Equator. *Anoplotermes* nests occur frequently in these mounds

12. Nest of *Apicotermes gurgulifex* from Angola (type colony)
(British Museum, Nat. Hist.)

13. Nest of *Apicotermes arquieri* from northern Nigeria, in vertical section

14 and 15. *Amitermes meridionalis*, the compass termites of north Australia. The long axis of the mound is invariably north–south

16. Mound of *Macrotermes natalensis* in sweet potato garden, Uganda, showing the openings to the "cellar" near ground-level

17. Mound of *Macrotermes bellicosus* in the highlands of Rwanda, showing the influence of climate in reducing external features

18. Queen cell of *Macrotermes*

were on average 3½ feet (115 cm) in diameter at the base and from 1½ to 2 feet (45 to 60 cm) high and, when cut open, showed three distinct regions—an outer wall about 3 inches (8 cm) thick of predominantly earth material, an inner wall of 5 to 6 inches (13 to 15 cm) noticeably more tough and woody, and finally, the inhabited portion consisting of thin-walled cells. Analyses of five mounds resulted as follows:

Region	Inorganic matter %	Organic matter %	Nitrogen %	Carbon %
Outer wall	52–81	19–47	0·13–0·35	7–25
Inner wall	8–20	79–91	0·49–0·69	43–47
Central part	6–14	86–94	0·58–0·75	47–53

More detailed analysis of one of the mounds showed that in the three regions cellulose formed 5, 7 and 8·5 per cent of the combustible matter, and lignin 24, 30 and 31·5 per cent respectively. The conclusion was drawn that the presence of cellulose in a more or less uniform proportion to lignin in all parts of the mound indicated that a proportion of the cellulose was generally left undigested to pass out with the lignin as excreta. In addition, since constructional work was observed to be carried out from the inside, it is suggested that the slightly higher lignin-cellulose ratio of the outermost layer is the result of further digestion when the material of the inside of the mound is eaten again to provide suitable building material.

The use of *Cubitermes* mounds for surfacing earth roads was general over large tracts of Africa where gravel was unobtainable, which suggests that such mounds would not improve agricultural land if put there in quantity. On the other hand, the additional nitrogen content of *Nasutitermes* and *Amitermes* mounds might outweigh the disadvantages of adding additional fine clay. Large numbers of small mounds are generally indicative of poor depth of soil, or low fertility, or both. The rate at which the associated termites destroy the natural mulch of dead vegetation appears to outweigh any advantage arising from the natural break-up of old mounds.

The Destruction of Termite Mounds

Termite mounds are not infrequently obstructions to mechanised agriculture, to the construction of railways, roads and other civil engineering projects and to the safety of aeroplanes on grass landing-strips. In addition their removal, or at least the destruction of the community within, may be desirable for the protection of buildings and crops. To level off a mound with a bulldozer, or in the case of a small one to break it up with a harrow or a heavy roller, does not necessarily destroy the termite colony, for a small nucleus of survivors below ground level may ultimately cause the mound to rise again. To be quite certain, the mechanical treatment is preferably supplemented with insecticide.

Insecticidal treatment to kill off a termite colony requires some knowledge of mound architecture, particularly when dealing with fungus-growing termites with their distinctive systems of wide passages within their mounds. It is essential to avoid dissipating the insecticide in the thick outer wall where there are no termites, so holes bored must reach into the central 'hive' and chemicals introduced through pipes—flexible plastic tubing being suitable for the purpose. Both liquid and gaseous insecticides may be wasted, however, if the hole ends in a broad shaft or the basement-like chamber usual in mounds of *Macrotermes natalensis*, since the termites are able to seal the narrow galleries leading from these into the living quarters at the first sign of danger.

For many years mound-building and subterranean nests of the fungus-growing termites in Africa and Asia have been eradicated by means of toxic smokes generated by pumping air over a sealed brazier in which a mixture of sulphur and arsenious oxide is fed to the glowing charcoal. Neat serviceable apparatus is obtainable for this purpose. Results obtained, in terms of the number of nests showing activity within a year of treatment, have varied greatly in different countries, no doubt according the skill and intelligence of the individual operator as well as to variations in the structure of the nests in different termite species. From a quarter to half an hour of constant pumping is necessary to ensure that the gas has penetrated an adequate proportion of the chambers and galleries, and deposited on the walls sufficient arsenic to kill passing worker termites who may have sheltered in safety. This and many other fumigants have an adverse effect on the fungus of the combs and so contribute to the weakening of the colony.

Benzene hexachloride having proved to be an effective insecticide against termites, Coaton (1947) devised an apparatus for burning BHC smoke generators in a pressure cylinder and leading the gas produced into termite nests. This proved both rapid and effective, but the cost of the smoke generator was too high for the method to be economic in general use.

The chlorinated hydrocarbon insecticides, benzene hexachloride, aldrin, dieldrin, chlordane and the like, in the form of water-miscible emulsions are proving effective for nest destruction. W. A. Sands (1962) has found the following procedure gives good results with the mounds of *Macrotermes bellicosus* in Northern Nigeria. A drilling tool was made by welding a $1\frac{1}{2}$-inch (4 cm) screw augur to a steel rod 4 feet (120 cm) long, and this was capable of making a hole through the hard outer covering of the mound through to the central hive. Three holes are enough for a normal mound 7 to 8 feet tall (2 to 2·5 m) (Plate 28) if well spaced. A length of plastic pipe is inserted in order that no solution is absorbed by the outer layer and wasted, and through this is poured 2 gallons (9 litres) of insecticide. The total of 6 gallons (27 litres) of solution needed for a mound is prepared by diluting $2\frac{1}{2}$ fluid ounces (70 cc) of Aldrin 40 per cent emulsifiable concentrate with water.

Petrol, carbon bisulphide and D-D soil fumigant (Shell) are among the other substances used to treat the nests of termites. They are, perhaps, best suited for emergencies, such as the control of small mounds on airstrips, or the subterranean *Odontotermes* that make funnel-like openings on the surface of farm roads and irrigation works. Care must be taken in handling these inflammable or corrosive substances. They have an advantage, however, in the small amounts required.

The removal of large termite mounds is a civil engineering problem, particularly in a broad band across Africa from Angola to Mozambique, where *Macrotermes goliath* flourishes. Photographs have been published of railway cuttings made through the middle of such mounds in the Congo. The more widely distributed species, *M. bellicosus*, *M. subhyalinus* and *M. natalensis* in Africa south of the Sahara and *M. gilvus* in south-east Asia, though they do not make such large mounds, nevertheless offer formidable obstacles to mechanized agriculture. They require to be removed in most cases before full use can be made of tractor-drawn ploughs and cultivators. Estimates of the number of *subhyalinus* mounds per acre in areas in Uganda, western Tanzania and Zambia were between $1\frac{1}{2}$ and 2. When preparing a large area of dry woodland in western Tanzania for the mechanical cultivation of groundnuts, it was found that it cost as much to level off the mounds as it had done to clear the bush, thus doubling the estimated cost of opening up the land, as the mounds had not been taken into account in the first case. The method devised for dealing with the mounds was simple. Mechanical soil augurs mounted on trucks were used to bore three holes around the lower part of each mound, and gelignite charges were introduced of such strength that on detonation the mound was not hurled bodily into the air, leaving a crater, but was shaken just enough for a bulldozer to be able to spread the soil around. The use of explosives has the additional advantage, it would appear, of killing all the occupants of the nest. If a mound is bull-dozed or hand-dug, the site should be sprayed with insecticide in order to eradicate the remnants of the colony as they come up from below to build again.

The question of queen removal as a means of destroying a colony has already been mentioned. Suffice it to repeat that the method is by no means as effective as it would at first appear, owing to the ability of termite communities to develop new substitute queens under favourable circumstances.

CHAPTER 5

Termites Injurious to Agriculture

The amount of damage that termites do to growing crops in the tropics is surprisingly small when one considers their ubiquity. In many cases such damage passes unnoticed since the amount of crop lost before the farmer begins to worry depends to a large extent on the general level of agricultural development in a particular area. Correct diagnosis is not always easy in agricultural problems and the termite may well be underestimated. Wyniger (1962) writes: 'It is well known that these cellulose-feeding insects prefer older plants, or young plants that are sickly or temporarily not thriving and flaccid. Coffee, cocoa, rubber, tea and other trees and shrubs are not attacked by termites even in regions where these insects abound, if they are growing under optimal conditions.' It does happen that economic returns can be obtained from crops not being grown under optimal conditions, particularly if adequate measures of plant protection are employed.

Immediate financial loss is the greatest spur to the adoption of control measures, as, for example in the death of young trees after labour has been expended in clearing the land and raising the seedlings. Next in interest come losses of plantation-grown annual crops, then peasant-grown perennial crops and finally peasant-grown annual cash crops. Locusts are probably the only pest taken seriously by peasant farmers. Harvester termites are common throughout subtropical dry grassland areas where they compete with man's flocks for the sparse grazing. Only in South Africa and Australia are they recognised as pests because they prevent full utilisation of the available grass by stock. Elsewhere the herdsman is content to share the grazing with the termites. Erosion due to overgrazing is the same whether it is caused by too many cattle or too many termites.

The natural habitat of dry-wood termites is the dry dead branches of living trees and in dead standing trees. The genus *Neotermes* has developed a taste for newer wood, thus becoming a pest in a number of cases such as on teak in Java, cocoa in West Africa and tea in Ceylon. Similarly some damp-wood termites of the genus *Coptotermes* have left their rotting logs in forests and woodlands to attack *Hevea* rubber and kapok in Java, *Eucalyptus citriodora* in the Seychelles and citrus in Queensland.

Delays in harvesting groundnuts, sunflower and maize arising from the demands of mechanised agriculture for a single operation, when

78

local conditions tend to produce irregular ripening, give ample opportunity for subterranean termites to cause damage. In Tanzania some years ago the loss of sunflower seeds was as much as 66 per cent, when termites felled green plants as well as those which were more obviously mature, putting the seed heads beyond the reach of the mechanical harvesters. Groundnut pods are liable to superficial damage by subterranean termites once they begin to ripen, and then they split and allow the groundnuts to escape during harvesting. Such losses can be minimized by developing even maturity in the crop.

Turning now from plants which are attacked while growing normally, there is the more prevalent problem of termite damage to plants which are temporarily embarrassed by drought or by some slight injury arising from careless hoeing, bad pruning or high winds. Consider the Englishman's traditional efforts to grow roses wherever he makes his home, the Arab's inclusion of a few coffee bushes in his seaside coconut plantation, or the German planter's collection of conifers—can it always be said that these plants were eaten by termites only because they were already moribund and could not have survived until the end of the dry season?

More indirectly, termites are harmful to growing crops by depriving them of mulches and vegetable residues before these are broken down far enough to be available to the plants. There are many areas where mulching has been demonstrated as a highly desirable practice, but impracticable because the termites eat up the mulching material almost as soon as it is put down. It appears that termite activity is greatest in those soils which would benefit most from liberal additions of plant residues, both as manure and as mulch. Perhaps this is one reason for the necessity for such large quantities of pen manure and compost being used to produce significant improvements in yield and in soil texture in many parts of the tropics.

So far as it has been possible to check the references, and from our experience, the termites dealt with below are either primary pests of the crops concerned, or their occurrence as secondary pests is of such regularity as to be of interest to the grower. Generally speaking only those records are used which give the species of termite involved.

Rubber

In parts of south-east Asia the rubber tree, *Hevea brasiliensis*, is damaged by the termite *Coptotermes curvignathus* to such a degree and with such regularity that there can be little doubt as to its status as a primary pest. In Malaya it was reported as far back as 1906 in an article by H. C. Robinson in the *F.M.S. Museums Journal*, since when much has been written about it. For a number of years it was known under the name of *Termes gestroi*, until the genus was split up, and it was decided that the Malayan species was different from *gestroi* of Burma and north-east India. There has been much speculation about the influence of external conditions on the susceptibility of the rubber tree to *Coptotermes* attack, but it now appears to be agreed that a tree does not necessarily have to be otherwise sick or damaged before termites will start operations. The nature of these operations is described by Beeley (1934) as follows:

'There is ample proof that *C. curvignathus* will attack apparently healthy young rubber trees and, if left undisturbed, can inflict fatal injury within three or four weeks' time. The seat of attack varies considerably and may be at a point a few inches above ground or at any point below ground level. The most usual point of entry is at a fork of the tap-root or near some hollow malformation of the tap-root at about nine inches below soil-level. As the attack is extended upwards above ground level a mud wall or casing is built around the trunk to protect the colony from other insects, birds, and heat. Beneath this mud casing the bark is attacked almost at once at many points, causing exudation of latex which mixes and coagulates with the attached mud, forming a rubbery mass, which can only be cleaned off with some difficulty when treatment is undertaken. Once an entry is gained, the insects commence mining vigorously in the wood of the tap-root, causing numerous long, radially-flattened galleries. These galleries are extensively interconnected and in time so weaken the tree that it is blown over by the slightest wind. In the case of buddings being attacked by white ants the upper limit of the mud wall may not extend beyond the union, the attack being concentrated on the snag.'

In the Malayan jungle *C. curvignathus* feeds on a variety of trees. Nests are not easy to locate as they are in large chambers hollowed out in stumps and tap-roots below ground level. Such chambers are divided up into 'floors' by thin horizontal layers of carton made from chewed and partly digested wood, and of a readily recognisable pattern. One colony of termites may have a number of subsidiary nests connected by galleries underground, and only by finding the queen can one be sure of having reached the primary nest. When the jungle is cleared for planting rubber, termites will remain in trees left for shade and in stumps, unless 'clean clearing' has been undertaken. Similarly when rubber is planted after another tree crop such as kapok, a similar danger exists. Attack is not customary if the land has been under annuals or food crops for a few years. In short the situation is akin to that with *Armillaria* and similar root diseases which spread into plantation crops from old stumps left behind when clearing. Termite attack is accelerated by fungus infection, injuries during weeding and drought, both climatic and physiological due to weed competition.

In Sumatra Dammerman (1913) considered *C. curvignathus* as a serious pest of rubber though later writers suggest that it is not so serious there as in Malaya.

In the Indo-China region serious damage to Hevea plantations is recorded by Bathellier (1927 and 1933) and, in greater detail, by Caresche (1937), who gives the species as *C. curvignathus*. Living trees in the jungle are attacked by the same termite, in particular those of the genera *Shorea* and *Dammara*. In rubber plantations, infested trees are found in groups. Attack is via the tap-root, and is especially severe on grafted trees. As the leaves of infested trees stay green even though much damage has been done to roots and trunk, attention may not be drawn to the attack until the tree is blown over in a storm.

The attack of *Coptotermes ceylonicus* on rubber in Ceylon is not regarded as serious. As in other countries there are many soil-inhabiting termites, particularly *Odontotermes* and *Microtermes*, which will feed on moribund or dead trees, but which are not primary pests.

In Brazil a *Coptotermes* was mentioned by Silvestri (1903) as damaging rubber in the Mato Grosso. Green (1916) states that it is said to attack wood exposed by tapping. Silvestri refers the insect to *C. marabitanas*, but it is now thought to be *C. testaceus*, which occurs also in Chile, Surinam, Venezuela and the West Indies, and which is known to destroy rubber trees weakened by leaf disease in Guyana.

The control of *Coptotermes* attack on rubber by the use of insecticides began with the fumigation of nests with sulphur dioxide. Later this was improved by the addition of arsenic, a mixture of gases being generated by pumping air over an enclosed charcoal burner to which the appropriate substances had been added—commonly a mixture of sulphur and arsenious oxide. Then fumigants such as carbon bisulphide and ortho-dichlorobenzene, and insecticidal dusts including Paris green, calcium arsenate and sodium silicofluoride were all tried in turn with varying degrees of success.

From the Rubber Research Institute (Newsam and Rao, 1958) comes the opinion that the chlorinated hydrocarbons—chlordane, aldrin and dieldrin—provide an economic solution to the termite problem in rubber plantations. At the low dosages necessary the cost of these insecticides allows for the treatment of every individual tree in an infested area, while their persistence in most types of soil provides protection over periods of at least three years. The low toxicity of these insecticides to mammals makes them much safer to handle than those previously used.

Emulsions of the insecticide chosen are diluted with water to a strength as follows:

chlordane	0·0375 per cent
aldrin	0·025 per cent
dieldrin	0·015 per cent

One pint (500 cc) of this is poured round each immature rubber tree, and 2 pints (1 litre) round mature trees because of their increased girth. A shallow channel is excavated around each tree to receive the insecticide, after first removing any earth sheaths or runways sticking to the trunk. Only in exceptional cases has reinfestation taken place within three years.

Cocoa

Indigenous dry-wood termites of the genus *Neotermes* are not uncommon in cocoa trees throughout West Africa; they are not generally regarded as a serious pest but rather as an insect taking advantage of the many opportunities that the cocoa tree provides in the way of dead wood. However, the results of a survey of twenty mature cocoa trees in Western Nigeria carried out by the West African Cocoa Research Institute in 1957 showed that 25 per cent of the areas of dieback and of wood of half an inch or more in diameter were infested by *N. aburiensis*. Damage was often relatively extensive and borings penetrated 6 to 8 inches (15 to 20 cm) into living wood. All colonies appeared to have originated from reproductives that had flown into dead wood. Kay (1960) suggests that some control efforts would appear to be desirable, especially the systematic pruning of all dead branches. On the three islands in the Gulf of Guinea that are important cocoa producers—Fernando Poo, São Thomé and Principe—the related *N. gestri* is considered of great economic importance through its invasion of the tree through inadequately treated wounds (Castel-Branco, 1963). Pairs of winged adults settle down to found new colonies in dead branches and wounds imperfectly calloused and the resultant communities move slowly downwards into the trunk, leaving the weakened branches to break off in storms.

Also in West Africa a number of subterranean termites have been recorded as building their shelter tubes from the ground up cocoa stems in search of wounds and dead wood. In São Thomé *Microcerotermes theobromae* is of some importance as a pest of older trees. On the mainland several species of *Microcerotermes* have been recorded as minor pests, including *M. edentatus* in the Ivory Coast, *M. solidus* in Ghana and, further afield, *M. parvus* in the Congo. *Schedorhinotermes putorius* is a much larger termite which nests at the foot of trees and builds shelter tubes over the trunks in search of wounds, becoming a secondary pest of cocoa. These shelter tubes are built of chewed wood; they have a rough exterior and are much larger than those of *Microcerotermes*. *Coptotermes sjostedti* behaves in a similar manner in the Ivory Coast. In Western Nigeria *Macrotermes subhyalinus* ring-barks seedlings,

19. Craters appearing above a subterranean nest of *Odontotermes badius* at the beginning of the rainy season prior to swarming, Kenya

20. Covered runways built up tree-trunk in Tanzania by related genera; left, *Odontotermes;* right, *Allodontermes*

21. Discarded wings of *Macrotermes subhyalinus* after swarming, Malawi

22. Termites in laboratory cultures; left, *Kalotermes jouteli* in piece of *lignum vitae* for mass rearing; centre, *Zootermopsis* in plate culture for observation; right, *Reticulitermes* in boiling tube with hole in base, method suitable for young colonies of moisture-loving species

23. Temporary trap for flying termites being constructed on mound of *Macrotermes subhyalinus* in Mal

young trees and basal chupons on mature trees, usually just after the rains have begun, and more frequently where coppiced trees have been earthed up, or where debris has been allowed to accumulate around the base of a tree. *Pseudacanthotermes militaris* has been observed behaving in a similar manner, though less frequently. Also in Nigeria an unidentified species of *Microtermes* was recorded as killing 20 per cent of young plants in a nursery by feeding on the roots and girdling the stems (Sands 1960a).

In Madagascar, *Bifiditermes madagascarensis* is the dry-wood termite associated with cocoa. Infestations begin in the usual way through wounds or via the branches of trees not in full vigour, and penetration into the main stem leads to premature death (Cachan, 1949).

Dry-wood termites have been reported as pests in a number of localities in the Pacific. In Samoa *Neotermes sarasini* was found by Damandt (1914) invading cocoa trees at a point below the collar and boring upwards through the heartwood into the branches, a direct reversal of the usual procedure. More recently specimens from that island have been identified as *N. samoanus*. Appreciable damage is done by *N. papua* in New Guinea, where the shade tree *Leucaena glauca* is also attacked (Smee, 1962). Unidentified species of *Neotermes* are reported from New Britain and New Ireland. Also in Samoa a species of *Microcerotermes* has been observed removing dead wood from old cocoa trees.

Tropical America has provided few reports of termite damage to cocoa. A species of *Neotermes* was recorded by Bondar (1939) in the Bahia province of Brazil. Another species of *Neotermes* occurs on the West Indian island of Grenada, entering neglected wounds and causing severe local damage.

The control of dry-wood termite attack is mainly a matter of taking such precautions as careful pruning of dead wood, the treatment of cut surfaces and wounds with a fungicide to promote rapid healing, and the removal of debris from the vicinity of tree bases. Smee (loc. cit.) suggests the opening-up of infested trunks and the introduction of aquous insecticidal emulsions, such as dieldrin at a strength of 0·05 active ingredient. For protection of young plants in nurseries, or when newly set out, see below under 'forestry'.

Tea

Tea is grown in areas of high rainfall, much of it at high elevations under somewhat temperate conditions. In consequence termites are less in evidence than in drier and warmer localities. Nevertheless heavy pruning and plucking induces much callus tissue, and not infrequently some dieback, which is attractive both to dry-wood and subterranean termites.

According to Eden (1958): 'Termites are a source of trouble in many tea districts. Those which consume only dead wood are not of vital importance because their control can be dealt with by bush sanitation methods aimed at removing dead branches which are a dangerous source of fungal infection. Those which will attack living tissues are serious pests. Of particular importance are those that ring the collar of tea and shade trees, thereby causing the total loss of mature plants that have taken years to grow.' Termite damage in tea nurseries is rare, presumably as a result of the care which is taken by most planters to ensure good growing conditions for the seedlings. Drought appears to be an important predisposing factor in the occurrence of termite damage in mature tea. Careless cultivation leading to the cutting of roots and minor injuries in the collar region induces subterranean termite attack.

In southern China and Formosa some local damage is caused by *Odontotermes formosanus*, a common ground-nesting termite which builds shelter tubes of earth over the stems of tea bushes in its search for dead wood. During periods of drought stems are ringed and the bushes wither and die, but such injury is sporadic in occurrence.

In north-east India and adjacent areas of East Pakistan where tea is grown extensively, there has long been some conflict of opinion on the significance of termite attack. Fifty years ago one observer in South Sylhet described the work of *Odontotermes* entering the heartwood through dead snags and, after eating this away, leaving only the sapwood with the interior filled with earth. With the drying out of this earth filling the sapwood also dried out, hindering the free circulation of sap and ultimately leading to the death of the bush. Hainsworth (1952) writing of this area states that 'in most cases the few termite runs scattered through a normal section appear to do very little damage and can be safely disregarded'. Further north in Assam three species of *Odontotermes* have been identified on tea bushes and their shade trees, viz. *O. assamensis*, *O. parvidus* and *O. redemanni*. However, in Assam attack by one or more unidentified species of *Microcerotermes* is considered by Das (1962) to result in a 15 per cent loss of crop annually. To this must be added the cost of replacing bushes that have died. These termites also feed on dead and diseased wood, but having gained a foothold they extend their galleries into living tissues and eventually cause the death of the infested bush. In this case there appears to be a connection between marginal rainfall for successful tea cultivation and the severity of termite attack. Das reports successful control of ground-dwelling termites with aldrin and dieldrin applied at a rate of 2·24 kg active ingredient/hectare (2 lb per acre), either as an emulsion or as a dust, provided that it is evenly distributed and worked into the soil soon after application. Insecticide application must be preceded by estate sanitation, including the removal of dead branches and the treatment of the cut surface with

paint, and clearing away from around the base of each bush any accumulation of debris and earth. Such measures are stated to be effective for
five years or more. In South India both roots and branches of apparently healthy tea bushes are attacked by *Coptotermes ceylonicus*, according to Rau (1939).

Tea in Ceylon is subject to attack by four dry-wood termites. *Postelectrotermes* (formerly *Neotermes*) *militaris* is widespread at elevations
between 3 000 and 5 000 feet (1 000 and 1 300) metres with *Kalotermes
jepsoni* found occasionally. At lower altitudes *Neotermes greeni* occurs
on tea but is more usually to be found in shade trees, and *Glyptotermes
dilatus* also occurs in lowland gardens. *P. militaris* differs from the
others in its ability to spread from one tea bush to another by way of
roots that have come in contact with each other in the soil, while apparently attacking shade trees only by the more usual way through wounds
and dead snags. Again, *P. militaris* can be found in apparently healthy
bushes and the other three species only after obtaining a foothold in the
usual way through dead branches. King (1938) points out that a healthy
tea bush can sustain dry-wood termite attack to the extent of having all
the heartwood of the main stem eaten away and replaced by callus
tissue, providing that there are no disease organisms present to weaken
the living wood and encourage the termites to feed on it. Termite
infested bushes are more liable to wind damage than those without any
infestation. Just how much economic damage results from these insects
has long been a debated question. More recently Ranaweera (1962) has
suggested that the problem has been over-estimated, while Fernando
(1962) is of the opinion that the damage done is, in fact, quite appreciable. Ranaweera describes the control methods advocated by the Tea
Research Institute of Ceylon as follows: 'At pruning time, the branches
of bushes showing galleries are cut back in at least two places per bush
to make sizeable entrance holes large enough to insert the spray nozzle
of a knapsack sprayer. Application of the insecticide is done the same
day immediately after cutting back, because termites quickly block the
holes so formed. Dieldrin—or chlordane—emulsion at the rate of one
or two pints ($\frac{1}{2}$ to 1 litre) per bush was forced into the galleries at about
70 lb (30 kg) pressure, using a pressure-retaining knapsack sprayer. . . .
Dosages have been standardised at 0·1 per cent dieldrin or 0·25 per cent
chlordane emulsion, one or two pints per bush.'

In Malaysia a subterranean termite, *Microtermes pallidus*, builds
shelter tubes up the stems of tea bushes and having gained entry by way
of a wound or patch of diseased bark, proceeds to tunnel through the
heartwood and branches. Branches thus weakened break off in storms.
Young plants are ringed at ground level after the manner of cutworm
damage. Injury to the stem by careless hoeing induces termite attack.
Similar damage by the related *Microtermes jacobseni* is reported from

Java. Also in Malaysia a certain amount of damage is done by larger ground dwelling termites, *Odontotermes javanicus* and *O. longignathus*.

Tea growing under marginal conditions in Africa is subject to the attentions of various species of *Odontotermes*. An unidentified species is responsible for much damage in Malawi where a considerable area is under tea. A small amount of ring-barking by *O. transvaalensis* has been reported from Rhodesia. In Uganda and Tanzania this genus has been responsible for the loss of young tea, a predisposing cause that has been noted being planting out with the taproot bent. Prolonged dry weather aggravates the symptoms of termite attack in tea gardens generally.

Coconuts

The coconut palm, *Cocos nucifera*, is found throughout the tropics within easy reach of the sea and so becomes liable to attack by a wide variety of termites. This is seldom of economic importance except, perhaps, where the crop is cultivated under estate conditions or where a local population is almost wholly dependent on it for food, usually in association with fishing. Attack falls into two distinct phases; on young plants up to the age of four years, including nursery seedlings, and on mature palms. Significant losses in nurseries occur in India and East Africa. Damage to mature palms is generally looked on as secondary to attack by other pests, or to mechanical injury and senility, except in Malaysia and certain Pacific Islands.

Along the west coast of India, coconut nurseries are subject to attack by the common ground-dwelling termite *Odontotermes obesus*, and where the soil is lateritic rather than sandy up to 20 per cent of the seedlings may be destroyed. As a rule the first sign of attack is the wilting of the central shoot, and inspection shows evidence of termite feeding at the collar or through the base of the nut (Nirula, Antony and Menon, 1953). Similar damage in Ceylon is attributed to *Odontotermes redemanni*. Also in Ceylon mature palms have been found with the trunks extensively hollowed out by *Coptotermes ceylonicus* (Jepson, 1931), and superficial attack by *Microtermes bugnoni* and *Nasutitermes ceylonicus*.

In the Seychelles *Coptotermes truncatus* and, to a less extent, a drywood termite, *Neotermes laticollis*, gain access to the interior of palms through holes made by the beetle borer *Melittoma insulare*. Two tree-nesting termites, *Microcerotermes subtilis* and *Nasutitermes nigritus*, nest on palms and while they act basicly as scavengers they are ready to exploit any wounds they may find. In Madagascar, *Nasutitermes laticeps* behaves in a similar manner.

Nurseries on the East African coast suffer from subterranean nesting termites, especially *Macrotermes subhyalinus*. Losses in Zanzibar have been recorded as high as 50 per cent. In Somalia *Odontotermes classicus* is recorded, while in Kenya and Tanzania unidentified species of this genus are known as minor pests. Young palms in Tanzania have been damaged by *Allodontermes morogorensis*. Records of damage in West Africa are few and relate to *Macrotermes subhyalinus* on seedlings in Nigeria.

In Malaysia and Java *Coptotermes curvignathus* attacks apparently healthy palms through wounds on the trunks or directly into the crowns. This termite nests below ground and builds covered runways of carton material up the trunks, using all available cover in the way of dead leaf-bases and fibre. The damage done depends on the amount of tunneling into the stems, and this is most extensive in neglected, old plantations (Corbett, 1932). Young palms in both countries are attacked by *Coptotermes sinabangensis* and *Globitermes sulphureus* in a similar manner. In Malaysia damage is also done by *Macrotermes carbonarius*.

On a number of islands in the Pacific where coconuts are the staple crop, dry-wood termites are of economic importance. *Neotermes rainbowi* was recorded long ago on Funafuti in the Ellice Islands excavating galleries in palms between three and six feet (1 to 2 m) from the base, which so weakened them that they broke off in the seasonal gales. (Headley, 1896). Seventy-five per cent of the palms on Suvarov Atoll in the Cook Islands were infested in 1941 and the loss of palms there and on neighbouring Pakapuka during subsequent storms caused serious concern for the local food supply. A related dry-wood termite, *Incisitermes immigrans*, attacks palms on Washington Island in the North Pacific. Two species of termites build their carton nests on the trunks of palms in the Solomon Islands, *Microcerotermes biroi* and *Nasutitermes novarumhebridarum*, but only serve to aggravate damage done by other agents. In the Philippines the tree-nesting termites are *Microcerotermes losbanosensis* and *Nasutitermes luzonicus* and their roles are similar to their relatives in the Solomons.

In Central America *Nasutitermes ephratae* has been observed on palms in Panama working into the living tissues between the sheath and leaf petiole of healthy trees. The globular nests of this termite are found just below the crowns of palms, and covered runways radiate out in all directions (Snyder and Zatek, 1924). *Coptotermes niger* also occurs in Panama as a secondary pest. *Nasutitermes costalis* is recorded from Puerto Rico and *N. rippertii* from Brazil as occasional pests of palms.

For controlling termites in coconut nurseries chlorinated hydrocarbon insecticides are being widely used, mixed with the soil before planting the seed nuts. Earlier practice in India and Ceylon was to place the coconuts on a layer of fine sand, or on a mixture of salt and cowdung in order to deter the termites. Sankaran (1962) recommends the use of

10 per cent benzene hexachloride dust at a rate of 100 kg/hectare (88 lb per acre) in India. Child (1964) observes that the same strength of insecticide at 50 kg/hectare (44 lb per acre) gave reasonably effective results, but 2 per cent dieldrin dust at 100 kg/hectare was better. The generally secondary nature of dry-wood termite attack suggests the protective value of good cultural practices in coconut plantations; avoidance of mechanical injury by cattle grazing, by cutting steps in the trunks to aid harvesting, and careless tractor driving, and the early treatment with a preservative paint of any such wounds.

Oil Palm

The oil palm is believed to be indigenous to tropical Africa, but its cultivation as an estate crop has developed largely in Malysia and Indonesia and it is from that part of the world that termite damage is reported. Three members of the Rhinotermitidae are recorded from Malaysia—*Coptotermes curvignathus*, *Schedorhinotermes longirostris* and *S. malaccensis*—and the first of these also from Indonesia. Not so important in the amount of damage done are two Amitermitinae—*Globitermes globosus* and *G. sulphureus*. 'Oil palms are not immune to the attacks of white ants and on properties of a peaty nature with surface and buried timber they may occasion considerable loss. *C. curvignathus* has been found tunnelling the trunk from base to crown causing not only malformed leaves but in some cases the death of the palm. When this insect is troublesome every effort should be made to clean the area of buried and surface timber as soon as economically and conveniently possible' (Bunting *et al.*, 1934).

Sugar Cane

Sugar cane is cultivated as an economic crop in so many different parts of the world and in consequence the list of termites feeding on it is long and varied. Appreciable damage is spasmodic in occurrence, and concern for the resulting loss of crop depends to a large extent on the development of the sugar industry in a particular area. There are three periods when canes are likely to be damaged by termites. The first of these is when the setts or seed-pieces are planted out in the fields. These setts are short lengths of mature cane with the pith exposed at each end, and are attractive to termites until the new shoots developing from buds at the nodes have grown tall and produced their own roots. The second period comes as the canes approach maturity. The third period comes at any time during the growth of the canes when the hard outer layer is broken by rodents, stem borers or other agents, thus providing termites with a means of access to the soft interior.

In India the main source of damage lies in early attack on the newly planted setts, which prevents maximum germination and results in poor stands. As many as 40 per cent of buds have been found to be destroyed and crop yields reduced by 33 per cent (Avasthy, 1967). Agarwala (1955) estimates that in the state of Bihar a loss of 2·5 per cent in tonnage of cane and 4·5 per cent in sugar output, valued at some £1 400 000 per annum, is caused by termites, mainly *Microtermes obesi*. On the other hand a statistical survey carried out at Pusa (Pruthi and Narayanan, 1939) where the termite concerned was *Odontotermes assmuthi*, showed that only one plot out of eight had a loss of more than 1 per cent of young plants. On experimental plots at New Delhi where *Odontotermes obesus* did most of the damage, loss of setts was 1·66 per cent in 1946 and 1·08 the following year (Narayanan and Lal, 1952). A number of other species of termites have been noted as minor pests, including *Trinervitermes heimi* foraging the leaves of growing cane. Severe damage to setts by unspecified termites is reported from Burma in areas of sandy soil.

In Queensland a particularly voracious termite, *Mastotermes darwiniensis*, is a major pest of cane in sandy localities. It forms large communities inside standing trees and travels long distances underground on foraging expeditions, attacking en route such unpromising substances as the lead and plastic sheathing of electric cables. Both setts and growing cane are attacked. Sporadic damage to cane by a number of other termites has been reported, including *Coptotermes acinaciformis*, *Schedorhinotermes intermedius* and *Amitermes herbertensis*.

Throughout the West Indies and Central America termites of the genera *Heterotermes* and *Nasutitermes* are of interest to the sugar industry. *Heterotermes* are small white termites with underground nests, and they attack newly planted setts, eating away the exposed pith and inner layers to leave a hollow tube before the developing buds have had time to develop adequate root systems. In addition they tunnel in old stools and kill the young suckers. Such damage is accentuated by poor growing conditions. Crop losses in Panama due to *Heterotermes tenuis* were given as 35 per cent (Snyder and Zetek, 1924), and this species is also prevalent in Jamaica and the Leeward Islands. In the Dominican Republic the genus is represented by *H. cardini*. In Venezuela *H. crinitus* attacks setts and bores into the stems and roots of growing cane (Guagliumi, 1962). *Nasutitermes* build their nests on trees and fence posts and travel long distances to reach food supplies. The soldiers are ant-like insects with pear-shaped heads and guard the long columns of workers that do the actual foraging. *Nasutitermes costalis* is regarded as a primary pest in Guadaloupe, causing serious losses of setts in the drier parts of the island and aggravating damage done by other pests. In Barbados the damage has been described as unspectacular but worthy of consideration. Infested fields there show a characteristic withered and browned appearance which disappears when the cane has been stimulated into new growth by rain, but less sugar is produced at harvest. A survey of seventy-six mature fields showed a crop loss of from 3 to 5 per cent in thirteen of them, and smaller losses in a further fourteen (Tucker, 1939). *N. costalis* is common from Cuba to Guyana. *N. cornigera* is found in the Leeward Islands and south to Guyana, *N. rippertii* from Jamaica and an unidentified species from Venezuela. Related termites are *Parvitermes pallidiceps* on cane in Haiti and *Velocitermes antillarum* in the Dominican Republic. *Microcerotermes exiguus* is recorded from sugar cane in Nicaragua.

In South America *Heterotermes* sp, *Cornitermes* sp. and *Nasutitermes globiceps* are found on sugar cane in Bolivia. In Brazil *Syntermes grandis*, *S. molestus* and *Procornitermes striatus* are recorded. In addition to the termites recorded above from Guyana, a small subterranean species, *Termes nigritus*, has been noted feeding on cane roots.

A minor pest of cane fields in the southern United States is *Reticulitermes flavipes*, better known for its attacks on building timbers.

In the Far East damage is done to plantations in the Philippines by *Heterotermes philippinensis*, *Coptotermes vastator*, *Microcerotermes losbanosensis* and *Macrotermes gilvus*, all of which will feed on setts. *M. gilvus*, which is widely distributed in south-east Asia, has been reported from Java, causing losses among setts of up to 5 per cent. In south China and Formosa *Coptotermes formosanus* is considered a serious pest and it has been introduced into Hawaii where it also feeds on cane. *Odontotermes formosanus* attacks young plants at ground level in Formosa, south China and the Ryuku Islands. *O. hainanensis* is a minor pest in south China, and *Nasutitermes parvonasutus* and *Capritermes nitobei* in Formosa.

Coptotermes havilandi has been accidentally introduced into Mauritius from south-east Asia, and it has been found in cane fields attacking stumps after harvest, as well as canes that have suffered damage by borers.

In many parts of the African continent termites have been recorded as damaging cane setts. Rouzaud (1962) lists them among the principal pests of sugar in the Congo, and Buyckx (1962) refers to *Ancistrotermes latinotus* as the cause of damage in Uele Province. In East Africa plantation grown cane has been attacked by *Odontotermes classicus* in Somalia, and by *Pseudacanthotermes militaris* in Kenya. Cane grown by peasant cultivators in Nigeria is attacked by *Amitermes evuncifer*, *Macrotermes subhyalinus*, and species of *Ancistrotermes* and *Microtermes* (Sands, 1960a).

Control of subterranean termite attack on sugar cane has been facilitated by the development of the persistent organochlorine pesticides. Luke and Ploeg (1950) controlled *Heterotermes* in the Dominican Republic by spraying setts in the furrow with aldrin emulsion at 2 lb a.i./acre (2 to 3 kg a.i./hectare) and dieldrin emulsion at 0·32 lb a.i./acre (0·35 kg a.i./hectare). In Queensland the damage done by *Mastotermes* has been reduced by 87 per cent or more with aldrin or heptachlor, each broadcast at 6 lb a.i./acre (6·6 kg a.i./hectare) and worked into the soil with two ploughings. Benzene hexachloride did not prove so effective (Wilson, 1969). Indian workers have obtained control of *Odontotermes* and *Microtermes* with dieldrin and chlordane (Reddy, (1962). However it has been found that heptachlor emulsion at 0·5 to 1 lb a.i./acre (0·5 to 1·1 kg a.i./hectare) provides an effective and economic control of termites with the additional advantage of a significant reduction in subsequent borer damage (Singh and Soneja, 1966). It is unfortunate that crude benzene hexachloride has phytotoxic effects on cane setts and plants, inhibiting the formation of both primary and secondary roots.

A treatment that serves the dual purpose of stimulating germination and protecting setts from termite attack is suggested by Muthuswamy and Aravamudhan (1958). Working in Bihar they demonstrated the advantage of dipping setts for ten minutes prior to planting in a solution of an organo-mercury fungicide and aldrin. They note, however, that in areas of great termite activity it was advantageous to spray the furrows with from 0·5 to 0·8 lb aldrin a.i./acre (0·6 to 0·9 kg a.i./hectare) in addition.

Fruit Trees

Fruit trees not under commercial cultivation are, like ornamental trees, rarely the objects of detailed entomological investigation. As citrus is, perhaps, the most widely cultivated fruit in the warmer parts of the world it has a high proportion of termite species observed causing injury. The problem in the tropics generally is not unlikely to be similar to the position in Natal as described by Fuller (1912)—'Although there are termites which build laborious earth-covered runways up the trunks of trees and feed on the bark they do not endanger thereby the life of the tree. ... Yet in an extreme case ... where dense scrub has been hastily cleared and burnt and the land ploughed up and planted to fruit trees, scarcely one tree was left, including oranges, mangoes and avocados.' In India, according to Sankaran (1962), the common subterranean termite *Odontotermes obesus* damages all kinds of fruit trees.

In southern Europe and the islands of the Mediterranean, the dry-wood termite *Kalotermes flavicollis* attacks a wide variety of fruit trees including fig, olive, pear and, perhaps most important, vines. In the case of vines the immediate effect of infestation is not catastrophic, but the plants are weakened and their useful life may be shortened by as much as ten years. This increases the rate at which vineyards require to be replanted. In the Banyuls district at the eastern end of the Pyrenees it was estimated that 80 per cent of the vines were infested, mainly those over ten years old (Ferrero, 1959). In Sardinia infestation of vineyards is equally extensive (Prota, 1962). No satisfactory control measures on a field scale appear to be in use.

Commercial plantings of citrus in the subtropics appear to be less affected by termites than those nearer the equator. In Israel the effect of *Reticulitermes lucifugus* is, in the words of Bodenheimer (1951), 'limited and passing damage'. Citrus under irrigation in Australia is occasionally injured by *Coptotermes acinaciformis* and *C. frenchi.* The unusual behaviour of a dry-wood termite, *Paraneotermes simplici-cornis*, attacking the tap-roots of newly-planted citrus in Texas is recorded by Dean (1954). In tropical countries generally, ground-dwelling termites are more numerous and damage to young citrus more frequent. In northern Australia *Mastotermes darwiniensis* is locally significant. In tropical Africa *Macrotermes bellicosus* and *M. subhyalinus* are reported from Nigeria, and *Odontotermes latericius* from Mozambique. Citrus growing in Arabia depends on control of *Microcerotermes diversus* in irrigated gardens (Ayoub, 1959). In Malaysia *Coptotermes curvignathus* attacks the bark at the collar and also the roots. *Coptotermes testaceus* causes similar damage in Surinam, while elsewhere in South America Guyana reports *Nasutitermes costalis* and Brazil *Rugitermes occidentalis* as pests.

Records of termite attack on date palms are not numerous. Some years ago 22 per cent of palms on an experimental farm in Mauritania were found to be damaged by an undetermined species. In Libya *Anacanthotermes ochraceus* has been recognised as the cause of loss. *Microcerotermes diversus* is widely distributed in Arabia feeding on dead leaf bases, and should it encounter uncalloused surfaces it is liable to penetrate into the central core of the palm stem and weaken it. Similar behaviour has been noted with *Odontotermes nilensis* in the Sudan, where in northern districts severe outbreaks have been reported.

Among other tropical fruits grown commercially, the avocado is damaged by dry-wood termites, in Brazil by *Rugitermes occidentalis* and in the Philippines by *Neotermes malatensis*, while subterranean termites penetrating the trunk through dead branches include *Coptotermes niger* in Panama, *Nasutitermes costalis* in Puerto Rico and *Schedorhinotermes lamanianus* in Tanzania. Guava in Brazil is host to two dry-wood termites, *Neotermes castaneus* and *N. wagneri*. Mango is rarely affected, but *Coptotermes heimi* has been noted in India and *Coptotermes cur-*

vignathus in Indonesia, both affecting young trees, while *Neotermes gardneri* was found in India in the branches of older trees. Litchi trees in south China have been damaged by a dry-wood termite *Cryptotermes declivis* and the ubiquitous *Coptotermes formosanus*. Mulberry trees in India and Pakistan are sometimes attacked by *Coptotermes heimi*, and from Baluchistan comes a somewhat unusual report of attack by a harvester termite, *Anacanthotermes macrocephalus*.

In localities where termite attack is possible, it would be desirable to plant out young fruit trees in plastic containers with an organochlorine insecticide incorporated in the soil, as described for forest trees in a later chapter. In Arabia Ayoub (1959) obtained satisfactory control of *Microcerotermes* by adding various organochlorine compounds to irrigation water used in newly planted gardens, but this method is hardly likely to find favour generally at the present time.

Cotton

Termite damage to seedling cotton by subterranean nesting species is not uncommon on farms in Africa and Asia. Usually this is of little significance to the farmer since it is customary to plant a number of seeds in each hole and thin out the seedlings later. In areas of marginal rainfall young plants may be attacked when drought conditions set in, but extra growth by the surviving plants will minimise the loss of crop as a rule. Thus most of the reports of termite damage to cotton come from research stations and government controlled farms where records are kept.

In the Gezira area of the Sudan, where cotton is grown under irrigation, the tap-roots of young plants are subject to attack by *Microtermes thoracalis*. Crowther and Barlow (1943) found that on average 31 per cent of plants were attacked but the loss in yield was only 3 per cent. In restricted localities attack reached 80 per cent, with a more significant reduction of yield. Current protective measures given by Gameel (1969) are seed treatment with dieldrin at a rate of 1 kilo a.i./hectare (0·9 lb a.i./acre) and 6 kilo (13 lb) Agrocide 3 mixed with sawdust applied to the soil at green ridging, again per hectare. In the Tokar Delta area near the Red Sea, where cotton is grown on flood land without irrigation, 'termites are a serious factor in that they attack plants at almost any stage of growth, boring into the stem at, or below, ground level and channelling in or eating the tip of the root, thus causing wilting, and eventually death' (Pearson, 1958).

In tropical Africa a number of the smaller fungus-growing termites, *Ancistrotermes* and *Microtermes* species, damage young cotton by entering the stem at ground level and working up and down the centre, causing the plant to wilt and, later, blow over in high winds. On lateritic soils in western Tanzania a predisposing cause to this pattern of attack is the rubbing of the stems against the hard earth during windy weather. *Ancistrotermes equatorius* attacks cotton in Uganda, while in countries further south this genus is represented by *A. latinotus*. An unidentified *Ancistrotermes* is also present in the Uele district of the Congo associated with *Coptotermes sjoestedti* (Buyckx, 1962). *Microtermes aluco* is recorded from West Africa, *M. kasaiensis* from Zambia, and from Tanzania a species as yet unidentified. Young cotton in Somalia has been damaged by *Coptotermes amanii*. Mature cotton plants in East Africa are attacked by various species of *Amitermes* and *Microcerotermes* but this is of little or no economic importance, however it does interfere significantly with attempts to establish perennial cottons for experimental purposes. In drier parts of Tanzania and Malawi severe defoliation may occur locally in the vicinity of nests of the harvester termite, *Hodotermes mossambicus*.

In Arabia, particularly in the extreme south, irrigated cotton is liable to be attacked by *Microcerotermes diversus*, a small subterranean termite widely distributed in the tamarisk bushes to be found in dry river beds. This attack is similar to that described above for *Microtermes* in East Africa.

Cotton in India is subject to damage by two omnivorous termites, *Odontotermes obesus* and *Trinervitermes biformis*. In Rajasthan the loss of crop may be considerable (Bhatnagar, 1962). In Gujarat control measures resulted in a 33 per cent increase in yield (Patel, 1962).

In the province of Yunnan in China several species of *Odontotermes* are reported as causing occasional damage to cotton (Cheo, 1948).

Control of *Odontotermes* in India was achieved by drilling in with the cotton seed BHC dust (0·0675 per cent gamma) at a rate of 56 kg/hectare (50 lb/acre), according to Patel. In the Congo, Buyckx recommends a 2·5 per cent dieldrin dust or a 10 per cent chlordane dust at 30 kg/hectare (26 lb/acre) prior to planting. Harvester termites are controlled by baiting with chopped grass or hay that has been dipped in a solution of dieldrin or sodium fluorsilicate and then dried in the sun. This bait is broadcast lightly over the threatened areas.

Wheat

The yield of wheat in India has been estimated to be reduced about 6 per cent by *Microtermes obesi*, which feeds on the roots of young plants and causes them to wilt. Individual localities suffer a greater loss. Seed treatment with insecticide before sowing increased yields by 43 per cent on a research station in Gujerat (Patel, 1962). Two mound-building termites, *Trinervitermes rubidus* and *T. biformis*, which usually feed on grasses are known to turn their attention to wheat.

In the upland areas of Tanzania the roots of young wheat are damaged by *Microtermes vadschaggae*. In Rhodesia termite damage is enough to justify insecticide applications in some localities. Harvester termites are liable to feed on wheat at all stages of its development in parts of South Africa, causing substantial crop loss.

Wheat in Brazil is damaged by *Procornitermes triacifer*, according to Gonçalves and Silva (1962).

Control of *Odontotermes* in India has proved satisfactory when organochlorines are applied to the soil prior to sowing—aldrin 5 per cent dust at 60 kg/hectare (53 lb/acre), chlordane 5 per cent dust at 40 kg/hectare (35 lb/acre), and BHC 10 per cent at 30 kg/hectare (26 lb/acre). Aldrin was noted as stimulating germination (Ghose, 1964). In Rhodesia, aldrin and dieldrin wettable powders were satisfactory as seed dressings.

Rice

Upland rice in various parts of the world is subject to root damage by small subterranean termites, while others that normally feed on grasses may turn their attentions to the growing and maturing plants. In Japan losses are caused by *Coptotermes formosanus* and to a less extent by *Capritermes nitobei*. In Formosa *Odontotermes formosanus*, *Capritermes nitobei* and *Procapritermes mushae* have been recorded, only the first of these being a pest. In Brazil *Procornitermes araujoi* feeds on roots and later on ripening stems, and *Syntermes molestus* also on roots. In Nigeria *Macrotermes bellicosus* attacks the roots of seedlings, while *Macrotermes subhyalinus* cuts the stems as the plant ripens and feeds on the fallen seed heads resulting in losses of from 15 to 20 per cent of crop on observation plots. Also in Nigeria the grass feeding *Trinervitermes ebenerianus* may invade the paddy and defoliate an area completely. There appear to be no specific recommendations for successful control of termites in rice.

Groundnuts

The commercial production of groundnuts is undertaken mainly by peasant farmers in areas of low rainfall. Termite damage occurs during periods of drought in the growing season, when subterranean termites penetrate the stems near ground level and hollow them out, causing the plant to wilt. Later, as the crop ripens, the outer layers of the seed-pods are gnawed allowing the entrance to the seed of fungi which lead to the development of poisonous substances in the groundnuts. In addition, seed-pods superficially damaged do not harvest in a satisfactory way with machinery.

Crop losses of up to 10 per cent were recorded in Northern Nigeria, more particularly in erect-growing, heavy cropping varieties (Sands, 1960a). *Amitermes evuncifer* and *Microtermes* sp. are recorded from Nigeria, *Ancistrotermes crucifer* and *Microcerotermes* sp. from the Gambia, and *Odontotermes vulgaris* and *Trinervitermes ebenerianus* from Senegal. In the Sudan the more serious damage is done by *Odontotermes nilensis* and *Microtermes thoracalis*, while *Macrotermes subhyalinus* and *Eremotermes nanus* are of less frequent occurrence. In the north-east Congo some loss of crop is regularly due to *Ancistrotermes latinotus*. The attempt to grow groundnuts on a large scale some years ago in Tanzania ran into trouble with mechanical harvesting due to the pods having been weakened by various *Odontotermes* and *Microtermes*.

In India, some damage is done to growing plants by *Odontotermes obesus*, and to a lesser extent *Trinervitermes biformis*. In south China ripe pods are eaten by *Coptotermes formosanus*.

Insecticidal control of termites on groundnuts is not widely practised. Indian workers recommend the use of BHC at 1 to 2 kilo gamma/hectare (0·9 to 1·8 lb/acre) or aldrin dust in the drills at 0·5 kilo a.i./hectare (0·5 lb a.i./acre). Seed treatment with aldrin at 28·5 grammes a.i. per kilo (5 oz per 10 lb) of seed has given satisfactory protection in heavily attacked localities in the Sudan (Schmutterer, 1961). BHC applied to the drills when sowing proved effective in protecting the ripening pods from attack in Tanzania.

Miscellaneous Food Crops

There are comparatively few records in the literature of termite damage to food crops grown by peasant farmers, such damage being more in the nature of a regular small loss of crop rather than the more spectacular incidence of locusts or army worm. However, Bigger (1966) has shown that in southern Tanzania annual food crops such as maize, sorghum, soya bean and sunflower, together with the root-crop cassava were all liable to some damage. For example, maize losses over a five-year period averaged 27 per cent loss of stand, and protective measures gave increases in yield of from 330 to 500 kilo per hectare (300 to 450 lb per acre). Pigeon pea was attacked in its second year. Termites concerned belong to the smaller fungus-growing genera, *Microtermes*, *Ancistrotermes* and *Allodontermes*. Maize in Rhodesia is subject to attack, more in the drier areas and on poor soils, by *Macrotermes*, *Odontotermes* and *Microtermes* (Rose, 1962). In the Congo, *Ancistrotermes latinotus* feeds on the stems of ripening maize. Termite attack on the prop roots and the stem near ground level results in the maize plant blowing over under the weight of the ripening cobs. Maize in northern Tanzania is locally subject to defoliation by the harvester termite, *Hodotermes mossambicus*.

Cassava cuttings in Nigeria are liable to be eaten by termites before they have become established, and losses of up to 40 per cent due to *Pseudacanthotermes, Odontotermes, Ancistrotermes* and *Microtermes* were observed by Sands (1962a). Yams are damaged as setts and later by tunnelling in the mature tubers, but outbreaks are sporadic and the overall effect is not economic (Coursey, 1967).

Odontotermes obesus in India is a pest of maize and plant mortalities of 22 per cent are reported by Agarwala and Sharma (1954). Losses in potatoes caused by this termite may be as much as 6 per cent (Kumar, 1965). Sugar beet in Iraq has been damaged by *Microcerotermes diversus*. In south China *Coptotermes formosanus* feeds on a variety of root crops including sweet potato, cassava and colocasia; *Odontotermes hainanensis* attacks cassava and pineapples. Potatoes are attacked by *Heterotermes tenuis* in Jamaica and the tubers rendered unfit for sale.

The use of insecticides to protect food crops from attack by termites is dependent on the economic status of the farmer, and the relatively high cost of insecticides. Bigger found that aldrin worked into the soil of the planting ridges at a rate of 0·5 kilo a.i./hectare (0·4 lb a.i. per acre) increased the yield of maize 200 to 400 kilo/hectare (180 to 350 lb/acre), in Tanzania. In India, Agarawala and Sharma found that aldrin at 0·2 kilo a.i./hectare (0·18 lb a.i./acre) increased maize yields by just under 200 per cent. In East Africa and Rhodesia seed dressings of maize with dieldrin wettable powder have given good results.

Pastures

A number of termites feed almost exclusively on grasses of various kinds, while others include dried grass in their diet at the appropriate season. Whether or not they are regarded as pests depends on the extent to which they compete with domestic animals for the available grazing, and to the extent that such competition worries the stock-owner (Plate 29). Harvester termites of the genera *Hodotermes* and *Anacanthotermes* belong to the more arid parts of Africa, north and south, to Arabia through Persia and on to Russian Turkestan in the north and to Pakistan and north-west India in the south. The so-called Snouted Harvester Termites, characterised by the pear-shaped heads of the soldiers, belong to the Nasutitermitinae and inhabit the less arid grasslands of Africa and Asia, while in Australia most of the grass-feeding termites belong to the Amitermitinae.

In Africa south of the Limpopo River, *Hodotermes mossambicus* occurs in the drier parts of the Orange Free State and the Transvaal 'bringing about the complete denudation of grass cover . . . at the end of the winter and in early spring' (Coaton, 1947). It appears that over-grazing resulting from competition between cattle and termites aids the establishment of new termite colonies by providing more bare patches of earth into which the alate pairs can disappear, while increased human activity reduces greatly the number of such natural enemies as the ant-bear, red meercat, plover and bustard (Plate 30). According to Nel (1968) seriously infested veld can recover without the use of chemical control measures if given complete rest from grazing, while chemical control without enlightened farming practices has little positive effect. The Snouted Harvester, *Trinervitermes trinervoides*, is present in somewhat damper areas and, according to Hartwig (1955) will remove about 20 per cent of the grass from veld with a good cover and up to 60 per cent where the cover is poor.

In arid areas of the Indian subcontinent a harvester termite, *Anacanthotermes macrocephalus*, is active, with *Trinervitermes biformis* replac-ing it as the rainfall increases. Other species of *Anacanthotermes* are present in Iran, Iraq and Afghanistan without, apparently, arousing any interest. In Turkmenia, U.S.S.R., however, *Anacanthotermes ahngerianus* is considered a pest of pastures with dense grass cover and losses of up to 20 per cent are mentioned by Ghilarov (1962).

Grazing areas in Australia are inhabited by a number of small-mound termites belonging to two purely local genera *Drepanotermes* and *Tumu-litermes*, and the widespread genus *Amitermes*. They aggravate the prob-lem of overgrazing by stock and kangaroos, which in turn leads to progressive soil erosion. Research is in progress, particularly on *Dre-panotermes rubiceps* and *Amitermes neogermanus*.

From South America comes a single reference to termite damage in the grasslands of Minas Gerais, Brazil, where the losses caused by *Corni-termes cumulans*, a nasute harvester, have warranted investigation.

The reduction of termite populations in grassland depends on the nesting habits of the particular termite. The mounds of *Cornitermes* were poisoned with aldrin or telodrin emulsions (Amante, 1962). Small mound builders such as *Trinervitermes* in South Africa are destroyed by breaking up the mounds by mechanical means, such as by dragging a 1 in (2 cm) steel cable over the land with a tractor or oxen. Coaton (1962) describes in detail his method of eradicating *Microhodotermes* in the Karoo; the tops of their low mounds are sliced off with a spade and 6 fl. oz (180 ml) of aldrin 6 per cent emulsion introduced into the exposed passages with a sheep dosing syringe. *Hodotermes* nests are subterranean, and difficult to locate so the only practical method of attack is by poison baiting. Coaton (1958) used chopped hay and wheat

24. *Macrotermes goliath* mound in south-west Tanzania

25. *Macrotermes goliath* mound as source of pottery clay

26. Mound of *Macrotermes natalensis* sectioned to show interior construction, Uganda

27. *Macrotermes natalensis* mound with the nest portion isolated from the outer wall, which has been occupied by *Pseudacanthotermes spiniger*

    (Dr P. R. Hesse)

28. Chemical treatment of termite mounds; boring holes in *Macrotermes* mound in northern Nigeria prior to introducing dieldrin emulsion

29. Grazing damaged by *Odontotermes* in Kenya; the bare patches of soil
tend to become eroded

30. Veld denuded by *Hodotermes mossambicus* at Vryburg, Cape Province.
The soil dumps indicate the openings to the subterranean nest

(P. C. Joubert)

31. The results of termite
    attack on young
    Eucalyptus plantations,
    eastern Nigeria

32. *Heterotermes* damage to wattle in St. Helena,
    the weakened branches split in high winds

33. Termite damage to two-year-old *Eucalyptus* trees, Nigeria

chaff dipped in a 1·2 per cent solution of sodium fluosilicate in water. This is dried and stored until required for spreading over the pastures during the cool weather when harvester termites are active.

TERMITES RECORDED AS AGRICULTURAL PESTS

RUBBER

Glyptotermes dilatus (Bugnion & Popoff)	Ceylon
Coptotermes ceylonicus (Holmgr.)	Ceylon
Coptotermes curvignathus (Holmgr.)	Malaysia, Indonesia
Coptotermes testaceus (L.)	Brazil, Guyana
Ancistrotermes guineensis (Silv.)	Nigeria

COCOA

Neotermes aburiensis Sjöst.	West Africa
Neotermes gestri Silv.	Fernando Po, São Thomé, Principe
Neotermes papua (Desn.)	New Guinea
Neotermes sarasini (Holmgr.)	Samoa
Neotermes samoanus (Holmgr.)	Samoa
Neotermes spp.	New Ireland, New Britain, Brazil
Bifiditermes madagascarensis (Wasm.)	Madagascar
Schedorhinotermes putorius (Sjöst.)	West Africa
Coptotermes sjoestedti Holmgr.	West Africa
Microcerotermes edentatus Wasm.	Ivory Coast
Microcerotermes parvus (Hav.)	Congo
Microcerotermes solidus Silv.	Ghana
Microcerotermes theobromae (Desn.)	São Thomé
Microcerotermes sp.	Samoa
Pseudacanthotermes militaris (Hagen)	Nigeria
Macrotermes subhyalinus (Rambur)	Nigeria
Microtermes sp.	Nigeria

TEA

Kalotermes jepsoni Kemner	Ceylon
Postelectrotermes militaris (Desn.)	Ceylon
Neotermes greeni (Desn.)	Ceylon
Glyptotermes dilatatus (Bugnion & Popoff)	Ceylon
Coptotermes ceylonicus Holmgr.	Ceylon, South India
Microcerotermes spp.	India (Assam)
Pseudacanthotermes militaris (Hagen)	Malawi
Odontotermes assamensis Holmgr.	India (Assam)
Odontotermes formosanus (Shiraki)	China, Formosa
Odontotermes horni (Wasm.)	Ceylon
Odontotermes javanicus Holmgr.	Malaysia

Odontotermes longignathus Holmgr.	Malaysia
Odontotermes parvidens Holmgr.	India (Assam)
Odontotermes redemanni (Wasm.)	India (Assam), Ceylon
Odontotermes transvaalensis (Sjöst.)	Rhodesia
Odontotermes spp.	East Africa, Malawi
Odontotermes (*Hypotermes*) *obscuriceps* (Wasm.)	Ceylon
Microtermes jacobseni Holmgr.	Java
Microtermes pallidus (Hav.)	Malaysia

COCONUT

Incisitermes immigrans (Snyder)	Washington Island
Neotermes laticollis (Holmgr.)	Seychelles
Neotermes rainbowi (Hill)	Ellice Island
Coptotermes ceylonicus Holmgr.	Ceylon
Coptotermes curvignathus Holmgr.	Malaysia, Indonesia
Coptotermes niger Snyder	Panama
Coptotermes sinabangensis Oshima	Indonesia
Coptotermes truncatus (Wasm.)	Seychelles
Microcerotermes biroi (Desn.)	Solomon Islands
Microcerotermes bugnioni Holmgr.	Ceylon
Microcerotermes losbanosensis Oshima	Philippines
Microcerotermes subtilis (Wasm.)	Seychelles
Macrotermes subhyalinus (Rambur)	East Africa, Nigeria
Macrotermes carbonarius (Hagen)	Malaysia
Odontotermes classicus (Sjöst.)	Somalia
Odontotermes horni (Wasm.)	Ceylon
Odontotermes obesus (Ramb.)	India
Odontotermes redemanni (Wasm.)	Ceylon
Allodontermes morogorensis Harris	Tanzania
Nasutitermes ceylonicus (Holmgr.)	Ceylon
Nasutitermes costalis (Holmgr.)	Puerto Rico
Nasutitermes ephratae (Holmgr.)	Panama
Nasutitermus laticeps (Wasm.)	Madagascar
Nasutitermes luzonicus (Oshima)	Philippines
Nasutitermes nigritus (Wasm.)	Seychelles
Nasutitermes novarumhebridarum (Holmgr.)	Solomon Islands
Nasutitermes rippertii (Rambur)	Brazil

OIL PALM

Schedorhinotermes longirostris (Brauer)	Malaysia
Schedorhinotermes malaccensis (Holmgr.)	Malayasia
Coptotermes curvignathus Holmgr.	Malaysia, Indonesia
Globitermes globosus (Hav.)	Malaysia
Globitermes sulphureus (Hav.)	Malaysia

SUGAR CANE

Mastotermes darwiniensis Froggatt	Australia
Heterotermes cardini (Snyder)	Cuba, Dominican Republic
Heterotermes crinitus (Emerson)	Venezuela
Heterotermes paradoxus (Froggatt)	Australia
Heterotermes philippensis (Light)	Philippines
Heterotermes tenuis (Hagen)	Panama, West Indies
Heterotermes sp.	Bolivia
Reticulitermes flavipes (Kollar)	U.S.A.
Reticulitermes speratus (Kolbe)	Formosa, Hainan Island
Coptotermes acinaciformis (Froggatt)	Australia
Coptotermes formosanus Shiraki	China, Formosa, Hawaii
Coptotermes havilandi Holmgr.	Mauritius
Coptotermes heimi (Wasm.)	India
Coptotermes vastator Light	Philippines
Schedorhinotermes intermedius (Brauer)	Australia
Anoplotermes schwarzi Banks	Cuba
Amitermes evuncifer Silv.	Nigeria
Amitermes herbertensis Mjöberg	Australia
Amitermes latidens Mjöberg	Australia
Amitermes obtusidens Mjöberg	Australia
Eremotermes paradoxalis Holmgr.	India
Microcerotermes exigus (Hagen)	Nicaragua
Microcerotermes losbanosensis Oshima	Philippines
Microcerotermes serratus (Froggatt)	Australia
Termes cheeli (Mjöberg)	Australia
Termes nigritus (Silv.)	Guyana
Termes saltans (Wasm.)	Brazil
Capritermes nitobei (Shiraki)	China, Formosa
Pseudacanthotermes militaris (Hagen)	Kenya
Macrotermes barneyi Light	China
Macrotermes subhyalinus (Rambur)	Nigeria
Macrotermes estherae (Desn.)	India
Macrotermes gilvus (Hagen)	Indonesia, Philippines
Odontotermes assmuthi Holmgr.	India, Pakistan
Odontotermes badius (Hav.)	South Africa
Odontotermes classicus (Sjöst)	Somalia
Odontotermes formosanus (Sihraki)	China, Formosa, Ryuku Islands
Odontotermes hainanensis (Light)	China
Odontotermes obesus (Rambur)	India, Pakistan
Odontotermes taprobanes (Walker)	India, Pakistan
Ancistrotermes latinotus (Holmgr.)	Congo
Ancistrotermes sp.	Nigeria
Microtermes obesi Holmgr.	India
Microtermes sp.	Nigeria
Syntermes grandis (Rambur)	Brazil
Syntermes molestus (Burmeister)	Brazil
Procornitermes striatus (Hagen)	Brazil

Cornitermes sp.	Bolivia
Nasutitermes cornigera (Motsch.)	West Indies, Guyana
Nasutitermes costalis (Holmgr.)	West Indies
Nasutitermes globiceps (Holmgr.)	Bolivia
Nasutitermes parvonasutus (Nawa)	Formosa
Nasutitermes rippertii (Rambur)	Jamaica
Nasutitermes sp.	Venezuela
Parvitermes pallidiceps (Banks)	Haiti
Velocitermes antillarum (Holmgr.)	Dominican Republic
Trinervitermes biformis (Wasm.)	India
Trinervitermes heimi (Wasm.)	India

FRUIT TREES

Mastotermes darwiniensis Froggatt	Australia (citrus)
Kalotermes flavicollis (F.)	France, Italy (fig, pear, olive)
Neotermes castaneus (Burm.)	Brazil (guava)
Neotermes gardneri (Snyder)	India (mango)
Neotermes malatensis (Oshima)	Philippines (avocado)
Neotermes wagneri (Desn.)	Brazil (guava)
Paraneotermes simplicicornis (Banks)	U.S.A. (citrus)
Rugitermes occidentalis (Silv.)	Brazil (avocado, citrus)
Cryptotermes declivis Tsai & Chan	China (litchi)
Anacanthotermes macrocephalus (Desn.)	Baluchistan (mulberry)
Anacanthotermes ochraceus (Burm.)	Libya (dates)
Reticulitermes lucifugus (Rossi)	Israel (citrus)
Coptotermes acinaciformis (Froggatt)	Australia (citrus)
Coptotermes curvignathus Holmgr.	Malaysia, Indonesia (citrus, mango)
Coptotermes formosanus Shiraki	China (litchi)
Coptotermes frenchi Hill	Australia (citrus)
Coptotermes heimi (Wasm.)	India (mulberry, mango)
Coptotermes niger Snyder	Panama (avocado)
Coptotermes testaceus (L.)	Surinam (citrus)
Schedorhinotermes lamanianus (Sjöst.)	Tanzania (avocado)
Microcerotermes diversus Silv.	Arabia (citrus, date, guava)
Macrotermes subhyalinus (Rambur)	Nigeria (citrus)
Macrotermes bellicosus (Smeath.)	Nigeria (citrus)
Odontotermes hainanensis (Light)	China (apricot, peach)
Odontotermes latericius (Hav.)	Mozambique (citrus)
Odontotermes obesus (Rambur)	India (fruit generally)
Odontotermes nilensis Emerson	Sudan (date)
Nasutitermes costalis (Holmgr.)	Guyana (citrus)
	Puerto Rico (avocado)

VINE

Kalotermes flavicollis (Fabr.)	Europe, North Africa
Reticulitermes lucifugus (Rossi)	Europe, North Africa

COTTON

Hodotermes mossambicus (Hagen)	South and East Africa
Coptotermes sjoestedti Holmgr.	Congo
Coptotermes amanii (Sjöst.)	Somalia
Amitermes sp.	Tanzania
Microcerotermes diversus Silv.	Arabia
Microcerotermes parvulus (Sjöst.)	Tanzania
Microcerotermes parvus (Hav.)	East Africa
Odontotermes obesus (Rambur)	India
Odontotermes latericius (Hav.)	Mozambique
Odontotermes sp.	China
Ancistrotermes equatorius Harris	Uganda
Ancistrotermes latinotus (Holmgr.)	Tanzania, Zambia, Rhodesia, Congo
Microtermes aluco (Sjöst.)	West Africa
Microtermes kasaiensis (Sjöst.)	Zambia
Microtermes thoracalis Sjöst.	Sudan
Microtermes sp.	Tanzania
Trinervitermes biformis (Wasm.)	India

WHEAT

Hodotermes mossambicus (Hagen)	South Africa
Microtermes obesi Holmgr.	India
Microtermes vadschaggae (Sjöst.)	Tanzania
Procornitermes triacifer (Silv.)	Brazil
Trinervitermes biformis (Wasm.)	India
Trinervitermes rubidus (Hagen)	India

RICE

Coptotermes formosanus (Shiraki)	Japan
Capritermes nitobei (Shiraki)	Japan, Formosa
Procapritermes mushae Oshima	Formosa
Macrotermes subhyalinus (Rambur)	Nigeria
Macrotermes bellicosus (Smeath.)	Nigeria
Odontotermes formosanus (Shiraki)	Formosa
Procornitermes araujoi Emerson	Brazil
Syntermes molestus (Burm.)	Brazil
Trinervitermes ebenerianus Sjöst.	Nigeria

GROUNDNUTS

Coptotermes formosanus (Shiraki)	China
Amitermes evuncifer Silv.	Nigeria
Eremotermes nanus Harris	Sudan
Microcerotermes sp.	Gambia
Macrotermes subhyalinus (Rambur)	Sudan
Odontotermes badius (Hav.)	South Africa
Odontotermes latericius (Hav.)	South Africa

Odontotermes obesus (Rambur)	India
Odontotermes nilensis Emerson	Sudan
Odontotermes vulgaris (Hav.)	Senegal
Odontotermes spp.	Tanzania
Ancistrotermes crucifer (Sjöst.)	Gambia
Ancistrotermes latinotus (Holmgr.)	Congo
Microtermes thoracalis Sjöst.	Sudan
Microtermes sp.	Nigeria
Trinervitermes biformis (Wasm.)	India
Trinervitermes ebenerianus Sjöst.	Senegal

PASTURES

Hodotermes erythreensis Sjöst.	Ethiopia, Somalia
Hodotermes mossambicus (Hagen)	East and South Africa
Microhodotermes viator (Latr.)	South Africa
Anacanthotermes ahngerianus	Turkmenia
Anacanthotermes macrocephalus (Desn.)	India, Pakistan
Psammotermes hybostoma Desn.	Libya
Amitermes neogermanus Hill	Australia
Drepanotermes rubriceps (Froggatt)	Australia
Cornitermes cumulans (Kollar)	Brazil
Trinervitermes biformis (Wasm.)	India, Pakistan
Trinervitermes trinervoides (Sjöst.)	South Africa

MISCELLANEOUS FIELD CROP;

Hodotermes mossambicus (Hagen)	Tanzania
Heterotermes tenuis (Hagen)	Jamaica
Coptotermes formosanus Shiraki	China
Microcerotermes diversus Silv.	Arabia, Iraq
Amitermes evuncifer Silv.	Nigeria
Eremotermes sp.	India
Pseudacanthotermes militaris (Hagen)	Nigeria
Macrotermes subhyalinus (Rambur)	East Africa, Rhodesia
Odontotermes hainanensis (Light)	China
Odontotermes latericius (Hav.)	Tanzania
Odontotermes obesus (Rambur)	India
Odontotermes zambesiensis (Sjöst.)	Tanzania
Ancistrotermes latinotus (Holmgr.)	Tanzania, Congo
Allodontermes tenax (Silv.)	Tanzania
Microtermes albopartitis (Sjöst.)	Tanzania
Microtermes redenianus (Sjöst.)	Tanzania
Microtermes vadschaggae (Sjöst.)	Tanzania

CHAPTER 6

Termites and Forestry

The influence of termites on tropical forestry is threefold; there is the destruction of seedlings and saplings required for afforestation, there is the reduction in yield of timber from forests where termites are active in mature trees, and there is the effect of termites on natural regeneration of woodlands. Foresters in general appear to agree with the view expressed by MacGregor (1950). 'There is nothing in published literature or unpublished reports to suggest that termites constitute a serious forest pest, except in the case of *Eucalyptus* plantations or in forest nurseries. The economic consequences in these cases, however, may be serious.'

Assessment of losses of timber due to termites is not easy, particularly in natural forests where selective felling is practised. In some cases there are outwards signs of infestation which enable loggers to avoid the more seriously affected trees. When trees are felled and signs of termite attack seen on the exposed surfaces, the logs may be left where they are, and since logs arriving at the mill show only a small proportion of rejects, the full extent of the losses goes unappreciated. There are records of appreciable economic loss from primary termite attack in natural forest only from eucalyptus forests in Queensland and New South Wales, where logs are rendered unsuitable for milling by *Coptotermes*. In British Honduras, where similar damage is done to mahogany and pine by another *Coptotermes*, it has recently been shown that the termites are secondary to invasion by a wood-rotting fungus, which in turn follows some mechanical injury to the bark. Years of selective felling in that country have led to an unnatural accumulation of termite-damaged trees.

Minor damage to indigenous trees appears to be reported more by entomologists than by foresters, but this has a practical bearing when the introduction of exotic trees is under consideration. The best documented instance of economic damage to plantations of introduced trees is that of dry-wood termite attack on teak in Indonesia.

A wave of afforestation projects began some twenty years ago in the dry woodland and savanna areas of Africa, India and, to a less extent, South America, with the intention of providing shelter belts, building poles and fuel for the rapidly expanding indigenous populations. In general the genus *Eucalyptus* was preferred to such genera as *Cassia*, *Albizzia* and *Gmelina* because of its more rapid growth potential. It soon became apparent, however, that in those areas where they were required most urgently eucalypts as transplants and young saplings were being killed by termites (Plates 31 and 33). Since it was widely held that termites were secondary pests unable to feed on healthy plants, the primary cause of death was sought elsewhere; drought was commonly blamed, while in Zambia it was concluded that the ecological conditions which favoured the development of *Brachystegia* woodland were themselves antagonistic to *Eucalyptus*. Some high losses were recorded; in Cameroon they reached 100 per cent with *Eucalyptus saligna* and from 60 to 80 per cent with other species; in the drier areas of Uganda between 50 and 70 per cent of transplants were regularly lost; in Northern Nigeria *E. camaldulensis* had a failure rate of between 68 and 74 per cent in the first eighteen months and 86 per cent after thirty months. Improved nursery practice and the use of organochlorine insecticides has solved this problem to a large extent.

It is convenient to deal with the incidence of termite damage to trees on a geographical basis. Control measures will be considered as a whole, followed by a note on the influence of termites on natural regeneration.

Africa

Serious pests of forest nurseries in tropical Africa, as listed by Parry (1956), are termites, cutworms, crickets and the larvae of chafer-beetles. While most kinds of trees are liable to termite attack, eucalypts are especially susceptible. Later, when the young trees come to be planted out in the field, termites are the main obstacle to success. Parry gives the following as being resistant to termites under adverse conditions: *Cassia siamea, Albizzia lebbek, Jacaranda* spp., *Casuarina* spp., *Gmelina* spp. and *Callitris* spp. In many cases the reports of losses in eucalypt plantations do not specify the termite responsible. Throughout tropical Africa, however, it is almost exclusively the work of members of the subfamily Macrotermitinae, the fungus-growing termites with nests in mounds or just below ground: *Microtermes, Ancistrotermes, Odonto-termes, Macrotermes* and *Pseudacanthotermes*. Particularly destructive are the smaller representatives, such as *Ancistrotermes amphidon* in Uganda, *A. crucifer* in Nigeria and *A. latinotus* in Zambia.

Records of termite attack on mature trees are few in number. In East Africa a dry-wood termite, *Glyptotermes kawandae*, bores in *Xymalos*. The earth runways of various *Macrotermes* and *Odontotermes* are commonly found on the trunks of trees seeking wounds and dead branches, but serious damage appears to be confined to amenity plantings in townships subjected to barbarous pruning techniques employed by local authorities. *Schedorhinotermes lamanianus* is active on *Delonix, Dal-*

bergia and *Manihot* in coastal areas, and *Coptotermes amanii* on *Samanea*. Wattle plantations in Natal are subject to local attacks by *Macrotermes natalensis* and *Odontotermes badius*, and Fuller (1912) describes the injury to apparently healthy trees.

On the island of St Helena a subterranean termite, *Heterotermes perfidus*, known only from that one locality, is found in plantations of *Acacia longifolia*. The heartwood of the older trees is hollowed out, shortening their life and reducing the yield of firewood. Since this tree grows quickly from fallen seed, termite attack is of little significance. More concern is felt there for the loss of ornamental specimens of *Araucaria*, *Cupressus* and *Acacia* which blow over in gales after being weakened by termites.

India, Pakistan and Ceylon

Damage to the roots of young trees in the first three years of their life is described by Beeson (1941), who mentions *Eucalyptus* as being most seriously affected and other susceptible trees as *Shorea*, *Tamarix*, *Tectona* and *Terminalia*. The only termite mentioned specifically is *Odontotermes feae*, but no doubt other species of this common genus are concerned as well.

Dry-wood termites are becoming recognised as forestry pests in the Indian subcontinent. *Bifiditermes beesoni* attacks *Ficus bengalensis* in India and *Acacia*, *Dalbergia*, *Eriobotrya* and *Zizyphus* in West Pakistan. Ahmad (1962) lists these genera together with *Salix* as hosts of *Neotermes pishinensis* in West Pakistan. *Neotermes gardneri* is found in India on *Artocarpus*, *Litsea*, *Pterosporum* and *Woodfordia*. In Ceylon, according to Fernando (1962), the commonest termite associated with living trees is *Postelectrotermes militaris*. It has already been mentioned as a pest of tea and rubber, and it also feeds on *Albizzia* and *Grevillea* used as shade trees in these plantations; other hosts are *Artocarpus*, *Eucalyptus* and *Cedrela*. Also in Ceylon, but less injurious, are other dry-wood termites *Neotermes greeni* and *Glyptotermes dilatus*.

An unusual record comes from Baluchistan, where one of the Asiatic harvester termites, *Anacanthotermes macrocephalus*, attacks *Salix*.

A subterranean termite, *Reticulitermes chinensis*, feeds on the roots of *Pinus longifolia* in plantations in Assam at elevations of 4 000 feet (1 200 m). It bores upwards through the roots, preferring those under 0·5 in (15 mm) in diameter, filling the galleries with earth and leaving the bark intact (Kapur, 1962). *Coptotermes* is a related genus found in warmer situations; *C. heimi* is recorded from a wide range of trees in India, and *C. ceylonicus* similarly in Ceylon. In the Seychelles mature *Eucalyptus* trees are damaged by *Coptotermes truncatus*.

Odontotermes is a genus well known as a scavenger of woody debris on the forest floor throughout the subcontinent. A number of species are known to attack living trees for reasons not always clear. These include *O. redemanni*, *O. wallonensis* and *O. parvidens* in India and Burma. Also in Burma *O. xenotermitis* attacks teak plantations, together with *Globitermes audax* and *Hospitalitermes birmanicus*.

South-East Asia

The dry-wood termite *Neotermes tectonae* has been recognised as a serious pest of plantation teak in Java for many years. Kalshoven (1930) found that plantations between twenty and thirty years old had between 50 and 75 per cent of trees infested. In addition, examination of other trees in the vicinity showed infestation rates varying from 10 per cent for *Grewia celtidifolia* and *Cassia fistula* to 14 per cent for *Artocarpus integra* and *Albizzia* spp. and 35 per cent for *Glochidion obscurum*. Winged adult termites settle on snags or dead branches of teak trees within, or on the underside of, the crown, and establish their colonies in cracks or in chambers excavated in dead wood. The developing colonies penetrate further into the trunk, excavating galleries in sound wood. Infested trunks develop characteristic swellings several metres from the ground. Some six years elapse before a colony produces winged adults capable of infesting other trees. In later papers Kalshoven (1952, 1954) deals with some of the silvicultural aspects of *Neotermes* attack, indicating that infested trees that have been girdled are best felled within eight months, and certainly before the second rainy season, in order that the numbers of flying termites emerging are kept to a minimum. In trees that have been felled and left on the forest floor the termite colonies decline rapidly, especially if the logs have been split, though there may be some that will survive until the following season, producing their quota of adults and so spread the infestation.

In Indonesia *Coptotermes curvignathus* as a pest of forest trees was studied by Kalshoven (1962, 1963). This termite has already been mentioned as affecting rubber. Among the trees found to be infested in Java and Sumatra were *Albizzia*, *Artocarpus*, *Bombax*, *Canarium*, *Mallotus* and *Oroxylon*. A distinct preference for leguminous trees was noted, while attack on teak was rare and secondary to dry-wood termite injury. Records of trees attacked in Malaysia include *Campnosperma*, *Intsia*, *Koompassia*, *Ochanostachys*, *Shorea* and *Styrax*.

China and Japan

Forest nurseries in south China are damaged by *Odontotermes hainanensis*. *Eucalyptus* seedlings generally are liable to be lost, with the exception of two species which show some resistance, *E. maculata* and *E. citriodora*. Young trees of *Cunninghamia lanceolata* and *Pinus masoliana* are attacked in the field.

Standing trees in the Canton Province of China are damaged by *Coptotermes formosanus*, including *Eucalyptus*, *Salix*, *Albizzia* and *Ficus*. In Japan this termite is a serious problem in forests of the cedar, *Cryptomeria japonica*, damaged heartwood being found in 53 per cent of trees over twenty-five years old by Nakajima and Shimizu (1959).

Australasia

In New Guinea young plantations of hoop pine, *Araucaria cunninghamii*, are attacked by *Coptotermes elisae* and the necessity for infilling causes dislocation of planting programmes. Older plantations of this tree and also kauri, *Agathis* spp. are attacked. *C. elisae* occurs in *Araucaria klinkii* in primary forest (Gay, 1963).

Afforestation in Australia's Northern Territory is being handicapped by a unique and voracious termite, *Mastotermes darwiniensis*. Introduced pines are susceptible at all ages. In view of its resistance to *Odontotermes* and similar termites in Africa and Asia, *Gmelina* was unexpectedly found to be an easy prey to *Mastotermes*. Elsewhere in Australia there appears to be no termite problem in young plantings, even with introduced pines.

The indigenous eucalyptus forests of Australia are subject to termite attack which results in a serious loss of timber probably unequalled elsewhere in the world, according to Greaves (1960). *Coptotermes acinaciformis* is mainly responsible, and has been the subject of detailed investigations in recent years. Colonies become established in living trees and eventually the heart-wood is eaten out to form a hollow pipe, part of which may house the termite nest while the rest is filled with a mixture of soil and excreta. Incipient colonies appear to be able to survive only in dead wood, so it is assumed that initial infestation takes place through old fire scars or other wounds imperfectly calloused over. Developing communities move inwards towards the centre of the tree, and the presence of mature nests is usually indicated by a swelling of the trunk. Once established, a colony can then send out columns of foraging workers able to penetrate the bark of undamaged trees. Surveys have shown infestations as high as 75 per cent of mature standing timber (Greaves, 1962). *C. acinaciformis* is active mainly in warm coastal forests.

Other termites infesting trees are as follows: *Mastotermes darwiniensis* in tropical Australia; *Neotermes insularis* in the east from Torres Strait to Victoria; *Porotermes adamsoni*, a primitive damp-wood termite restricted to the alpine forests of the south-east; *Coptotermes frenchi* widely distributed at altitudes between 1 000 and 2 000 feet (300 and 700 m), and *Coptotermes brunneus* in Western Australia.

Central and South America

In South America afforestation with eucalyptus in the state of São Paulo, Brazil, has been hampered by attack from three species of termites, *Procornitermes striatus, Syntermes insidians* and *S. molestus*. These primitive nasute termites fill the role played by *Odontotermes* and related genera in Africa and Asia in feeding on seedling and sapling trees. Damage to more mature eucalypts by *Heterotermes tenuis* is reported from Brazil.

Mahogany and pines in Central America are attacked by *Coptotermes niger*. A high proportion of the standing timber in the forests of British Honduras, where selective felling has been practised for many years, has the heart-wood hollowed out into a pipe. Logs so affected are rejected by sawmillers. As in Australia, nests are indicated by massive swellings high up the trunks. Plans for reafforestation introduced the question of possible termite damage to new plantings. Williams (1965) found that an essential precursor of *Coptotermes* attack on *Pinus caribea* in British Honduras was the presence of a brown-rot fungus, *Lentinus pallidus*, which in turn is secondary to mechanical injury, usually fire. In neighbouring Mexico and Guatemala, however, pines were found attacked in the absence of the fungus. In these countries it would appear that the heartwood has a low resin content, whereas in British Honduras the resin and turpentine content is high enough to repel *Coptotermes* until fungus attack breaks down some, at least, of these substances. The exotic *Gmelina* is attacked by *Coptotermes* in British Honduras without prior fungus infection.

In a survey of forest insects in Puerto Rico, Martorelli (1945) lists three termites injurious to living trees. Two are dry-wood termites, *Incisitermes snyderi* with eleven host species recorded on Mona Island, and *Glyptotermes pubescens* restricted to high altitude forest with three host species. *Nasutitermes costalis*, an arboreal nesting termite known locally as 'el comején', has 108 host trees recorded and in the author's words 'is perhaps our most destructive termite and the damages done to trees every year have not been determined yet but presumably are worth consideration'. Logs of *Guiacum* from the Dominican Republic have reached England heavily infested with a dry-wood termite, *Neotermes jouteli*. In view of the reputation for hardness enjoyed by the heart-wood of lignum vitae, it is not surprising that almost all the galleries were found in sap-wood.

In Bermuda, a study of the pests and diseases of the rapidly disappearing local cedar, *Juniperus bermudiana*, brought to light the damage done by *Kalotermes approximatus*. More than 40 per cent of trees examined were found to be infested, representing a serious loss of timber as well as a real menace during hurricanes. This termite was also found in *Citharexylum*, *Melia* and *Persea* (Waterston, 1937, 1938).

North America

In the more arid districts of California the desert willow, *Chilopsis*, is host to two termites—*Paraneotermes simplicicornis*, a dry-wood termite which, unexpectedly, hollows out the tap-root, and *Heterotermes aureus* which feeds on bark.

Mediterranean and Middle East

Reference has been made already to dry-wood termite damage to fruit trees in southern Europe, and the insect responsible, *Kalotermes flavicollis*, is also to be found in trees grown for timber or ornamental purposes in many countries bordering the Mediterranean and Black Sea. In Italy it has been found in chestnut, plane, robinnia and elder; in Israel in *Populus alba*; and in Egypt in *Casuarina*.

The common subterranean termite of southern Europe, *Reticulitermes lucifugus*, is recorded from time to time killing ornamental trees. A study of avenue trees in the vicinity of Pisa, northern Italy, by Venturi (1965), suggests that this termite represents a potential threat to the distinctive Tuscan landscape. Along one main road, examination of some 2 000 trees, mainly plane with some sycamore maple, showed 40 per cent with signs of termite attack and 120 individual trees dead and acting as *foci* of infection. In the Pisa Botanic Garden, attack was observed on eucalyptus, magnolia, myrtle and *Liquidambar*. The main predisposing cause appears to be the entrance of water into wounds caused by careless pruning and by mechanical injury or animals breaking the bark.

In Arabia *Microcerotermes diversus* is widely distributed in the indigenous *Tamarix*. It attacks exotics such as *Casuarina* in addition to fruit trees. It is also reported from ornamental trees in Persia. In southern Arabia a dry-wood termite *Epicalotermes aethiopicus* lives in indigenous acacias.

Termites and Natural Regeneration

The regeneration of woodland by natural seeding and by coppicing can be hindered by the feeding activities of ground-dwelling termites, especially in semi-arid areas or during a prolonged drought. This will reduce considerably the production and length of useful life of eucalyptus pole plantations, and similar ventures, if measures are not taken after cutting to protect stumps with some simple wood preservative. Such action keeps away termites and other organisms until new shoots have had an opportunity to develop root systems of their own. In Africa and Asia, various species of *Macrotermes, Odontotermes* and *Microtermes* are active in this way as part of their general role in removing woody debris, while in the West Indies and Central America it is done by *Nasutitermes* working from their arboreal nests.

Natural regeneration of woodlands cleared by primitive agricultural-ists with their system of shifting cultivation is similarly hindered. Young trees are ring-barked at the collar as a matter of course and termite attack soon follows. There is nothing one can do about this as the nuisance is greatest where the land is poorest and the care for the land least obvious. In certain circumstances, however, termite action may facilitate natural regeneration. Reference has been made in an earlier chapter to the influence of termite mounds on vegetation. Broad-based mounds of some species of *Macrotermes* in Africa and Asia provide conditions for the growth of shrubs and trees, by raising areas of more fertile soil above the surrounding ground level, setting in motion a cycle of vegetation change which can ultimately restore the original woodland. This has been discussed by Cufodontis (1955), who concludes that in view of the tremendous problems, both technical and financial, in organising tree planting to make good the widespread deforestation in tropical Africa there are grounds for hope in the processes of natural regeneration based on termite mounds.

Termite Control in Nurseries and Young Plantations

Termite attack in nurseries and young plantings is usually more in evidence with exotics than with native trees, and especially when grow-ing conditions are marginal. Eucalyptus has, so far, been the main sufferer since it has been tried out in so many different countries to pro-vide shelter belts, building poles and firewood.

Termite damage may be secondary to disease, drought, uneven water-ing, mechanical injury or bad planting. Silvicultural methods which ensure healthy and uninterrupted growth must have first consideration and the introduction of plastic containers for seedlings has been a considerable step forward.

The arrival of organochlorine insecticides, from DDT onwards, stimulated interest in the possibility of protecting seedlings and newly planted trees until they had outgrown the normal hazards of termite attack. Wettable powders and emulsions of benzene hexachloride and chlordane, followed by aldrin and dieldrin, were used in nursery beds, and later when planting out these were again used to spray the roots before soil was returned to the planting holes. Encouraging results were reported from Brazil and from many parts of Africa, but there were failures too, and some lack of precision about the amount of insecticide required to provide efficient protection. An investigation was undertaken by the Termite Research Unit in cooperation with the Forestry Department in Northern Nigeria, the results of which were described by Sands (1960b, 1962). It was fortunate that the use of polythene film in tubular form was being developed at this time for the propagation of tree seed-lings, replacing the older nursery beds, seed boxes, clay pots and the like. The new method allowed more accurate dispensing of insecticides in potting mixtures, enabled the young trees to be planted out with their barrier of treated soil intact and, most important of all, provided a method of transplanting with minimal check on growth. In order that a minimum amount of insecticide is used to provide satisfactory results it is necessary to ensure thorough mixing in the potting soil, and for this purpose a mechanical aid was found desirable. A small cement mixer does this work well. Dieldrin 2 per cent dust was used at a rate of 10 oz per cubic yard of potting mixture (370 g per cubic metre) sufficient for 500 pots. On biological assay this was found to be equivalent to 5 kilo/hectare (4·4 lb/acre) in the top 150 mm (6 in) of soil. For large-scale operations, however, the Forestry Department increased the amount of dieldrin $2\frac{1}{2}$ times. According to Wimbush (1962) the potting mixture was made up of 4 parts river sand and 3 parts of compost with ammonium sulphate, superphosphate and dieldrin 2 per cent dust each 880 g added to every cubic metre of mixture (3 lb per cubic yard). In 1961 the cost of the dieldrin dust worked out at 3 shillings per thousand trees. The pots were of black tubular polythene film gauge 250, gusset formed and perforated with two pairs of drainage holes near the bottom. When opened and filled with soil this gave a pot 8 inches (200 mm) high by 3 inches (75 mm) diameter.

The protection afforded by soil treatment in this manner lasts at least eight years so far as the insecticide is concerned, which is far longer than necessary for a tree to outgrow the risk of attack by subterranean termites. However this presupposes that the barrier of treated soil around the base of the plant remains intact, and furthermore that there is insufficient soil movement to cover the base of the plant with a layer of untreated soil that would allow safe passage for termites to the collar. In practice the careful setting out of the plastic film pots sufficiently high to minimise the danger of soil wash, and the preservation of the complete barrier of treated soil around the young tree has given adequate protection in the field for the three or four years necessary to ensure a reasonable stand.

TERMITES AS FORESTRY PESTS

IN NURSERIES AND ON YOUNG TREES

Mastotermes darwiniensis Froggatt	tropical Australia
Coptotermes elisae (Desn.)	New Guinea
Amitermes evuncifer Silv.	Nigeria, Uganda
Microcerotermes massaiaticus Harris	Kenya
Pseudacanthotermes militaris (Hagen)	Nigeria
Macrotermes subhyalinus (Rambur)	Nigeria, Uganda
Macrotermes natalensis (Hav.)	Uganda
Odontotermes feae (Wasm.)	India
Odontotermes hainanensis (Light)	China
Odontotermes sp.	Uganda
Ancistrotermes cavithorax (Sjöst.)	Uganda
Ancistrotermes crucifer (Sjöst.)	Nigeria
Ancistrotermes latinotus (Holmgr.)	Zambia
Microtermes spp.	Nigeria, Uganda
Procornitermes striatus (Hagen)	Brazil
Syntermes insidiens Silv.	Brazil
Syntermes molestus (Burm.)	Brazil

ON MATURE TREES

Mastotermes darwiniensis Froggatt	tropical Australia
Kalotermes approximatus Snyder	Bermuda
Kalotermes flavicollis (Fabr.)	Mediterranean coast
Incisitermes snyderi Light	Puerto Rico
Bifiditermes beesoni (Gardner)	India, W. Pakistan
Epicalotermes aethiopicus Silv.	Arabia
Neotermes gardneri (Synder)	India
Neotermes greeni (Desn.)	Ceylon
Neotermes insularis (Walker)	Australia
Neotermes jouteli (Banks)	Dominican Republic
Neotermes tectonae (Damm.)	Indonesia
Postelectrotermes militaris (Desn.)	Ceylon
Postelectrotermes pishinensis (Ahmad)	W. Pakistan
Glyptotermes dilatus (Bugnion)	Ceylon
Glyptotermes kawandae Wilkinson	Uganda
Glyptotermes pubescens Snyder	Puerto Rico
Paraneotermes simplicicornis (Banks)	U.S.A.
Anacanthotermes macrocephalus (Desn.)	Baluchistan
Porotermes adamsoni (Froggatt)	Australia
Heterotermes aureus (Snyder)	U.S.A.

34. Internal damage to mature
    Cupressus trees by *Heterotermes*,
    St. Helena

35. Covered runways constructed
    by *Microcerotermes diversus* on
    ornamental acacia to wounds
    and scars, Iran
    (The Iranian Oil Operating Companies)

36. Tree seedling being destroyed
    by *Odontotermes boranicus* in
    dry country, northern Kenya

37. *Cryptotermes dudleyi* in wood-work of house, Tanzania

38. Railway sleeper damaged by *Anacanthotermes vagans* in Iran

(The Iranian Oil Operating Companies)

Heterotermes perfidus Silv.	St Helena
Heterotermes tenuis (Hagen)	Brazil
Reticulitermes chinensis Snyder	India (Assam)
Coptotermes acinaciformis (Froggatt)	Australia
Coptotermes amanii (Sjöst.)	East Africa
Coptotermes brunneus Gay	Australia
Coptotermes ceylonicus Holmgr.	Ceylon
Coptotermes curvignathus Holmgr.	Indonesia
Coptotermes elisae (Desn.)	New Guinea
Coptotermes formosanus Shiraki	Japan
Coptotermes frenchi Hill	Australia
Coptotermes heimi Wasm.	India
Coptotermes niger Snyder	Central America
Schedorhinotermes lamanianus (Sjöst.)	East Africa
Microcerotermes diversus Silv.	Arabia, Persia
Globitermes audax Silv.	Burma
Macrotermes natalensis (Hav.)	South Africa
Odontotermes latericius (Hav.)	South Africa
Odontotermes parvidens Holmgr.	India, Burma
Odontotermes redemanni (Wasm.)	India
Odontotermes wallonensis (Wasm.)	India
Odontotermes xenotermitis (Wasm.)	Burma
Nasutitermes costalis (Holmgr.)	Puerto Rico
Hospitalitermes birmanicus (Snyder)	Burma

CHAPTER 7

Timber

Dead wood, a term which in the present context embraces timber, is the staple food of a large number of the more common termites. Those termites which are found in standing trees have been discussed in the preceding chapter on forestry problems. Since the termites destructive to timber in use are all to be found in buildings, they are listed in Chapter 8. Here it is proposed to deal with the problem as it is influenced by the nature of the timber.

Some timbers are well known for their resistance to pests and the organisms of decay, others may be made resistant by treatment with wood preservatives. There remains a third class which are not naturally resistant and which are not amenable to preservative treatments as at present practised. Utilisation of new timbers and new preservatives depends on efficient testing under local conditions, and this is discussed here. Termite resistance in timbers is not a simple property, but depends on the kinds of termites to which they are exposed, as well as the conditions under which the timbers are employed (Plates 38, 39).

Natural Resistance

Throughout the tropics certain timbers have local reputations for resistance to termite attack, founded on generations of practical experience. Such timbers are usually indigenous, but some are imported as in the case of mangrove which has for centuries been carried from East Africa to the countries around the Persian Gulf. West Indian mahogany, Burmese teak and African iroko are examples of durable timbers whose reputations have carried them far from their original homes. Some timbers have not maintained their reputations under different conditions in new countries, or where new varieties of termite have appeared.

On the question of natural durability in timber Smith (1949) stresses the importance of environment and the weakening effect of fungi under damp conditions, especially at temperatures between 75° F and 90° F (24°–32° C). His results indicate the great variability of samples, even from the same log, and how for practical purposes it is inadvisable to classify timbers other than into the broadest groups of relative durability.

Durability in the face of termite attack is a synthesis of many properties in a timber, not least of these being resistance to fungi, because such attack will almost certainly open a way for termites. Of immediate interest to insects there are three properties, viz.: palatability, repellency, and opportunity.

PALATABILITY

This appears to be governed to a large extent by the proportion of lignin present. Lignin and cellulose are the major constituents of wood, but whereas the cellulose can be digested and used as food by the termites, the lignin is all excreted. According to Wolcott (1946) lignin is neither toxic nor repellent to *Cryptotermes brevis*, and it formed 90 per cent of the excreta when these termites fed on a wood of high lignin content (45 per cent) as compared with 50 per cent when they fed on wood with only 23 per cent lignin. Among unpalatable timbers of high lignin content are:

West Indian mahogany, *Swietenia mahogani*	46–46 per cent
Fustic, *Chlorophora tinctoria*	48 per cent
Maga, *Montezuma speciosissima*	52 per cent

For highly susceptible timbers, Wolcott gives the following lignin contents:

Flamboyante, *Delonix regia*	21 per cent
Humboldt's willow, *Salix humboldtiana*	23 per cent

Hardwoods have a higher proportion of lignin in their heartwood than in the sapwood. Furthermore there are, in sapwood, starches and sugars which render it more palatable than the heartwood of the same tree. Temperate-zone hardwoods are low in lignin content, as are conifers generally. Closely related species may differ significantly in lignin content, and in palatability, so it is difficult to generalise from generic names.

REPELLENCY

Specific chemical substances are present in some woods in sufficient quantities to drive away termites. In other woods the amount present is only sufficient to repel the termite after it has eaten a minute particle. Once again it is the heartwood that usually has an effective concentration of repellent substance. Extracts of resistant heartwoods have been used to impregnate palatable softwoods and so render them termite-repellent for long periods. These extracts have been analysed, and in some cases it has proved possible to synthesise likely constituents in quantity in order to test them individually. Much of the testing has been carried out by Wolcott (1958) using *Cryptotermes brevis*, and he has shown that Chlorophorin, which occurs in the timber iroko (*Chloro-phora excelsa*), is effective as a one-half per cent solution, in which the test pieces are dipped for ten minutes, for more than $4\frac{1}{2}$ years. Pinosylvin and its derivatives, from *Pinus sylvestris*, was shown to be similarly effective at a dilution of one-hundredth of one per cent. In view of the lack of resistance to termite attack shown by *Pinus sylvestris* timber, one can only assume that Pinosylvin is present in exceedingly small amounts in the tree. Tectoquinone from teak (*Tectona grandis*) was considered by Wolcott to be the active agent in this resistant timber, and experiments with it showed that a 0·5 per cent solution protected flamboyante wood for over nine years against dry-wood termites. However, workers in Australia (Rudman *et al.*, 1958) show that pure Tectoquinone is not effective against *Coptotermes lacteus* and *Nasutitermes exitiosus*, or against fungi, and cannot be regarded as the real source of resistance in teak. No doubt the active chemical was present as an impurity in Wolcott's material and is, in fact, effective at dilutions of the order of those effective for Pinosylvin.

Not unexpectedly the distribution of these repellent substances in the living tree is uneven, and the durability of timber therefrom is liable to be affected by the age of the tree, the conditions under which it was grown, and also the part of the tree from which it was cut. Such variations are the more significant as the average content of repellent substance approaches a minimum. Reference has already been made to the great difference between heartwood and sapwood of the same tree, and the maximum effect is generally found in the outer layers of the heartwood. Coniferous woods are generally of low resistance, but there is considerable variation in the group as shown in tests with dry-wood termites. *Picea sitchensis*, the Sitka spruce, is among the most susceptible woods, while the heartwood of *Pinus occidentalis*, the Cuban pine, almost equals mahogany in its resistance. Age is of importance in the accumulation of repellent substances, much of our present-day troubles arising from the exhaustion of virgin forests with their old mature trees, and the almost universal use of young second-growth trees for timber.

Resins of the right sort and in adequate amounts will make a timber unpalatable. This was particularly evident in the pitch-pine of earlier years when the timber of *Pinus palustris*, *P. elliottii* and *P. caribaea* had a well-deserved reputation for resistance to dry-wood termites in the southern United States, the islands of the Caribbean and in coastal West Africa. Timber from second-growth woodlands is no longer 'fat' with resin, and not at all resistant to termites. A good example of the durability of pitch-pine may be seen in the old Fourah Bay College building at Freetown, Sierra Leone. Built around 1850, this building was quite free from termites in 1955, although much damage is apparent in buildings of later date there.

Essential oils make timber repellent, as for example the cedarwood oil in species of *Cedrela*, and the camphor in *Cinnamomum camphora*. Such substances tend to be lost easily on exposure to sun and air, and unless allied to high lignin content or similar property, the durability of the timber decreases rapidly.

OPPORTUNITY

This is intended to cover the very various factors making up the environment in which the timber is required to be durable, and details of which are necessary in considering claims for termite resistance.

Termites vary greatly in their habits, particularly their food preference, and in their geographical distribution. Thus there are localities where termite attack is much more intense than in others, either because conditions are favourable for termites as a whole, or because of the presence of a voracious species. A timber may acquire a reputation for termite resistance in one area, and fail when tried in another. There are more termites, both individually and in variety, in the tropics than in more temperate climates, and there is no doubt that the average time required for termites to seek out and destroy a piece of wood is far less in, say, Tanzania and Malaya than it is in the Cape Peninsula or Cyprus. In the tropics there is much variation and as a result of the high proportion of humus-feeding termites in rain forests termite damage is slower there than in dry woodlands and savannas, as is seen when comparing the results of field trials in Northern Nigeria with those of coastal areas in Eastern Nigeria. With regard to the effect of the particular species of termite present, a good example is found in *Mastotermes darwiniensis* of a voracious species with a limited range causing much more rapid damage in the north of the Australian continent than is general elsewhere in its absence.

When a timber has been tested for termite resistance with favourable results, full consideration should be given to the opportunities for damage during the course of the test in assessing the chances of the timber being similarly resistant elsewhere. Time and a hot damp climate tend to work in favour of the termites, leaching away or changing the composition of the substances which are the basis of natural resistance in timbers.

SOME RESISTANT TIMBERS

Lists of timbers resistant to termite attack have been published by a number of workers over the past forty-five years, among the earlier being Oshima for Formosa and the Philippines, Snyder for the U.S.A. and Panama, Foxworthy in Malaya and Beeson in India. Wolcott, in

Puerto Rico, has studied the timbers of many countries in relation to the West Indian dry-wood termite. The available information has been assembled in great detail by Bavendamm (1955) and listed for ease of reference under botanical names, in botanical families, and according to country of origin. For present purposes a list has been prepared of those hardwoods included in the British Standard Nomenclature of Commercial Hardwoods (B.S. 881 : 1955) which are reputed to show reasonable resistance to termite attack. For secondary timbers or woods of purely local interest it will be necessary to consult Bavendamm, or original papers of a later date.

TERMITE-RESISTANT COMMERCIAL TIMBERS

Botanical species	Source of supply	Standard name
Achras sapota L.	Central America	sapodilla
Adina cordifolia Benth. & Hook.	India, Burma, Thailand	haldu
Afzelia africans Smith	West Africa	afzelia
A. bipindensis Harms.	,,	,,
A. pachyloba Harms.	,,	,,
A. quanzensis Welw.	East Africa	,,
Baikiaea plurijuga Harms.	Rhodesia	Rhodesian teak
Brachylaena hutchinsii Hutch.	East Africa	muhuhu
Carapa guianensis Aubl.	West Indies, Tropical and Souther America	crabwood
Cedrela mexicana Roem.	West Indies, Tropical America	Central American cedar
C. toona Roxb.	India, Burma, Thailand	Burma (etc.) cedar
C. toona var. *australis* C.DC.	Australia	Australian cedar
Chlorophora excelsa Benth. & Hook.	West and East Africa	iroko
C. tinctoria Gaud.	West Indies and Tropical America	fustic
Chloroxylon swietenia DC.	Ceylon, India	Ceylon satinwood
Cordia alliodora R. & P.	West Indies and Tropical America	salmwood
Cylicodiscus gabunensis Harms.	West Africa	okan
Cynometra alexandri C. H. Wright	Uganda	muhimbi
Dalbergia latifolia Roxb.	India, Java	Indian rosewood

Botanical species	Source of supply	Standard name
D. stevensonii Standl.	British Honduras	Honduras rosewood
Daniellia orgea Rolfe ex Holl.	West Africa	orgea
Dicorynia paraensis Benth.	Guianas, Brazil	basralocus
Diospyros spp.	Tropical Africa	African ebony
Distemonanthus bentham-ianus Baill.	West Africa	ayan
Eperua falcata Aubl.	Tropical South America	wallaba
Erythrophleum guineense G.Don.	Tropical Africa	missanda
Eucalyptus creba F. Muell.	Australia	ironbark
E. marginata Sm.	,,	jarrah
E. sideroxylon A.Cunn.	,,	ironbark
Eusideroxylon zwageri Teijsm. & Binn.	Borneo, Indonesia	billian
Guaiacum officinale L.	West Indies and Tropical America	lignum vitae
Hopea odorata Roxb.	India, Burma, Thailand, Indo-China	thingan
Hopea spp.	Malaya	merawan
Hura crepitans L.	West Indies and Tropical America	hura
Hymenaea courbaril L.	West Indies and Tropical America	courbaril
Intsia bijuga O.Ktse. } *I. palembanica* Miq. }	Malaya, Borneo, Indo-nesia, New Guinea	merbau
Lagerstroemia hypoleuca Kurz.	Andaman Islands	Andaman pyinma
Lophira alata Banks	West Africa	ekki
Manilkara, see *Achras*		
Millettia laurentii De Wild.	Congo	wenge
Mimusops djave Engl.	West Africa	moabi
Mora excelsa Benth.	Guianas, Trinidad	mora
Ocotea rodiaei Mez.	Guyana	Demerara green-heart
Olea welwitschii Gilg. & Schil.	East Africa	loliondo
Peltogyne spp.	West Indies and Tropical America	purpleheart
Piptadenia africana Hook.	West and East Africa	dahoma
Piratinera guianensis Aubl.	Tropical America	snakewood
Pterocarpus angolensis DC.	East and Southern Africa	muninga
P. indicus Willd.	East Indies	amboyna
P. macrocarpus Kurz.	Burma, Thailand	Burma padauk
P. soyauxii Taub.	West Africa	African padauk
Robinia pseudoacacia L.	Europe, U.S.A.	robinia

Botanical species	*Source of supply*	*Standard name*
Sarcocephalus diderrichii De Wild.	West Africa	opepe
Shorea spp.	East Indies	meranti, seraya
(there is considerable variation in resistance to termites among the species in this genus, and their precise status is difficult to ascertain from the literature)		
Swietenia mahagoni Jacq.	West Indies	American mahogany
Tectona grandis L.	India, Burma, Thailand, Java	teak
Tristania conferta R.Br.	Australia	brush box

Wood Preservation

Timber may be protected from attack by termites, as it is from other wood-boring insects and from fungi, by a variety of processes which aim at introducing adequate amounts of chemicals which are poisonous or repellent and keeping them in the timber over long periods of time. Three points have to be considered:

1. Choice of a chemical, or formulation of several chemicals, which will be effective against the termites of a particular area, and under the particular condition in which the treated timber will be employed.
2. Knowledge of the local termites involved so that an effective level of impregnation may be assured.
3. Choice of timber with reference to its absorptive power (or degree of resistance to wood preservative) and suitability for the impregnation process available.

A more detailed treatment of this subject will be found in Findlay (1962).

CHEMICALS FOR WOOD PRESERVATION

The search for new chemicals likely to protect timber from termites goes on all the time. Field testing of their efficiency, as opposed to laboratory tests, is a slow process, with the result that there is always a time-lag in obtaining this essential practical proof of their value. Such tests are necessary, especially with regard to the decomposition of the chemical under the tropical sun and in conditions of high humidity, and to its loss by leaching when the timber is in contact with soil moisture. While creosote has been in use as a wood preservative for over a hundred years, and Dr Wolman patented his original formula—a mixture of sodium fluoride and dinitrophenol—in 1907, pentachlorophenol has only been in commercial use since 1933. The rapidly expanding group of chlorinated hydrocarbons is of even later origin.

The following list is intended only as an indication of the various types of wood preservatives in use and is based on British Standard Code of Practice, CP 112.100. Proprietary preparations vary in their constituents and so they are not mentioned here, but their value may be assessed from the amount of active material if this is stated by the manufacturer.

Further particulars of these chemicals and their suitability for use under various conditions will be found in the publications of the British Standards Institution, the Forest Products Research Laboratory, the Timber Development Association, British Wood Preserving Association, and similar bodies in other parts of the Commonwealth.

I. Coal tar creosote.
II. Organic solvent preservatives—
  naphthenates, metallic and chlor-; pentachlorophenol, and organic derivatives.
III. Water-soluble preservatives—
  sodium pentachlorophenate; copper, chrome and/or arsenic; fluor, chrome, arsenic; compounds of boron, sodium fluoride, zinc, etc.

There are three broad divisions of the conditions under which building timbers are required to remain resistant to termite attack:

1. In contact with the ground, and subject to leaching by soil moisture.
2. Exterior work, not in direct contact with the ground but exposed to sun and rain.
3. Interior work.

Creosote is perhaps the best known of all wood preservatives. Because of its odour and incompatibility with painting, it is more or less restricted to the first of these divisions. Organic solvent and water-soluble preservatives are variously used in all three divisions, with a bias in favour of oil-borne preservatives for timber in contact with the ground. The efficiency of the impregnation process is, in practice, probably of greater importance than the type of preservative used.

METHODS OF IMPREGNATING TIMBER

The various wood preservatives are applied in four quite different ways:

1. Brushing, spraying and dipping.
2. Hot and cold open-tank method.
3. Pressure impregnation in closed tank.
4. Diffusion.

Brushing, spraying and dipping do not, as a rule, produce any great depth of penetration and the resulting protective layer is accordingly fragile. A combination of highly absorptive timber and preservative formulated for low viscosity will give the best results, more particularly with fabricated units such as window frames and with furniture. As a protective treatment for woodwork already in position, brushing and spraying are the only practical methods, and like painting require to be repeated at intervals. One has only to saw through a piece of timber which has been brushed or dipped with cold creosote to see how thin a protective layer may result from such applications. Brushing and spraying are referred to again later with reference to treatment of termite-infested buildings.

Dipping in open tanks is an improvement on brushing, and since it requires only simple equipment it is possible under circumstances which would rule out more complex procedures. Soaking in low-viscosity pre-servatives for forty-eight hours is about the optimum period. Facilities for draining back into the tank surplus fluid from each batch of treated timber are essential to prevent wastage. Only seasoned timber of a sort known to absorb preservatives is worth treating. This method is useful for farm posts and for joinery work. Absence of fire hazard makes the use of the more volatile oils possible (Plate 41).

The hot and cold open-tank treatment requires more equipment in the form of at least one tank with a source of heat. In its simplest form this may be an old oil drum over an open fire. An open fire limits the choice of preservative to water-soluble mixtures, or with a little care creosote and pentachlorophenol in the heavier petroleum oils. In this way farm poles and joinery work may be treated. Large tanks with flues or steam coils for heating are an improvement, but are more complicated to run. The idea is to heat up the timber in the preserving fluid for two hours or more, depending on the cross-section of the timber, at a temperature in the region of 200° F (93° C), and then, when it is heated right through, the timber is removed to an adjacent tank of cold fluid, or the heat is removed and the tank allowed to cool overnight. Contraction of air in the cell during cooling draws preservative into the timber. The depth of penetration achieved is variable and it is advisable that all cutting, boring and making of joints be completed before treatment. If water-soluble preservatives are used, time must be allowed for treated timber to season again before it is put into use.

Pressure impregnation is a highly technical matter requiring special equipment, the main feature of which is a closed tank or cylinder large enough to accommodate timber in the mass. There are a number of systems employed, making use of heat, pressure and vacuum to obtain the desired standard of absorption. The finished product is generally judged by the retention of active preservative expressed as weight per cubic foot. For example, it is usual to specify a creosote retention of 10 lb per cubic foot (160 kg per cubic metre) for timber that will be in contact with the ground, while if pentachlorophenol as a 5 per cent solution in oil is employed, a retention of 8 to 10 lb per cubic foot (120 to 160 kg per cubic metre) is suggested for outside work and 6 lb (100 kg per cubic metre) for internal work. The question of the absorptive capacity of various timbers is discussed below (Plate 42).

Impregnation by diffusion is a process whereby preservatives are introduced into green timber immediately after sawing. This cuts out transport charges to and from a central pressure impregnation plant, since it can be undertaken as an on-the-spot treatment at 'bush' saw-mills as well as at larger establishments. It is claimed that some timbers which are impervious to pressure treatment will respond to diffusion. The process was developed originally for protecting timber against fungi and boring beetles, but some of the chemicals used have proved to be of value against termites. Boron compounds have lately been shown to be effective against dry-wood and moist-wood termites because, it is believed, they kill off the intestinal protozoa on which these termites depend for the digestion of cellulose. As the process is suitable for the treatment of veneers immediately after peeling from the log, it offers a potentially simple method of producing termite-proof plywoods.

The green timber is dipped in a tank containing a concentrated water solution of the preservative, or passed on an endless belt through a spray tunnel, or else the preservative is sprayed on to the timber while it is being stacked, and then it is stored under conditions of reduced ventilation to allow it to dry slowly and allow the chemicals thus applied to the surface layers to diffuse naturally through the timber. This process of diffusion takes time, and there must be sufficient sap in the timber to permit of this.

A diffusion process of a different type is applicable to timbers *in situ*. This has been patented recently in the U.S.A., and involves the use of a semi-stable highly viscous oil-in-water emulsion containing penta-chlorophenol which is applied to the wood in a thick layer. The outside of this layer soon dries to form a protective crust under which the oil and pentachlorophenol diffuse slowly into the dry timber below.

THE IDENTITY OF THE LOCAL TERMITES

Termites vary greatly in their susceptibility to different wood preservatives, with the result that a dosage effective in one locality may prove inadequate in another. Gay and Wetherly in Australia have shown that while 0·27 per cent by weight of pentachlorophenol gave good protection against the local *Nasutitermes*, 2·16 per cent permitted *Coptotermes* to do some damage in laboratory tests. On the other hand borax was effective against *Coptotermes* at from 0·46 to 0·56 per cent, while *Nasuti-termes* was able to tolerate up to 1·09 per cent. With a water-soluble proprietary preservative, 'Tanalith U', significant difference in the minimum lethal doses for two species of *Coptotermes* was found, *C. acinaciformis* being more tolerant than *C. lacteus*. It is worth noting that these workers have found that Australian termites require higher retentions in in the treated timber of boric acid, zinc chloride and 'Tanalith U' than have been found to be effective against the woodworm *Anobium* in New Zealand.

SUITABILITY OF TIMBERS FOR IMPREGNATION

As a broad generalisation it may be said that only sapwood can be impregnated successfully, while heartwood is difficult or impossible to treat irrespective of whether or not it is naturally resistant to termite attack. It is mostly softwood that is impregnated commercially. Hardwood poles are frequently treated with perservative in order to make the sapwood durable and thus allow the poles to have a reasonable length of life. As in all generalisations in biology, there are variations to be taken into account in practice, among the more noteworthy of these being the high resistance to penetration by preservatives of the sapwood of Canadian spruce, Douglas fir, and cypress. Among the pines there is great variation in their uptake of preservative from the highly absorbent *Pinus patula* to the resistant *P. gregii* and *P. halepensis*, though in general the genus may be considered as amenable to impregnation. Eucalypts vary but are, on the whole among the more difficult timbers to impregnate. From the detailed account of pressure treatments for wood preservation given by MacLean (1952) and from the report on the protection of buildings in South Africa (National Building Research Industry, Pretoria, 1950) lists have been compiled of common timbers whose sapwood is difficult to impregnate and those whose heartwood is easy to impregnate (see below).

Since the termite resistance of treated timber depends on its retention of a minimum quantity of a particular preservative for a depth which will provide an effective barrier, with some allowance for fair wear and tear over a period of time, a measure of the retention achieved should be available with each batch of the timber. It is not enough to know that the timber has been subjected to a particular treatment, unless it is clear that the timber is of a variety and nature amenable to impregnation in that manner as a result of periodical tests.

SOME COMMON TIMBERS WITH SAPWOOD DIFFICULT TO IMPREGNATE

softwoods

Cedrus deodara	cedar (deodar)
Chamaecyparis lawsoniana	Port Orford cedar
Cupressus lusitanica	cypress
Cupressus torulosa	cypress
Picea species	Canadian spruce
Pseudotsuga taxifolia	Douglas fir
Thuya plicata	western red cedar
Tsuga canadensis	eastern hemlock

hardwoods

Afzelia quanzensis	East African afzelia
Chlorophora excelsa	iroko
Entandophragma cylindricum	sapele
Khaya ivorensis	African mahogany
Liquidambar styraciflua	American red gum
Piptadenia africana	dahama
Pterocarpus angolensis	muninga
Syncarpia glomulifera	turpentine
Tectona grandis	teak

SOME COMMON TIMBERS WITH HEARTWOOD EASY TO IMPREGNATE

hardwoods

Betula verrucosa	European birch
Fagus grandifolia	American beech
Fagus sylvatica	European beech
Fraxinus americana	American ash
Fraxinus pennsylvanica	American green ash
Nyssa aquatica	tupelo
Nyssa sylvatica	,,
Quercus species	American red oak
Tilia americana	basswood

Simple Field Testing for Termite Resistance

There are so many different kinds of timber used in constructional work, so many wood preservatives on the market, and not a little variation in the habits of termites in different countries, that the architect or engineer is frequently without the precise information on termite resistance that he would desire. Small-scale trials have to be carried out locally to provide this information, and the following suggestions are offered in order that they will stand up to critical examination and their results may be compared with other trials. These notes on what are commonly known as 'termite graveyard tests' are grouped under three heads: proving of the site; layout and conduct of test; and ancillary, or supporting data.

PROVING OF THE SITE

It does not appear always to be obvious that much time and trouble will be saved if the site chosen for the test is first proved, or shown to have an adequate supply of wood-feeding termites available. After clearing the site of vegetation and levelling-off, slabs or stakes of a timber known to be eaten freely by the local termites should be partially buried in the soil at regular intervals over the area. In the absence of a susceptible local wood, 'deal' boards from packing cases or stakes of *Eucalyptus saligna* are satisfactory for this purpose. During dry weather, termite attack will be accelerated by watering the plot occasionally, or providing a light cover of grass or wood shavings. When there are signs of general termite activity, the stakes should be removed at random and inspected until it becomes apparent that over 75 per cent of them are damaged, when all the stakes are then removed. The time taken for this to be reached should be noted and used as a minimum for the subsequent trials. Parts of the site where attack is greatest should be noted for use in case the whole area cleared is not required.

The time taken to prove a site will vary. It is likely to be least in dry countries, during their brief rainy season. Areas within the closed canopy of lowland tropical rain forest should not be chosen as here termite attack on timber is usually slow until rotting is well established, but cultivated areas outside the forest are suitable. Cold weather tends to drive termites deeper into the soil and reduces their activity near the surface, as also may happen with extreme drought. Summer rainfall favours termite attack. In the bushveld of the Transvaal, it has been found advisable to make the initial inspection after fourteen days, and in the right season of the year a period of six weeks may prove adequate for a trial. In tropical Africa, generally speaking, a trial will run for about three months. Care must be exercised when mulching or watering the plot to accelerate termite attack that the test slabs do not rot away before they are attacked by insects.

The termites which make the largest mounds are unlikely to be the most active species in destroying timber. The surface of large mounds is not a suitable site for field tests, and the flat ground around the base of such mounds may produce less activity than some place midway between two mounds. Some of the fastest wood destruction goes on in places where the termites build small mounds or none at all. The reliable wood destroyers are small insects whose colonies are not concentrated in a series of closely packed chambers, but are spread out with long inter-communicating corridors.

LAYOUT AND CONDUCT OF TEST

Some degree of uniformity in the wood samples to be tested is desirable. Stakes 3 by 3 inches (8 by 8 cm) or slabs of one-inch planking cut to a width of about 6 inches give roughly the same area of surface exposed. They can be from 6 to 12 inches (15 to 30 cm) long, of which two-thirds is buried in the soil. It is desirable to mark the slabs or stakes with metal labels, as these will remain behind should the wood have been eaten away completely between inspections. If the label disappears as well, destructive agencies other than termites may be suspected.

An orderly arrangement of the slabs in a test plot facilitates inspection and checking and increases the value of the results, particularly if a 'Latin Square' type of layout is adopted. A convenient type of Latin Square is one made up of twenty-five slabs, five of each of five different treatments, arranged in five rows to form a square, with one representative of each treatment in each row, horizontal or vertical, thus:

A	B	C	D	E
B	E	A	C	D
C	D	E	A	B
D	A	B	E	C
E	C	D	B	A

Any letter may represent the untreated control, leaving space for four treatments. A smaller square is not useful, and if the trial is a simple one of one kind of timber treated in one particular manner then the layout suggested would be:

A	attractive local timber or deal
B and D	untreated timber
C and E	treated timber

There are other satisfactory ways of laying out tests, but the 5 by 5 Latin Square, repeated as often as is necessary to include all the required treatments, is simple and one that can be recommended to those not well versed in experimental statistics (Plate 40).

The question of protecting the slabs from excessive rain or sun is bound up with that of inducing rapid attack, as mentioned above. Watering in a dry climate will not only attract termites, but by compacting the surface of the soil will tend to keep away ants, which are the termites' worst enemies. It is not unknown in dry sandy soils for ants to keep termites away from parts of a test plot and so make the results most unreliable. Light grass shelters or perforated tins may be desirable to modify extreme climatic conditions, but are generally only necessary when testing wall boards, plywood, fabrics and the like.

The length of time which a trial must be allowed to run will be indicated by the time taken when proving the site. It varies so much with local conditions that no suggestions can be offered, other than the rather obvious one that time must be allowed for the known susceptible timber to be well eaten.

Test slabs should not be pulled out of the ground at frequent intervals in order to see how things are going on, and then replaced. Such disturbances may scare away the termites and will reduce the rate of attack. The desirable arrangement is to have two similar plots arranged adjacent to each other, one of which can be removed and inspected at the earliest likely time, and the other remain in reserve for later inspection should the first one prove too early. Some attention should be paid to the season when the test is carried out. When problems such as leaching or decomposition of the protective medium are being considered, the length of the experiment will be increased greatly, and a number of replications are necessary that can be inspected during the course of the trial without affecting the remaining slabs. Extensive damage to slabs becomes apparent when the portions remaining above ground fall over.

Results are best expressed as simply as possible. Suggestions for categories into which the slabs are placed after inspection are:

1. Undamaged.
2. Superficial attack only, obviously discontinued.
3. Damaged.

Subdivision of group 3 seems unnecessary in this type of experiment since it is merely a matter of time for 'slight damage' to develop into 'heavy damage', if it has started at all during the short time that has elapsed.

ANCILLARY DATA

It is desirable, when presenting the results of a trial, to give some idea of the kinds of termites to which the wood has been exposed. This information is already available for some parts of the tropics, but not in all. When slabs are removed for inspection they may be shaken over a sheet of white paper and if there are any termites about they will fall out and be easy to collect. Preserved in spirit or formalin, they can then be sent for identification.

Particulars of the climate during the course of the trial should also be noted. It is clearly not possible to compare results of one trial conducted in the season of maximum termite activity with another carried out in a period of general inactivity.

39. Subterranean termite damage to untreated electricity pole, Nigeria

40. Timber testing plot or "graveyard" in Uganda

41. Tank for dipping timber in preservative, Jamaica

42. Cylinder for pressure impregnation of timber, Trinidad

Laboratory Testing for Termite Resistance

Laboratory tests of the natural resistance of timbers and of the relative efficiency of chemicals as wood preservatives are of great practical value in permitting the screening of a large number of samples in a relatively short time. They enable minimum lethal doses and similar quantitative matters to be determined with accuracy. On the other hand they require laboratory facilities and trained staff, which are not always available. Official organisations with facilities for testing with termites exist in France, Switzerland, Germany and Australia. Laboratory tests for research purposes are carried out in a number of countries by commercial firms, forestry laboratories and universities.

European laboratories employ one or other of the two termites native to the Mediterranean area, *Kalotermes flavicollis* and *Reticulitermes lucifugus*. According to Gösswald (1956), *Kalotermes* is the better test insect because the individuals are specially resistant to adverse conditions, there are few difficulties in maintaining laboratory cultures, and finally it is an aggressive feeder under laboratory conditions. On the other hand, *Reticulitermes* is much more fertile, new colonies are readily made by splitting up an old one, and larger numbers of insects can be used in tests to produce more massive effects.

Kalotermes flavicollis, the yellow-necked dry-wood termite, lives in communities of rarely more than 500 individuals. It bores into the dead wood of vines and various trees, and under certain circumstances into building timbers. There is no true worker caste, the nymphs of the later instars collecting and distributing food to the community. Development under natural conditions is slow and subject to seasonal fluctuations. At a constant temperature of 25° C, and in high relative humidity, the progeny of a pair of young adults will be from twenty-five to fifty-five after twelve months. While the first two larval instars are fairly regular in occupying twenty-four to thirty-one days, later development is highly variable. Winged adults do not appear as a rule until a colony is at least two years old.

The technique for testing with *K. flavicollis* is given in detail by Gösswald and includes the following points. The tests are conducted at 27° C and 98 per cent RH in special glass containers. These containers consist of a lower dish containing potassium sulphate paste to maintain the humidity, on which rests a glass ring with a metal gauze base to contain thirty nymphal termites and the piece of material under test, and finally a glass cover. Dead and dying termites are removed daily and replaced with fresh ones, during the three weeks of the test. If the results obtained are sufficiently promising, the same sample is then subjected to 150 termites for a further period of three weeks.

Reticulitermes lucifugus, the Mediterranean moist-wood termite, lives in large communities numbering several thousand. Their social organisation is well developed and for test purposes it is necessary to use a team of workers, nymphs and soldiers. Development is greatly influenced by temperature, the optimum being 25° C (77° F) when a primary colony will number about fifty workers and one or two soldiers after one year. Secondary colonies are easily established by removing from an established community a suitable selection of the different castes, including several nymphs which will become substitute reproductives in due course.

Testing with *R. lucifugus*, as carried out at the Centre Technique Forestier Tropical, Nogent-sur-Marne, consists of using a piece of the test material as a base and attaching to it with paraffin wax a glass cylinder 8 cm by 2 cm (3 in by 1 in). The cylinder is then filled with clean moist sand to one-third of its height and pieces of pine sapwood which have already been attacked by termites are inserted. Approximately 100 termites are now introduced, made up of two soldiers, about 10 nymphs and the balance workers. This is all put away in an incubator and maintained at 20° C (77° F) and between 90 and 95 per cent RH for six weeks. At the end of this time the test slab is removed for examination.

A detailed account of the method of laboratory testing developed by the Division of Entomology, C.S.I.R.O., Canberra, is given by Gay and his associates (1955). They use three species of termites, *Nasutitermes exitiosus*, *Coptotermes lacteus* and *C. acinaciformis*. In the United States, *Reticulitermes flavipes* and *R. hesperus* are widely used in laboratory tests.

Different methods of rearing termites in the laboratory are shown on Plate 22.

CHAPTER 8

Termite Damage to Buildings

Termite damage to buildings is such that within the wide limits of their geographical distribution, already described, these insects will in time destroy any unprotected timber used in construction work or as fittings, unless it has been rendered unpalatable or is naturally resistant to termites. Furthermore, since the function of most buildings is to provide shelter and protection for man and his possessions, it is not enough that the buildings themselves are constructed throughout of materials which cannot be attacked but they must also protect the contents from attack if they are to merit the label 'termite-proof'. Woodwork does not need to be in contact with the ground to become infested, since subterranean termites will build their tubular runways from the soil over brickwork, up the interior of cavity walls, and in similar situations for very long distances to reach roof-beams or ceiling boards. Dry-wood termites, on the other hand, will fly direct into the roof of a building and start their colonies in timber far removed from the ground. They have been found in isolated plugs of softwood set high up in concrete walls to support electric fittings. Few situations could be said to be out of their range.

While it is not possible to estimate the annual loss caused by termite attack on buildings throughout the world, some idea of the magnitude of the problem can be got from the figures available. According to Ebeling (1968) 'termites cost the U.S. public approximately half a billion dollars per year'. For Australia the annual cost has been estimated by Hickin (1969) at around A\$7 million, of which A\$3 million goes to termite control operators mainly in the state of Queensland. In general, however, governments and other large organisations are reluctant to break down their building repair costs in order to provide a precise figure for termite damage. In 1943 the government of Jamaica included in its census a question relating to the presence of termites in the homes of each family. Analysis of the returns from the fourteen parishes showed that the percentage of dwellings infested varied from 45·1 in Manchester to 80·9 in Westmorland, with an overall average for the island of 61·2. Of all the houses stated to be in good condition, 40 per cent had termites present, while in the category 'bad condition' termites were in 73 per cent.

The West African Building Research Station inquired into the cost of repairing termite damage to government and para-government buildings in the four British West African territories in 1955 and gave as their estimate £250 000 per annum, or 10 per cent of the estimated value of the buildings. In 1953 the annual expenditure on repairs to government buildings in the Federation of Malaya was estimated to be just over £75 000. In Bermuda, the cost of repairing termite damage to the cathedral at Hamilton over the period 1939 to 1951 (interrupted by the war) was £15 576. Such estimates are for tropical countries where termite activity is at its greatest. Outside the tropics, termites are less voracious. The damage which they do to farm buildings in the southern states of the U.S.A. is estimated to cost in repair bills about 1 per cent of the gross value of the property annually. In comparing this with the 10 per cent of tropical countries it is necessary to remember the greater value and density of building in the U.S.A.

There has undoubtedly been an increased appreciation of the importance of termite damage to buildings in recent years. This is primarily due to the impact of rising costs of repairs and maintenance. The actual amount of damage done has also increased because of the greater opportunities which the termites have been given by large building programmes in many tropical countries, especially where low-cost housing projects are more concerned with the number of 'units of housing' rather than future costs of upkeep. Changes in architectural style and local building practice have not infrequently been made without due regard to the risk of termite attack. Finally the spread of injurious termites from one country to another still continues, with all the complications this may entail in established methods of protection and control.

Increased numbers of buildings, together with changes in building practice, have resulted in termites becoming a nuisance in countries where hitherto they have passed unnoticed. In Aden and other parts of the Middle East, for example, houses were traditionally built of mud brick or masonry, with thick walls and an absolute minimum of timberwork. Local timber was rarely available and imported timber was chosen for its termite resistance, generally teak and, for roofing poles, mangrove. The apparent freedom of these buildings from termites—damage being restricted to fittings such as carpets, books and a limited amount of ornamental work in softwoods—led to a disregard for the potentialities of the local subterranean termites when modern buildings were planned. In West Africa many of the older houses on the coast are bungalows of imported pitch-pine set high above the ground on masonry pillars. These pillars made it difficult for the subterranean termites to build their runways up from the ground without being observed, while the pitch-pine of those earlier days proved very resistant to dry-wood termites. Much the same is true of the West Indies. In south-east Asia, bungalows were commonly built up on pillars of local hardwood, and much hardwood was used in their construction. Nowadays, pillars are no longer fashionable or are omitted in order to reduce building costs, and houses are built of brick or masonry directly on the surface of the ground, with local or imported softwoods, and never a thought for the termites.

A factor which militates against the use of termite-resistant hardwoods even in the countries where they exist is their greatly enhanced value for export. Much of the increase in termite damage to buildings in East Africa is due to the decline in the use of the local timber *mvule* (*Chlorophora excelsa*) in favour of imported timber and fabricated carpentry work. In addition, the slow ageing of hardwoods used for structural work and for furniture renders them increasingly susceptible to dry-wood termites, so that one finds increasing sign of damage in the older buildings in Zanzibar and the East African coast due to *Cryptotermes dudleyi* as time goes on. In the Caribbean area termite damage is on the increase because of the decline in the natural resistance of pitch-pine, now that primary forests in the producing countries are practically exhausted and almost all timber now comes from secondary growths which have no special resistance to termites—in fact are rather attractive to them.

The Nature of Termite Damage

The general picture of termite damage to buildings is straightforward; the worker termites remove all palatable wood excepting only the outer layers which are left to provide the shelter and freedom from disturbance that are necessary to termites. There are, however, considerable differences in detail among the different groups of termites as already outlined.

Dry-wood termites eat out galleries in the timber and these provide accommodation for the king and queen, the soldiers, and the various young stages of the community. The community is found in the vicinity of maximum feeding activity at any time. In course of time their galleries coalesce to form large cavities. At intervals the working nymphs make small holes to the exterior, the size of woodworm holes, through which they eject the accumulated faecal pellets. Small heaps of this ejected frass accumulate beneath infested woodwork and provide the first indications of dry-wood termite infestation. If these indications are ignored, the presence of the termites may continue to be unsuspected until such time as the structure is subject to some unusual strain such as during an earthquake, a hurricane, or perhaps just a party. Since colonies of dry-wood termites consist of only a few hundred individuals, and as they usually start from a single pair of flying adults, the rate at which the infestation builds up is slow; but given time the number of colonies will increase to the limit of the food supply (Fig. 24.1).

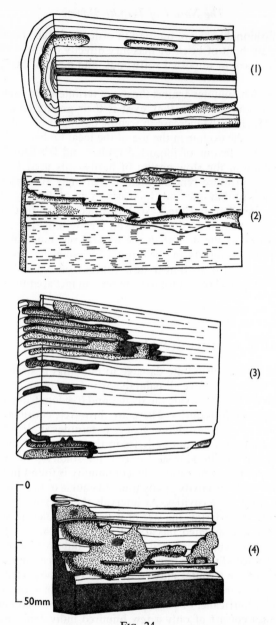

FIG. 24
Typical termite damage to building timbers: 1. *Kalotermes*, dry-wood termite; 2. *Reticulitermes*, moist-wood termite; 3. *Coptotermes*, tropical moist-wood termite; 4. *Odontotermes*, ground-dwelling termite filling excavations with soil

Subterranean termites, on the other hand, have fixed nests from which the workers move out in search of food, and to which they return with their spoil. Distances of one hundred yards (thirty metres) may be travelled by the small workers with their loads of wood. Communities of subterranean termites number many thousands of individuals, and those which make the distinctive large mounds in the tropics are estimated to run into millions. For this reason, the rapidity and scale of their attack on new buildings is much more spectacular than that of dry-wood termites. Typical of subterranean-termite infestation is the presence of soil or a mixture of sand and chewed wood in the excavated timber, while earthen tubes or covered ways are constructed over impenetrable foundations and walls to provide lines of communication between nest and food. When timber is in direct contact with the ground, the termites prefer to approach it from below through tunnels in the soil and so enter without any outward signs. A wall of mud bricks, or of masonry with mud mortar, or built with a continuous cavity, will provide a direct and unsuspected route to timber roof-members. When there is some impenetrable obstacle to negotiate, the termites resort to covered ways on the outside until the timber is reached. The size and manner of construction of these covered ways is a clue to the sort of termite involved.

Subterranean termites belonging to the family Rhinotermitidae nest in old tree stumps, buried timber and similar situations and their work is characterised by the thin laminae of wood left behind to divide up the excavations into a series of floors, and by the presence of sponge-like masses of pale-coloured wood pulp in the larger galleries. The gallery walls and the inner lining of the covered ways have a pale spotted appearance, like dried oatmeal porridge. The covered ways are constructed with chewed wood, and perhaps a little sand. *Coptotermes* damage in the tropics and *Reticulitermes* damage in the temperate zone is frequently diagnosed as 'dry rot' (Fig. 24.2 and 3).

The remaining subterranean termites of the family Termitidae, including all the mound-building species and the fungus-growing termites of Africa and Asia, tend to remove wood *en masse*, filling the spaces within the remaining thin outer layer with packed earth to maintain to some degree the rigidity of the structure. Woodwork below ground or encased in masonry tends to disappear entirely. The ability of these small blind worker termites to leave only the thinnest of outer layers to hide them from observation is quite inexplicable. So is their ability to appreciate the need for some internal support, either in the form of ribs of wood left uneaten or of soil mixed with saliva to set like mortar (Fig. 24.4).

The Kinds of Termites Attacking Buildings and their Distribution

Of the 1 800 different species of termites so far described, 148 have been recorded at one time or another as damaging buildings in various parts of the world. Of these, 80 are to be regarded as potentially serious pests, in that they appear to infest buildings regularly in at least one particular area, necessitating repair work. More species may be added to the list as records are obtained from some of the less developed parts of the tropics. The 80 injurious species are distributed among the various families of termites as follows:

	species
Mastotermitidae—the Australian *Mastotermes*	1
Kaltotermitidae—the dry-wood termites	14
Hodotermitidae—the harvester termites	3
Rhinotermitidae—moist-wood subterranean termites	37
Termitidae—ground-dwelling, mound-building and tree-nesting termites	25

In the Northern Temperate Zone, roughly between latitudes 46° and 30° north, timberwork is damaged by termites of the genus *Reticulitermes*, belonging to the family Rhinotermitidae or moist-wood termites. In southern France and countries bordering on the Mediterranean and Black Sea, *Reticulitermes lucifugus* is present. After a gap due to the cold high plateau of Turkestan and Tibet, *R. speratus* appears in China and Japan. In North America the genus is represented by *R. hesperus* in the west and *R. flavipes* in the east, both species just crossing the border into Canada.

South of 30° north latitude, dry-wood termites become serious pests, especially four species of *Cryptotermes*—*brevis*, *cynocephalus*, *dudleyi* and *domesticus* (Plates 37 and 45). Some of these have travelled so far along the main sea routes in timber, furniture and the like that it is difficult to suggest where they originated. Under warmer conditions *Heterotermes* replaces *Reticulitermes*, but the larger and more vigorous genus of moist-wood termites, *Coptotermes*, predominates in the Far East, Australia and tropical America (Plate 43). Of the Termitidae, *Macrotermes* and *Odontotermes* are active in Africa, India and south-east Asia, where the mounds of the larger species are a typical feature of the landscape in many parts (Plates 49 and 50). The genus *Nasutitermes*, whose soldiers have characteristic pear-shaped heads and whose nests are frequently attached to tree trunks and fence posts, are locally of importance in Ceylon, Mauritius, parts of Australia, and much of Central America and the West Indies.

A list of the termites recorded as damaging buildings is given on p. 150

and on p. 155 they are assembled according to their geographical distribution. Common names for termites are of little more than local value, and are positively misleading when transferred from one continent to another. For instance the 'small mound termites' of Africa and Asia have close relatives in Australia and South America that produce the most impressive structures. To use the scientific name of the genus is the way to avoid confusion since sophisticated methods of pest control demand precise knowledge of the particular insect involved. This is particularly important when dealing with existing termite infestations in buildings, and in adapting traditional building styles to reduce the risk of attack. Furthermore, identification is essential for the exchange of information about termite control measures in order to avoid disappointment when it is found that control measures successful in one country do not work in another. For example, boron compounds kill intestinal protozoa at concentrations too low to affect the termites themselves, and their use leads to death by starvation of those kinds of termites which possess intestinal protozoa, while those that do not depend on protozoa continue unaffected unless the concentration of boron is greatly increased.

Measures to Prevent Termite Damage to Buildings

The cost of measures designed to reduce the risk of termite damage to a building must be considered in relation to the probable cost of repairs and replacements if these are not employed, bearing in mind also the anticipated or desired economic life of the new building. Within the tropics, and much of the adjoining subtropics, the only localities likely to be free from potential house-destroying termites are rolling sand-dunes, salt marshes and high ground over 1 800 metres above sea level. Furthermore, houses built of concrete, metal and glass are not necessarily termite-proof unless they have been designed to deny access to termites capable of damaging wooden furniture, decorative fabrics, books and the like. Merely to avoid having any timber in the structure is not the answer (Plate 44).

Briefly the measures necessary are as follows:

Design

Avoidance of excessive moisture by siting and planned drainage, by care in arranging ventilation, by the use of basements or by raising the structure on piers and bearers rather than on dwarf walls;
arrange adequate facilities for inspection;
use of mechanical barriers, such as metal caps and concrete slabs, and the provision of protected expansion joints in concrete-slab floors.

Construction

Site clearance of nests and the removal of all woody material such as tree roots and contractors' rubbish liable to attract termites (Plate 48); soil poisons to provide a chemical barrier, especially for slab-on-ground constructions where subsequent inspection is impossible;

all timber to be naturally resistant or to have been adequately impregnated after seasoning;

attendance to detail, avoiding cracks in walls, seeing that wood frames do not penetrate below the concrete of floors, having no steps or other additions that are not themselves adequately termite-proof, taking care that the soil is not filled back too close to, or even above, the ant-proof course in foundation walls.

Mechanical Barriers

CONCRETE SLAB

For small buildings such as prefabricated low-cost housing, on level sites it may be practicable to cover the site with a slab of concrete large enough to allow an apron not less than six inches (15 cm) wide continuously around the proposed structure. Providing that precautions are taken to prevent cracking, such a slab will prevent ground-dwelling termites from reaching the building except by building runways over the apron where they can be seen and destroyed. This method is used, for example, in Malaya with the prefabricated schools made by the Forestry Department from pressure-impregnated local timbers. If the slab is to be poured in sections then the soil below the joint should be treated with an insecticide, and a termite-proof jointing compound used to fill the gap (Plate 53).

METAL CAPS OR 'ANT GUARDS'

Buildings on hardwood or masonry pillars are protected with metal caps on the top of each and every pillar. These prevent termites from working up through the pillar or from building their runways over the surface to reach the constructional timbers above (Plate 46). Caps are made of metal which does not corrode rapidly, is tough enough to resist casual damage, and is capable of being worked into the desired shape. Zinc, copper and some alloys are eminently suited to this purpose, while galvanised iron is much cheaper. In Australia 24-gauge galvanised iron is generally recommended for guards. The cap must fit easily over the top of the pillar with projecting sides not less than 2 inches (50 mm) all round bent downwards at an angle of 45°. If it is not stamped out from the flat, the cap must have the corners cut and soldered. The completed article resembles an inverted baking tin. Termites building their runways up the surface of the pillar are unable to negotiate the projecting edge of the guard. If the bearers of the building are bolted to the pillars, care must be taken to seal the gap between the edge of the hole through the metal cap and the bolt by coating the top of the pillar with a layer of bitumen before placing the cap in position. If possible, use should be made of a long bolt bent to link the bearer with the side of the pillar, and thus passing outside the metal shield (Fig. 25).

When the building is raised above ground level on dwarf walls a continuous metal cap may be laid above the damp-proof course with a projecting portion on each side. Interior walls must not be omitted from the protecting plan. If the floors are of wood on beams, then the projecting strips of metal are bent down at 45° on both sides of the wall. Joints and corners should be securely lapped or soldered. If the floors are cast as concrete slabs on earth fill, the interior projecting strip of metal should be left unbent and incorporated into the floor slab to seal the junction between it and the wall.

Adequate crawl space is essential in buildings with suspended wooden floors to permit of easy inspection. In Africa and tropical Asia there are a number of ground-dwelling termites, not necessarily species which habitually make large mounds, which will build up heaps of earth in the space below the floor that eventually reach the woodwork and provide the termites with direct access to it. Alternatively the heaps of earth may be constructed against an interior wall to cover over a section of the protective metal shield. Such constructions take time and will be destroyed before they enable any damage to be done if regular inspection is provided for.

CONCRETE BARRIER

On foundation walls of brick or masonry an effective termite barrier is provided by a continuous cast concrete slab, usually about 3 inches (75 mm) thick and projecting 2 to 3 inches (50 to 75 mm) at both sides. Where local conditions suggest any risk of cracking as a result of subsidences, some reinforcement of this slab is indicated. Again it must be emphasized that interior walls must have this protection. Slabs should not be broken to allow pipes to pass through them, nor may waste pipes and the like be allowed to touch the projecting edges or they will form bridges over which the termites can bypass the barrier (Fig. 26; Plate 47).

With slab floors cast between the foundation walls, care must be taken to avoid crevices at the junction with the concrete barrier. This may be achieved by having a clean gap filled with termite-proof jointing compound, acting as an expansion joint. Alternatively, the soil below the gap may be thoroughly treated with insecticide.

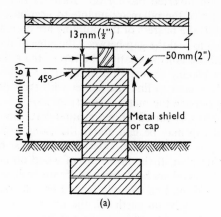

13mm (½")

50mm (2")

45°

Min. 460mm (1'6")

Metal shield or cap

(a)

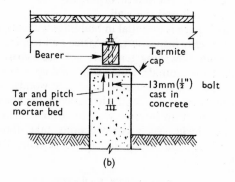

Bearer

Termite cap

Tar and pitch or cement mortar bed

13mm (½") bolt cast in concrete

(b)

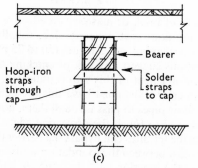

Bearer

Hoop-iron straps through cap

Solder straps to cap

(c)

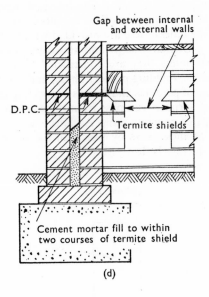

(d)

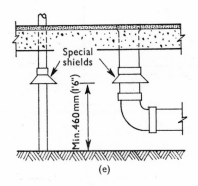

(e)

FIG. 25

Metal termite shields; constructional details in Australian buildings
(Reproduced by courtesy of the Director, Commonwealth Experimental
Building Station)

BRIDGING

With buildings on piers or piles it is an error in design, or subsequent management, to enclose any part of the sub-floor area for washrooms, garages and the like unless these are provided with termite-proof foundations (Plate 52). Similarly steps and staircases must have termite-proof foundations unless they are constructed so as to leave a gap between them and the building proper. These, and other additions to a building in the way of pergolas and frames supporting creepers, provide bridges over which termites can pass from the soil into the building in spite of metal caps or concrete slabs. Architects might well draw their clients' attention to these ways by which all the value of anti-termite design may subsequently be lost.

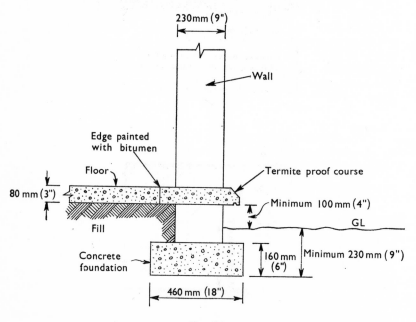

Fig. 26

Termite-proof course for a 9-inch (230 mm.) block wall
Notes: 1. Preferably the outside of the termite-proof course should be chamfered and throated as shown.
2. Foundation concrete to be 1:3:6 mix.
3. Floor and termite-proof course to be 1:2:4 mix.
(Reproduced by permission of the Director, Building Research Station, D.S.I.R.)

Bridging may also result from the installation of piping for various utilities, apart from actual damage to caps and barriers. Freestanding pipes may be fitted with metal flanges bent down at 45° to act as termite guards. Pipes passing through concrete floors may have metal collars which on being set into the slab will prevent crevices being formed by the concrete shrinking away from the pipe. Alternatively, the soil below may be thoroughly poisoned to provide a chemical barrier to the passage of termites.

CHEMICAL BARRIERS

The use of chemicals to produce a layer of soil lethal or repellent to termites is a useful method of protecting temporary or low-cost structures when the cost of structural termite barriers is out of proportion to the value of the building. Site poisoning is also an insurance against faulty workmanship and other factors leading to failures in termite-proofing in buildings of a more permanent nature. Such chemicals are usually applied in the form of solutions in fuel oil or water, or as emulsions in water. Among those in use in different parts of the world are:

creosote oil	DDT
sodium arsenite	benzene hexachloride
pentachlorophenol	chlordane
sodium pentachlorophenate	dieldrin
copper naphthenate	

The length of time over which these chemicals remain effective depends on a number of factors, including soil type, exposure to weather and the kind of termite involved. It is an important practical point, but one that cannot be dealt with satisfactorily on the data as yet available. From South Africa it is learnt that pentachlorophenol and copper naphthenate have remained effective as undercover soil poisons for nine years. In Australia there have been some differences according to the localities, but on one site where there was a variety of termites present an effective period of five years was given by creosote, pentachlorophenol, sodium pentachlorophenate, and chlordane. In the United States of America (Hetrick, 1957) benzene hexachloride, chlordane and dieldrin have given complete protection for periods of up to seven years so far, though in Panama a somewhat shorter life has been found.

The application of soil poisons on the building site must be done methodically. If a watering-can is used, it is useful to have a template which will mark out the area this volume will cover—for instance a 2-gallon can of 5 per cent pentachlorophenol solution would serve for 25 square feet, and the template could mark out an area 5 feet by 5 feet, whereas a similar can of $2\frac{1}{2}$ per cent solution would require a template of half the area, say 4 feet by 3 feet. In metric terms 10 litres of 5 per cent solution would serve for 2·5 square metres, with the template adjusted accordingly. Foundation walls are treated when they have reached ground level, and before the trench on either side is filled in. A second dose is customary when about half the fill has been returned.

DOSAGE

The following rates of application have been gathered from a number of sources. Local conditions and individual preferences govern the choice of oil- or water-borne insecticides, as well as the dilution of the solution. Oil is a more costly carrier than water and there is a tendency to use oil solutions at greater strength, and in consequence smaller volume, than those with water.

copper naphthenate
    5 per cent in fuel oil at 4–8 gall./100 sq. ft. (2–4 litres/1 sq. metre)
pentachlorophenol
    5 per cent in fuel oil at 4–8 gall./100 sq. ft. (2–4 litres/1 sq. metre)
    or emulsion in water at 4–8 gall./100 sq. ft. (2–4 litres/1 sq. metre)
sod. pentachlorophenate
    $2\frac{1}{2}$ per cent. in water at 12–20 gall./100 sq. ft. (6–10 litres/1 sq. metre)
sodium arsenite
    10 per cent. in water at 12–20 gall./100 sq. ft. (6–10 litres/1 sq. metre)
benzene hexachloride
    0·8 per cent (gamma) in fuel oil or emulsion in water at 12–20 gall./100 sq. ft. (6–10 litres/1 sq. metre)
chlordane
    1 per cent infueloil or emulsion in water at 12–20 gall./100 sq. ft. (6–10 litres/ 1 sq. metre)
DDT
    8 per cent in fuel oil at 12–20 gall./100 sq. ft. (6–10 litres/1 sq. metre)
dieldrin
    0·3 per cent as emulsion in water at 10 gall./100 sq. ft. (5 litres/1 sq. metre)

The rates of application given above refer to the treatment of levelled sites and prior to the casting of slab floors. For foundations the volumes indicated would be applied to 100 running feet or 2 metres respectively of trench, and two applications given.

Protection Against Dry-wood Termites

Measures discussed so far have all been directed against ground-dwelling termites, which may be prevented from entering a building by protective barriers. The small but important group of dry-wood termites have no connection with the soil since they live in dry, dead branches of

43. Roof beams of building attacked by *Coptotermes amanii*, Tanzania

44. Built-in furniture damaged by *Microcerotermes diversus* at Abadan, Iran
(The Iranian Oil Operating Companies)

45. Roof posts of building heavily infested with *Cryptotermes dudleyi* showing accumulation of frass around the base, Tanzania

46. Termite runways on concrete foundations of temporary building in Ghana, no termite proofing measures having been taken

47. External view of concrete termite-proof course on dwelling-house, Malawi

trees and in seasoned timber. They spread by means of small swarms of flying termites which appear at intervals during the rains. New buildings become infested wherever structural timbers or furniture present an end grain, crevice or split which will allow a foothold to a pair of flying termites. Mechanical barriers being out of the question, the only satisfactory answer is to use timber that is naturally termite-resistant or which has been treated with a suitable wood preservative.

The acme of folly is to use wood from an old building in a place where dry-wood termites are known to exist. More commonly, however, dry-wood termites are introduced into new buildings in furniture that has come from an infested house or warehouse without fumigation or other treatment.

Large areas within the continental land masses appear to be free from injurious dry-wood termites, but coastal districts and islands generally are not so fortunate. While the natural rate of increase of dry-wood termites is such that damage is rarely apparent during the early years of a building's life, once damage is noticed, however, it is reasonably certain that the infestation is widespread. The advantages of ensuring freedom from dry-wood termites by using impregnated timber throughout a building are emphasised if some prominent public building has suffered damage and the cost of repair has been well publicised. Otherwise people are tempted to consider only the more rapidly appearing ground-dwelling termites in their plans for protective measures against termites.

Control of Termites in Buildings

Before attempting to eradicate termites in buildings and taking measures to prevent further trouble, it is essential to know what kinds of termites are involved. Only with some knowledge of the habits of the termites and an understanding of local building practices are the control measures likely to be effective and economic. The main division is, once again, between subterranean and dry-wood termites. It may be desirable to attack the nests of ground-dwelling termites some distance away from the building on the lines already detailed in an earlier chapter dealing with mounds. It should be ascertained, however, which of the mounds or underground nests are worth attacking from the point of view of removing any threat to buildings.

Skilled operators are not easy to find in the tropics nor, it must be added, are they generally in demand, with the result that termite-control measures are not infrequently palliative and unnecessarily expensive. All of which serves to emphasise the desirability for measures to protect buildings from termites to be considered in the design and construction.

TREATMENT OF BUILDINGS INFESTED WITH GROUND-DWELLING TERMITES

It is necessary, first of all, to find out where the termites are entering the structure. The link is then destroyed by removing the debris, wooden supports or the like and inserting a barrier, structural, chemical or both, to prevent further movement. Once the building has been effectively sealed off the termites within the building will die in time without any further action being taken against them. An exception to this may be found in the case of some species of *Coptotermes* and related moist-wood termites which are able to make their nests in structural timbers away from the ground, if such timbers are kept abnormally damp by leaking water-pipes, proximity of damp soil as in window-boxes and verandah tubs, or some similar reason (Plate 49). Such nests must be located and treated, and the predisposing cause removed.

Chemical treatment of the soil through which termites must pass to reach the buildings is the usual method employed. Suitable chemicals are to be found among those already listed above for site poisoning in new buildings. Choice of chemicals is limited when buildings are in occupation and gardens have been developed. Water emulsions of chlordane and dieldrin are officially recommended in the United States for use against *Reticulitermes* because of their relatively low toxicity to plants and because water emulsions generally are less liable to creep up walls and spoil decorations than are oil emulsions. Chlordane used as a 1 per cent emulsion and dieldrin as a 0·5 per cent emulsion are both well above the minimum strengths for efficient application and no good is likely to come from using them stronger. They need to be used with the reasonable care and respect due to poisons. Rubber gloves should be worn by the operators and care taken to keep the solution away from the skin, especially from spray or splashing which might reach the face.

To treat a house built on a concrete slab, or with concrete floors resting on an earth fill, holes require to be made through the slab into the fill below, or bored horizontally through the foundation walls from the outside just below the level of the base of the slab. Mechanically operated drills are necessary for this work. Holes through the slab are suggested 1 foot or 18 inches (30 to 45 cm) apart along a line 6 inches (15 cm) from the interior face of the wall. Holes through the outer foundation walls could, with advantage, be at 4 to 5 foot (1 to 1·5 m) intervals if pressure equipment is available for injecting the insecticidal solution. A dosage of 1 gallon of solution per yard (5 litres per metre) of foundation is desirable, after which the exterior foundation walls are exposed by digging a trench about 15 inches (40 cm) deep and emulsion applied at the same rate before the soil is returned.

In a house with suspended floors and adequate crawl-space, trenches are dug along both sides of all foundation walls and the solution applied as before. Such treatment must include porches, verandahs and staircases. An extra dose is suggested around washing slabs, waste-water outlets and other places liable to remain damp.

When applying emulsion to a trench, a proportion of the dose should be sprinkled or sprayed on and then covered with some 6 inches (15 cm) of soil which is then well tamped down. More soil is returned and the process repeated until the trench is filled once more.

When there is any doubt about the complete success of constructional measures or soil poisoning in isolating an infested building from the ground, it is advisable to treat as much as possible of the woodwork near ground level with a preservative. Good penetrative power is important since it is not always possible to reach all sides of the woodwork. Organic solvent type preservatives with pentachlorophenol or one of the chlorinated hydrocarbon insecticides as active agent are in general use for this type of work, usually with additives to promote penetration and to prevent 'blooming'—the growth of crystals on the surface. Needless to say, all replacements of damaged woodwork should be given a thorough coating of preservative before they are placed in to position.

Fumigation to Control Dry-wood Termites

Buildings that have become infested with dry-wood termites may have their woodwork treated piecemeal with wood preservatives in the hope that sufficient depth of penetration will be achieved to kill all the termites present. With skill and patience much may be done, especially if the greater part of the building is of stone or concrete, but if the building is mainly of timber construction the problem may be too great to be dealt with in this way. Furniture infested with dry-wood termites is a source of danger to new buildings, in addition to the loss that its own destruction would entail. Treatment of furniture with wood preservatives on a large scale as a control measure is laborious since it entails the removal of polish, varnish or paint from the surface as a preliminary to applying the insecticide. In such cases fumigation is suggested to eradicate the dry-wood termites.

Methyl bromide is used as a fumigant for the control of woodboring insects, such as powderpost, furniture and death-watch beetles. Tests carried out at the Pest Infestation Laboratory, Slough, have shown that dry-wood termites (*Kalotermes*) and damp-wood termites (*Zootermopsis* and *Reticulitermes*) are killed by concentrations of methyl bromide that are effective against these other pests. Control of dry-wood termites in structural timbers and furniture is a technological matter to ensure that the methyl bromide reaches the termites.

The Division of Wood Technology of the New South Wales Forestry Commission has shown that at temperatures of 60° F (16° C) and over, 2 to 3 lb of methyl bromide per 1 000 cubic feet (1 kilo per 20 cubic metres) over twenty-four hours will penetrate softwood to a depth of 2 inches (5 cm) and kill powderpost beetles. A variety of Australian hardwoods were treated successfully at 3 lb/1 000 cubic feet (1 kilo per 20 cubic metres). These results were obtained both in fumigation chambers and under plastic tarpaulins, with shipments of timber and with prefabricated wooden buildings in the flat.

Current practice in the United States is to cover the whole building in a tent of plastic tarpaulins and introduce methyl bromide at a minimum of 3 lb/1 000 cubic feet (1 kilo/20 cubic metres), depending on the efficiency of the tent as a gas holder, the temperature, and the complexity of the structure, for twenty-four hours. This is a highly skilled job. Methyl bromide is highly poisonous to animals and plants, and in addition it is liable to react with a variety of materials, including foam rubber, woollens, leather and fats, giving them a most unplesant odour.

Furniture may be fumigated in a similar manner, either in a fumigation chamber or a well-sealed room. Using methyl bromide the amount suggested is 2 lb per 1 000 cubic feet, or 1 kilo per 30 cubic metres for fifteen to twenty hours at a temperature of 70° F (21° C) or over.

Fumigation kills the termites present, but does nothing to prevent reinfestation at any time after a few days. Serious damage by dry-wood termites to structural timbers is likely to take a number of years to build up if the only source of reinfestation is the flying termite. Consideration should be given to the possibility of delaying reinfestation indefinitely by brushing or spraying with a wood preservative the exposed surfaces of all woodwork not already painted. No great depth of penetration need be aimed at in this operation, but particular attention should be paid to cracks and joints and exposed end grain, for these are the places sought out by the flying termites to give them quick access to the interior of the timber.

Termites Injurious to Building Timbers
—Systematic List

This list has been compiled from the records of the Termite Research Unit and from published accounts of damage to woodwork in buildings. The distribution given is that of recorded damage and is not necessarily that of the termites themselves. An asterisk signifies that a particular termite causes significant damage according to reports at present available.

family MASTOTERMITIDAE
Mastotermes darwiniensis Froggatt   tropical Australia

family KALOTERMITIDAE dry-wood termites

Bifiditermes mutubae Harris	Uganda
Cryptotermes brevis (Walker)	U.S.A. (Florida, Louisiana), Bermuda, Bahamas, West Indies, Guiana, Colombia, Brazil, Peru, Chile, Madeira, St Helena, West Africa (Gambia to Nigeria), Uganda, South Africa, Madagascar, Hong Kong
Cryptotermes cavifrons Banks	Bahamas, Cuba, Puerto Rico, Haiti, Guatemala
Cryptotermes cynocephalus Light	Malaysia, Philippines
Cryptotermes domesticus (Haviland)	Malaysia, Vietnam, China, Japan, Pacific Islands, Ceylon
Cryptotermes dudleyi Banks	Malaysia, Philippines, Ceylon, East Africa, Seychelles, Colombia, Trinidad
Cryptotermes havilandi (Sjöstedt)	West Africa (Sierra Leone to Nigeria), Brazil, Trinidad, Barbados
Cryptotermes longicollis Banks.	Panama
Cryptotermes pallidus (Rambur)	Mauritius
Cryptotermes perforans Kemner	Ceylon
Cryptotermes rospigliosi Snyder	Peru
Incisitermes immigrans (Snyder)	Ecuador, Peru
Incisitermes incisus (Silvestri)	Venezuela
Incisitermes marginipennis (Latreille)	Mexico, Guatemala
Incisitermes minor (Hagen)	U.S.A. (California, Arizona)
Incisitermes repandus (Hill)	Fiji
Incisitermes schwarzi (Banks)	U.S.A. (Florida)
Incisitermes snyderi (Light)	U.S.A. (south-east), Bahamas, Cuba
Kalotermes brouni Froggatt	New Zealand
Kalotermes flavicollis (Fabr.)	Europe (Mediterranean coast), Turkey
Kalotermes sinaicus (Kemner)	Israel
Marginitermes hubbardi (Banks)	U.S.A. (California, Arizona), Mexico
Neotermes assmuthi (Holmgren)	India
Neotermes castaneus (Burmeister)	West Indies (St Lucia)
Neotermes chilensis (Blanchard)	Chile
Neotermes laticollis (Holmgren)	Seychelles
Postelectrotermes praecox (Hagen)	Madeira

family HODOTERMITIDAE harvester termites

Anacanthotermes ochraceus (Burmeister)	North Africa (Algeria to Egypt), Sudan, Arabia
Anacanthotermes septentrionalis (Jacobson)	Iran, Afghanistan, Russia (Turkmenia)

Anacanthotermes vagans (Hagen)   Iran, Iraq, Afghanistan
Hodotermes mossambicus (Hagen)   South Africa
Microhodotermes viator (Latreille)   South Africa

family TERMOPSIDAE damp-wood termites

Stolotermes ruficeps Brauer   New Zealand
Zootermopsis angusticollis (Hagen)   U.S.A. (western states)
Zootermopsis nevadensis (Hagen)   U.S.A. (western states)

family RHINOTERMITIDAE moist-wood termites
subfamily Psammotermitinae sand termites

Psammotermes allocerus Silvestri   South Africa
Psammotermes voeltzkowi Wasmann   Madagascar
**Psammotermes hybostoma* Desneux   North Africa (Algeria to Egypt), Sudan, Bahrein

subfamily Heterotermitinae

Heterotermes aethiopicus (Sjöstedt)   South Arabia, Sudan
**Heterotermes aureus* (Snyder)   U.S.A. (south west), Mexico
**Heterotermes ceylonicus* (Holmgren)   Ceylon
**Heterotermes convexinotatus* (Snyder)   West Indies, Panama, Guatamala, Venezuela
**Heterotermes indicola* (Wasmann)   India, West Pakistan, Afghanistan, Ceylon
**Heterotermes malabaricus* Snyder   India
**Heterotermes perfidus* Silvestri   St Helena
**Heterotermes philippensis* (Light)   Philippines, Mauritius, Madagascar
**Heterotermes tenuis* (Hagen)   West Indies, Guyana, Brazil, Paraguay, Argentina, Peru
**Reticulitermes chiensis* Snyder   China
**Reticulitermes flavipes* (Kollar)   U.S.A. (eastern states), Canada, Germany (Hamburg), Austria (Hallein)
Reticulitermes fukienensis Light   China
**Reticulitermes hageni* Banks   U.S.A. (eastern states)
**Reticulitermes hesperus* Banks   U.S.A. (western states)
**Reticulitermes lucifugus* (Rossi)   Europe (southern), Madeira, Algeria, Turkey
**Reticulitermes speratus* (Kolbe)   Japan, Korea, China, Formosa
**Reticulitermes tibialis* Banks   U.S.A. (western states), Mexico
**Reticulitermes virginicus* (Banks)   U.S.A. (eastern states)

subfamily Coptotermitinae

**Coptotermes acinaciformis* (Froggatt)   Australia, New Zealand
**Coptotermes amanii* (Sjöstedt)   Somalia, Kenya, Tanzania, Malawi, Rhodesia
**Coptotermes ceylonicus* Holmgren   Ceylon, India
**Coptotermes crassus* Snyder   Mexico, Honduras, Guatemala

Coptotermes elisae (Desneux)	New Guinea
*Coptotermes formosanus Shiraki	Formosa, China, Hawaii, Pacific Islands, Ceylon, South Africa, U.S.A. (Gulf Coast)
*Coptotermes frenchi Hill	Australia
Coptotermes gaurii Roonwal & Krishna	Ceylon
*Coptotermes grandiceps Snyder	Solomon Islands
*Coptotermes havilandi Holmgren	Malaysia, Thailand, Madagascar, Mauritius, Jamaica, Brazil
Coptotermes heimi (Wasmann)	India, West Pakistan
*Coptotermes intermedius Silvestri	West Africa (Senegal to Nigeria)
Coptotermes lacteus (Froggatt)	Australia
*Coptotermes michaelsoni Silvestri	Australia (south-west)
*Coptotermes niger Snyder	Panama, Guatemala, British Honduras
*Coptotermes obiratus Hill	New Guinea, Papua
*Coptotermes pamuae Snyder	Solomon Islands
*Coptotermes sjostedti Holmgren	West Africa (Senegal to Cameroon), Congo, Angola, Uganda
*Coptotermes testaceus (L.)	Bahamas, West Indies, Venezuela, Guyana, Surinam, Brazil, Chile, Peru
*Coptotermes travians (Haviland)	Malaysia
*Coptotermes truncatus (Wasmann)	Seychelles, Madagascar
*Coptotermes vastator (Light)	Philippines, Hawaii

subfamily   Rhinotermitinae

Prorhinotermes inopinatus Silvestri	Guam
*Prorhinotermes simplex (Hagen)	U.S.A. (Florida), Cuba, Puerto Rico, Jamaica
Prorhinotermes tibaoensis (Oshima)	Philippines
Schedorhinotermes intermedius (Brauer)	Australia
*Schedorhinotermes lamanianus (Sjöstedt)	Tanzania, South Africa
Schedorhinotermes putorius (Sjöstedt)	São Thomé
Schedorhinotermes sarawakensis (Holmgren)	Sabah
Schedorhinotermes solomonensis (Snyder)	Solomon Islands
Schedorhinotermes translucens (Haviland)	Sarawak

family   TERMITIDAE   subterranean and mound termites
subfamily   Amitermitinae

Amitermes belli (Desneux)	India
Amitermes evuncifer Silvestri	Nigeria

Amitermes excellans Silvestri	Guyana
Amitermes herbertensis Mjöberg	Australia (Queensland)
Amitermes lönnbergianus (Sjöstedt)	Kenya
Amitermes obeuntis Silvestri	Australia (south-west)
Amitermes unidentatus (Wasmann)	Zanzibar
*Amitermes vilis (Hagen)	Iran, Turkmenia
Amitermes wheeleri Desneux	Mexico
Eremotermes sabaeus Harris	South Arabia
*Globitermes sulphureus (Haviland)	Malaysia, Thailand
Microcerotermes arboreus Emerson	Trinidad
*Microcerotermes diversus Silvestri	Israel, Arabia, Iraq, Iran
Microcerotermes exiguus (Hagen)	Venezuela
*Microcerotermes fuscotibialis Sjöstedt	Sierra Leone
*Microcerotermes losbanosensis Oshima	Philippines
Microcerotermes palestinensis Spaeth	Israel
Microcerotermes subtilis (Wasmann)	Seychelles
Microcerotermes turneri (Froggatt)	Australia (New South Wales)

subfamily Termitinae

Angulitermes dehraensis (Gardner)	West Pakistan

subfamily Macrotermitinae

*Allodontermes giffardi Silvestri	Sierra Leone
Allodontermes schultzi (Silvestri)	South Africa
Ancistrotermes cavithorax (Sjöstedt)	West Africa (Sierra Leone to Cameroon)
Macrotermes bellicosus (Smeathman)	West Africa
Macrotermes falciger (Gerstecker)	South Africa
Macrotermes gilvus (Hagen)	Malaysia, Philippines
Macrotermes natalensis (Haviland)	Central and South Africa
Macrotermes subhyalinus (Rambur)	West, Central and East Africa, Sudan
Microtermes aluco (Sjöstedt)	Ghana
Microtermes havilandi Holmgren	South Africa
Microtermes mycophagus (Desneux)	West Pakistan
*Microtermes redenianus (Sjöstedt)	Tanzania
Microtermes tragardhi (Sjöstedt)	Sudan
*Odontotermes badius (Haviland)	Tropical Africa
Odontotermes bangalorensis Holmgren	India
Odontotermes brunneus (Hagen)	India
*Odontotermes ceylonicus (Wasmann)	Ceylon
*Odontotermes feae (Wasmann)	India, East Pakistan, Burma
Odontotermes formosanus (Shiraki)	Formosa, Vietnam, Cambodia, Thailand
*Odontotermes horni (Wasmann)	Ceylon
Odontotermes kibarensis (Fuller)	Uganda
*Odontotermes latericius (Haviland)	East, Central and South Africa
Odontotermes nilensis (Emerson)	Sudan
*Odontotermes obscuriceps (Wasmann)	Ceylon

48. Excavations for foundations of
house in Sierra Leone cutting
through nest of subterranean
termites already present on
the site

49. Runways of *Odontotermes* from
infested wall-plate descending to
newly replaced window-frame
before decoration has been
completed, Nigeria

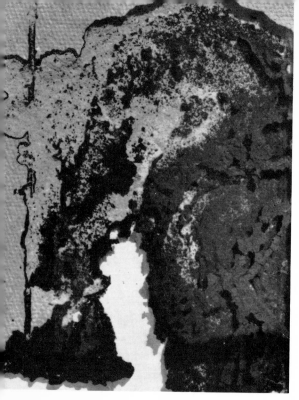

50. *Odontotermes* damage to fibre board partition within two years of building being completed, Kenya

51. Lighter at Sandakan, Sabah, heavily infested by *Coptotermes*

52. New house in British Honduras with floor-boards damaged by *Coptotermes*, which has gained access via the wash-room constructed between the concrete pillars at one corner of the building

53. Termite-proof prefabricated building for rural school, designed and constructed by the Forest Dept., Malaysia, from pressure-impregnated local soft-wood

54. Mattress cover damaged by termites during storage, Persian Gulf

55. *Macrotermes* damage to synthetic rubber covering of railway signals cable buried beside the track instead of being supported on posts, Rhodesia

56. Leather football and wooden cricket bat damaged by *Copto-termes* in a Singapore warehouse

Odontotermes pauperans (Silvestri) West Africa (Senegal to Nigeria)
Odontotermes redemanni (Wasmann) Ceylon
Odontotermes transvaalensis (Sjöstedt) South Africa

subfamily Nasutitermitinae

Naustitermes ceylonicus (Holmgren)   Ceylon
Nasutitermes corniger (Motschulsky)   Panama, Guatemala
Nasutitermes costalis (Holmgren)   West Indies, Guyana
Nasutitermes sp. (not *costalis*)   Peru
Nasutitermes ephratae (Holmgren)   Panama, Guatemala, West Indies
Nasutitermes exitiosus (Hill)   Australia
Nasutitermes globiceps (Holmgren)   Paraguay
Nasutitermes havilandi Desneux   Malaysia
Nasutitermes longipennis (Hill)   Australia (tropics)
Nasutitermes matangensiformis
  (Holmgren)   Vietnam
Nasutitermes nigriceps (Haldeman)   Mexico, Guatemala, Jamaica
Nasutitermes rippertii (Rambur)   Jamaica
Nasutitermes voeltzkowi (Wasmann)   Mauritius
Subulitermes mexicanus (Light)   Mexico

Termites Damaging Buildings—Regional List

EUROPE

Dry-wood termites

Kalotermes flavicollis (Fabr.)   Mediterranean coast

Subterranean termites

Reticulitermes lucifigus (Rossi)   France, Spain, Portugal, Italy, Yugo-
                                        slavia, Romania, Greece, southern
                                        Russia, Malta, Cyprus

Reticulitermes lucifugus var.
  santonensis Feytaud   France (Atlantic coast)
Reticulitermes flavipes (Kollar)   Germany (Hamburg), Austria (Hal-
                                        lein)

ASIA
Middle East

Dry-wood termites

Kalotermes flavicollis (Fabr.)   Turkey
Kalotermes sinaicus Kemner   Israel

Subterranean termites

*Anocanthotermes ochraceus
  (Burmeister)   Arabia

Anacanthotermes septentrionalis (Jacobson)	Iran, Afghanistan, Turkmenia
Anacanthotermes vagans (Hagen)	Iraq, Iran, Afghanistan
Psammotermes hybostoma Desneux	Bahrein
Reticulitermes lucifugus (Rossi)	Turkey, Israel
Heterotermes aethiopicus (Sjöstedt)	South Arabia
Heterotermes indicola (Wasmann)	Afghanistan
Amitermes vilis (Hagen)	Iran, Turkmenia
Eremotermes sabeus Harris	South Arabia
Microcerotermes diversus Silvestri	South Arabia, Iraq, Iran
Microcerotermes palestinensis Spaeth	Israel

Pakistan—India—Burma—Ceylon

Dry-wood termites

Cryptotermes cynocephalus Light	Ceylon
Cyptotermes dudleyi Banks	East Pakistan, India, Ceylon
Cryptotermes perforans Kemner	Ceylon

Subterranean termites

Heterotermes ceylonicus (Holmgren)	Ceylon
Heterotermes indicola (Wasmann)	Pakistan, India, Ceylon
Heterotermes malabaricus Snyder	India
Coptotermes ceylonicus Holmgren	Ceylon, India
Coptotermes exiguus (Holmgren)	Ceylon
Coptotermes formosanus Shiraki	Ceylon
Coptotermes gaurii Roonwal & Krishna	Ceylon
Coptotermes heimi Wasmann	West Pakistan, India
Coptotermes parvulus Holmgren	India
Amitermes belli (Desneux)	India
Angulitermes dehraensis (Gardner)	West Pakistan
Odontotermes bangalorensis Holmgren	West Pakistan, India
Odontotermes brunneus (Hagen)	India
Odontotermes ceylonicus (Wasmann)	Ceylon
Odontotermes feae (Wasmann)	India, East Pakistan, Burma
Odontotermes horni (Wasmann)	Ceylon
Odontotermes obscuriceps (Wasmann)	Ceylon
Odontotermes redemanni (Wasmann(	Ceylon
Microtermes mycophagus (Desneux)	West Pakistan
Nasutitermes ceylonicus (Holmgren)	Ceylon

Far East

Dry-wood termites

Cryptotermes brevis (Walker)	Hong Kong
Cryptotermes domesticus (Haviland)	China, Formosa, Thailand, Vietnam

Subterranean termites

Reticulitermes chinensis Snyder	China
Reticulitermes fukienensis Light	Hong Kong, China

Reticulitermes flaviceps (Oshima)	China
*Reticulitermes speratus (Kolbe)	Japan, Formosa, Korea
*Coptotermes formosanus (Shiraki)	Japan, Formosa, China, Hong Kong
Coptotermes havilandi Holmgren	Thailand
*Globitermes sulphureus (Haviland)	Thailand
Odontotermes formosanus (Shiraki)	Formosa, Vietnam, Cambodia, Thailand
Nasutitermes matangensis (Haviland)	Vietnam

Philippine Islands

Dry-wood termites

*Cryptotermes cynocephalus Light
*Cryptotermes dudleyi Banks

Subterranean

Heterotermes philippensis (Light)
Prorhinotermes tibaoensis (Oshima)
*Coptoterms vastator Light
Microcerotermes losbanosensis Oshima
Macrotermes gilvus (Hagen)

Malayan Region

Dry-wood termites

*Cryptotermes cynocephalus Light	Malaya, Java, Sumatra, Sarawak, Sabah
*Cryptotermes domesticus (Haviland)	Singapore, Java, Sarawak, Sabah
*Cryptotermes dudleyi Banks	Java, Sumatra, Sabah

Subterranean termites

Coptotermes havilandi Holmgren	Malaya, Java
*Coptotermes travians (Haviland)	Malaya, Java, Sumatra, Sabah
Schedorhinotermes sarawakensis (Holmgren)	Sabah
Schedorhinotermes translucens (Haviland)	Sarawak
Nasutitermes havilandi (Desneux)	Malaya

PACIFIC OCEAN

Dry-wood termites

Cryptotermes brevis (Walker)	Hawaii, Fiji, Marquesas
*Cryptotermes domesticus (Haviland)	Samoa, Solomon Islands, Fiji, New Guinea, New Britain
Incisitermes repandanus (Hill)	Fiji

Subterranean termites

*Coptotermes formosanus Shiraki	Hawaii, Guam, Midway, Marshal Is.
*Coptotermes grandiceps Snyder	Solomon Islands

Coptotermes pamuae Snyder	Solomon Islands
Coptotermes vastator (Light)	Hawaii
Prorhinotermes inopinatus Silvestri	Guam
Schedorhinotermes solomonensis (Snyder)	Solomon Islands

AUSTRALASIA

Dry-wood termites

| *Kalotermes brouni* Froggatt | New Zealand |

Subterranean termites

Mastotermes darwiniensis Froggatt	tropical Australia
Stolotermes ruficeps Brauer	New Zealand
Schedorhinotermes intermedius (Brauer)	Northern Territory, Queensland, New South Wales
Coptotermes acinaciformis (Froggatt)	Australia, New Zealand
Coptotermes elisae (Desneux)	New Guinea
Coptotermes frenchi Hill	New South Wales, Victoria, South Australia, New Zealand
Coptotermes lacteus (Froggatt)	Victoria, New South Wales, New Zealand
Coptotermes michaelsoni Silvestri	Western Australia
Coptotermes obiratus Hill	Papua, New Guinea
Microcerotermes turneri (Froggatt)	New South Wales
Amitermes herbertensis Mjöberg	Queensland
Amitermes obeuntis Silvestri	Western Australia
Nasutitermes exitiosus (Hill)	New South Wales, Victoria, South and Western Australia
Nasutitermes longipennis (Hill)	Northern Territory

NORTH AMERICA

Dry-wood termites

Cryptotermes brevis (Walker)	Florida, Louisiana
Incisitermes minor (Hagen)	California
Incisitermes schwarzi (Banks)	Florida
Incisitermes snyderi Light	California, Texas, Alabama, Louisiana, Mississippi, Florida
Marginitermes hubbardi (Banks)	California, Arizona

Subterranean termites

Zootermopsis angusticollis (Hagen)	Western states
Zootermopsis nevadensis (Hagen)	Western states
Prorhinotermes simplex (Hagen)	Florida
Heterotermes aureus (Snyder)	California, Arizona
Reticulitermes flavipes (Kollar)	Canada (Ontario), eastern states
Reticulitermes hageni Banks	Eastern states
Reticulitermes hesperus Banks	Western states, British Columbia
Reticulitermes tibialis Banks	Western states

Reticulitermes virginicus (Banks) Eastern states
Coptotermes formosanus Shiraki Gulf states

CENTRAL AMERICA AND CARIBBEAN

Dry-wood termites

Cryptotermes brevis (Walker) Mexico, Guatemala, West Indies from Jamaica to Trinidad

Cryptotermes domesticus (Haviland) Panama
Cryptotermes dudleyi Banks Panama, Trinidad
Cryptotermes crassus Snyder Mexico
Cryptotermes cavifrons Banks Guatemala, Bahamas, Bermuda, Cuba, Haiti, Puerto Rico

Cryptotermes havilandi (Sjöstedt) Trinidad, Barbados
Cryptotermes longicollis Banks Panama
Procryptotermes hubbardi (Banks) Mexico
Incisitermes immigrans (Snyder) Panama, Guatemala, Salvador
Incisitermes marginipennis (Latreille) Mexico, Guatemala
Incisitermes snyderi Light Panama, Cuba, Puerto Rico, Bahamas

Neotermes castaneus (Burmeister) St Lucia

Subterranean termites

Reticulitermes flavipes (Kollar) Mexico
Reticulitermes tibialis Banks Mexico
Heterotermes aureus Snyder Mexico
Heterotermes tenuis (Hagen) Panama, Guatemala, Bahamas, West Indies from Jamaica to Trinidad

Heterotermes convexinotatus Snyder Panama, Guatemala, Jamaica, Puerto Rico, Haiti, Virgin Islands

Prorhinotermes simplex (Hagen) Jamaica, Puerto Rico, Cuba
Coptotermes niger Snyder Panama, Guatemala, Brit. Honduras, Bahamas, West Indies

Coptotermes crassus Snyder Mexico, Honduras, Guatemala
Coptotermes havilandi (Holmgren) Jamaica
Amitermes wheeleri Desneux Mexico
Subulitermes mexicanus (Light) Mexico
Nasutitermes cornigera (Motschulsky) Panama, Guatemala
Nasutitermes ephratae (Holmgren) Panama, Guatemala, Guadeloupe, Montserrat, Trinidad

Nasutitermes costalis (Holmgren) West Indies, Guyana
Nasutitermes nigriceps Haldeman Mexico, Guatemala, Jamaica
Nasutitermes rippertii (Rambur) Jamaica
Microcerotermes arboreus Emerson Trinidad

SOUTH AMERICA

Dry-wood termites

Cryptotermes brevis (Walker) Venezuela, Guyana, Brazil, Chile, Peru

Cryptotermes dudleyi Banks   Colombia
Cryptotermes havilandi (Sjöstedt)   Brazil
Cryptotermes rospigliosi Snyder   Peru
Incisitermes immigrans (Snyder)   Ecuador, Peru
Incisitermes incisus (Silvestri)   Venezuela
Neotermes chilensis (Blanchard)   Chile

Subterranean termites

Heterotermes tenuis (Hagen)   Guyana, Brazil, Paraguay, Argentina, Peru
Heterotermes convexinotatus (Snyder)   Venezuela
Coptotermes havilandi Holmgren   Brazil
Coptotermes testaceus (Linnaeus)   Guyana, Surinam, Venezuela, Brazil, Chile, Peru
Amitermes excellens Silvestri   Guyana
Microcerotermes exiguus (Hagen)   Venezuela
Nasutitermes costalis (Holmgren)   Guyana
Nasutitermes globiceps (Holmgren)   Paraguay
Nasutitermes sp.   Peru

AFRICA
North Africa

Subterranean termites

Reticulitermes lucifugus (Rossi)   Morocco, Algeria, Tunis
Psammotermes hybostoma Desneux   Algeria, Libya, Egypt, Sudan
Anacanthotermes ochraceus
(Burmeister)   Algeria, Libya, Egypt, Sudan
Heterotermes aethiopicus (Sjöstedt)   Sudan

Tropical Africa

Dry-wood termites

Cryptotermes brevis (Walker)   Senegal, Gambia, Sierra Leone, Ghana, Nigeria, Uganda
Cryptotermes dudleyi Banks   Somalia, Kenya, Tanzania
Cryptotermes havilandi (Sjöstedt)   Sierra Leone, Ivory Coast, Nigeria
Bifiditermes mutabae Harris   Uganda

Subterranean termites

Coptotermes amanii (Sjöstedt)   Somalia, Kenya, Tanzania, Malawi, Rhodesia
Coptotermes intermedius Silvestri   Senegal to Nigeria
Coptotermes sjoestedti Holmgren   Senegal to Cameroons, Congo, Angola, Uganda
Schedorhinotermes lamanianus
(Sjöstedt)   Tanzania
Macrotermes bellicosus (Smeathman)   West Africa

Macrotermes natalensis (Haviland)	Central Africa
Macrotermes subhyalinus (Rambur)	West, East and Central Africa, Sudan
Odontotermes badius (Haviland)	throughout tropical Africa
Odontotermes kibarensis (Fuller)	Uganda
Odontotermes latericius (Haviland)	East and Central Africa
Odontotermes nilensis Emerson	Sudan
Odontotermes pauperans (Silvestri)	Senegal to Nigeria
Allodontermes giffardi Silvestri	Sierra Leone
Ancistrotermes cavithorax (Sjöstedt)	Sierra Leone to Cameroons
Microtermes aluco (Sjöstedt)	Ghana
Microtermes redenianus (Sjöstedt)	Tanzania
Microtermes tragardhi (Sjöstedt)	Sudan
Amitermes evuncifer Silvestri	Nigeria
Amitermes lonnbergianus (Sjöstedt)	Kenya
Amitermes unidentatus (Wasmann)	Zanzibar
Microcerotermes fuscotibialis Sjöstedt	Sierra Leone

SOUTH AFRICA

Dry-wood termites

Cryptotermes brevis (Walker)	south-east coast

Subterranean termites

Hodotermes mossambicus (Hagen)	widespread
Microhodotermes viator (Latreille)	Cape Province
Coptotermes formosanus Shiraki	Cape Province, Transvaal
Psammotermes allocerus Silvestri	south-west coast
Macrotermes natalensis (Haviland)	Transvaal, Natal, Zululand
Odontotermes badius (Haviland)	Transvaal, Orange Free State, Natal, South-West Africa
Odontotermes latericus (Haviland)	Transvaal, Orange Free State, Natal, South-West Africa
Odontotermes transvaalensis (Sjöstedt)	Transvaal
Allondontermes schultzi (Silvestri)	South-West Africa
Microtermes havilandi Holmgren	Transvaal, Orange Free State, Natal

INDIAN OCEAN

Dry-wood termites

Cryptotermes pallidus (Rambur)	Mauritius
Neotermes laticollis (Holmgren)	Seychelles

Subterranean termites

Heterotermes philippensis Light	Madagascar, Mauritius
Psammotermes voeltzkowi Wasmann	Madagascar
Coptotermes havilandi (Holmgren)	Madagascar, Mauritius
Coptotermes truncatus (Wasmann)	Madagascar, Seychelles
Microcerotermes subtilis (Wasmann)	Seychelles
Nasutitermes voeltzkowi (Wasmann)	Mauritius

ATLANTIC OCEAN

Dry-wood termites

Cryptotermes brevis (Walker)   Madeira, Ascension, St Helena
Postelectrotermes praecox (Wollaston) Madeira

Subterranean termites

Reticulitermes lucifugus (Rossi)   Madeira
Heterotermes perfidus Silvestri   St Helena
Schedorhinotermes putorius (Sjöstedt) São Thomé

CHAPTER 9

Damage to Materials other than Timber

Stories of termite damage to travellers' baggage and to household goods in countries through which they passed have long been an ingredient of 'travellers' tales' from the tropics. To attempt to separate fact from fiction might ruin a good anecdote, and it would be unwise to be too dogmatic about what a termite can and cannot chew. The exploratory urge of worker termites is virtually unlimited, and their patience extraordinary. Random search for anything edible appears to be limited only by hardness of the surface encountered, and ultimately by distance from the nest. Some confusion arises from the use of the terms 'attack' and 'eat' in consideration of termite damage. For example, serious inquiries have been received for information regarding 'termites eating glass' and 'termites attacking steel', for both of which there is some slight factual backing. Ground-dwelling termites, such as *Macrotermes* and *Odontotermes*, construct tunnels of earth over materials through which they cannot or do not wish to burrow their way and these they construct of grains of sand cemented with a damp mortar of clay and saliva. This saliva in contact with certain types of glass will, in time, etch the polished surface. This happened to microscope slides in East Africa when the cabinet they were in was damaged by *Odontotermes badius* and the labels eaten from the slides. The idea of termites being able to make their way through steel appears to have arisen from the case of a stainless-steel knife in the possession of the Division of Entomology, Canberra. It was found in a box of personal possessions sent from Malaya to Australia after the last war, which had been invaded by *Coptotermes*, with much building of earth and carton tunnels. When the blade of the knife was cleaned, a small hole was found to have been corroded right through: as in the cases where termites are claimed to have penetrated concrete, one must consider the likelihood of flaws in the material. Damage to materials may be considered under two heads according to their origin—organic and inorganic. From the viewpoint of termite nutrition these heads might be equally well called expected and unexpected.

Organic Materials—Paper, Fabrics, Leather, Rubber

Documents, books and cardboard are mainly cellulose and are natural food for termites. They are eaten by all the ground-dwelling and dry-wood species which are to be found infesting buildings, including *Reticulitermes* in Europe and U.S.A., *Coptotermes* in Australia, Asia and parts of Africa, *Macrotermes* and *Odontotermes* in Africa south of the Sahara, India and south-east Asia, *Mastotermes* in northern Australia, and *Cryptotermes* on tropical islands and the coasts of continents. In Colombia there is to be seen a monument erected in 1789 on which is inscribed 'a paternoster to Jesus that we may be free from termites' (Snyder, 1948). The unfortunate results on the development of indigenous cultures in many parts of the tropics through the constant destruction by termites of *objets d'art* in wood, and of records on wood and paper, is, perhaps, not widely appreciated. The effects of insects on human culture in Africa are discussed by Godwin (1958).

Fabrics of cotton, linen, jute, silk and rayon are eaten by most of the termites which normally feed on wood (Plate 54). Carpets are damaged in houses in the Middle East where floors of beaten earth or tiles without cement permit the movement of *Reticulitermes* up from the ground below. Carpets were found in Malaya damaged by *Cryptotermes* coming from the floorboards and timber joists. *Coptotermes* and *Odontotermes* are common in warehouses and goods awaiting shipment may be damaged, as, for example, is occasionally to be seen in bales of cotton cloth imported into this country.

Leather is eaten by termites. According to Colwill (1958) the method of tanning has a significant effect on susceptibility to attack; the grades known as 'chrome retan', 'semi-chrome' and 'full vegetable tan' are damaged while 'full chrome' is relatively immune (Plate 56).

Natural rubber offers no barrier to termites, though there is some doubt about its digestibility. Foam rubber in furnishings and as an insulating material is readily damaged. Latex products for sealing and jointing will be attacked if the formulation does not include an active repellent. Damage to electrical insulation is referred to below when cables are discussed.

Inorganic Materials—Metals, Plastics

Considered apart from any feelings of surprise and annoyance, the actual amount of damage done to metals by termites is small. Species of the genus *Coptotermes* have been recorded as penetrating the lead sheathing of electric cables in many parts of the tropics, particularly in the Far East and Central America, but the most persistent termite appears to be *Mastotermes darwiniensis* in northern Australia. Any metal which is soft enough to be scored by termite mandibles is liable to damage, the main factor being the presence of a particular termite with the will to continue eating its way through such unpromising material. One can appreciate the forces which compel a dry-wood termite to make a gallery outwards through a lead sheath, but it is not easy to suggest why *Mastotermes* and *Coptotermes* work inwards to reach what may be no more than a thin cotton layer round copper wire embedded in a plastic. Many cases of penetration of metal sheets, especially those used as termite shields in buildings, are in fact the effects of corrosion producing a passageway.

The increasing use of plastics in the tropics during recent years has brought to notice their susceptibility to termite damage. The incessant probing of worker termites foraging for food leads them to gnaw their way into materials of no nutritive value, although such activities are not necessarily a complete waste of time since undigested fragments are used in the construction of shelter tunnels. Any material exposed to termites which is not as hard as the jaws of these insects, or of repugnant taste, is liable to be attacked. Plastics used for sheathing electric cables, for water pipes and sanitary fittings, for dam linings and similar purposes in contact with the soil are naturally at greatest risk.

Industrial plastics cover a wide range of susceptibility to termites from the readily eaten plasticised polyvinyl chlorides and low density polyethylenes to highly resistant nylon. Laboratory tests with Australian termites on a large number of plastics are reported by Gay and Wetherly (1969). They found that resistance is closely correlated with surface hardness. There is little indication of positive repellency as a factor, although tricresyl phosphate as a plasticiser with polyvinyl chloride produced a product less susceptible to attack than when dioctyl phthalate was used. In the case of thermosetting plastics incorporating fillers, Gay and Wetherly suggest the potential value of employing some substance such as hard silica or zircon flour to produce a material physically resistant to termites. Another approach to which attention has already been paid is to incorporate a repellent insecticide and some success has resulted from the use of the organochlorines aldrin and dieldrin. Unfortunately these insecticides have fallen under suspicion as health hazards and while they may be acceptable in cable sheathing materials, they are less likely to be approved for water piping, packaging and the like.

Some degree of flexibility is desirable in plastics used for piping and cable sheaths and this conflicts with a sufficient degree of hardness to keep termites away. Actual thickness has been observed to prove a deterrent, but termites in different localities vary greatly in the amount of drive they exhibit in working through unpromising material and local trials would be necessary before this method could be used with confidence.

Plastic bonding agents for plywoods are of increased value if they make the final product termite proof. Radiation-processed plywoods have been studied by Affeltranger (1968) and it was found that polymethyl methacrylate produced a termite resistant plywood, whereas polyvinyl acetate bonded plywood was severely attacked. In the case of laminated beams, termites gaining entrance at the ends of the beams will not be prevented from working their way along whatever the bonding material is employed. Plastic paints are grazed from the walls of buildings in the Middle East by subterranean termites building their covered runways upwards in search of timber.

Packaging

Pest-proof packaging is a wider problem than that of keeping away termites, but in the tropics it is doubtful if any other single agent apart from the weather is so rapid in its action under normal conditions of storage. Buildings there which are used as warehouses and shops are, in general, not designed to be termite-proof and infestation by subterranean termites passes to packages in contact with floors, walls and structural timbers. Protection of wood and cardboard containers, of packing materials, and even of the labels on tins and jars may be necessary to ensure that the goods reach the consumer unspoilt.

Studies of the toxic and repellent effects of chemicals in volatile solvents and in wax for use on cardboard and kraft paper were made by Chamberlain and Hoskins (1949) in the U.S.A. Their test insects were *Zootermopsis angusticollis*, *Z. nevadensis* and *Incisitermes minor*. They found that repellency and toxicity were not associated in all cases. Of the chemicals then available, the most promising results were obtained with gamma benzene hexachloride (lindane) used at 1 per cent in wax. This protected cardboard boxes for more than eighteen months.

Consideration should be given to the desirability of treating packing cases with wood preservatives, especially for heavy machinery liable to be left in ports or on building sites for long periods. Much inconvenience was caused in Rhodesia some years ago when ground-dwelling termites destroyed large numbers of wooden barrels containing bitumen for road construction work, after they had been dumped along the site of the road. The cost of preservative treatment is of the order of 10 per cent of the cost of the actual timber used.

Cables

Since 1896, when telegraph cables in Indo-China were found to be damaged by termites, manufacturers and users of insulated cables in the tropics have been made aware, sooner or later, of this hazard. The risk of damage is greatest when cable is in contact with the ground, for it is then exposed to a variety of subterranean termites. Above ground, damage usually results from close contact with woodwork that has become infested with either subterranean or dry-wood termites.

Among the species that have been recorded as penetrating the lead sheathing of cables are *Coptotermes formosanus* in the Far East, *C. acinaciformis* in Australia, *C. havilandi* in Australia, and *C. niger* in Panama. It is doubtful, however, if any of these approach in severity of attack the northern Australian *Mastotermes darwiniensis*.

The development in recent years of plastics and synthetic rubbers for electrical insulation has added to the variety of substances to which termite damage has been reported. Telecommunications in Malaya, for example, have been hampered by this trouble, The enormous expansion of 'wired radio' in a number of countries has increased greatly the opportunities for termite damage by the use of plastic-coated wiring in buildings already infested with termites. Among the more striking instances of damage was that caused by ground-dwelling termites, *Macrotermes* or *Odontotermes*, in Rhodesia to railway-signal cable buried alongside the permanent way instead of being supported on short posts in the normal manner (Plate 55). The cable was $1\frac{1}{8}$ inches (28 mm) in diameter, of black synthetic rubber which had been removed over large areas by the termites to a depth of $\frac{1}{4}$ inch (6 mm) to expose the copper wires within. Usually damage to cables is in small localized patches and it is due to the entrance of moisture that the insulation breaks down. A detailed bibliography of damage to cables is given by Colwill (1958).

Physical protection in the form of brass or copper ribbon wrapped as an outer layer is expensive, and repellent insecticides are being sought for incorporation in the insulating compounds. One practical difficulty is to find chemicals which will not be decomposed at the temperatures under which the plastic is extruded. The Division of Entomology, Canberra, has reported favourably on the resistance of polyvinyl chloride to which has been added fractional percentages of aldrin and dieldrin. Manufacturers do not disclose their successes in this field, but it is understood that in addition to the chemicals already mentioned, metallic naphthenates are used.

Plastic-coated cables used above ground in the tropics are liable to be damaged by rodents and ants as well as by termites. A correct diagnosis is essential as a preliminary to control measures.

Notes on some Chemicals used in Termite Control

(a) Organochlorines

ALDRIN

Technical aldrin is a light brown, odourless solid consisting mainly of a complex organochlorine, HHDN, which on exposure slowly changes into HEOD, the major component of dieldrin (see below). Aldrin is insoluble in water and stable in the presence of strong alkalis and such acids as are normally to be met with in agriculture. It dissolves readily in organic solvents (e.g. 6 per cent by weight in kerosene, 26 per cent in fuel oil and 58 per cent in acetone).

Aldrin is marketed as dusts, wettable powders and emulsifiable concentrate for dilution with water. It is toxic to man and animals by ingestion, inhalation and by absorption through the skin, and reasonable precautions are necessary to protect operators and livestock. It is not harmful to plants.

BENZENE HEXACHLORIDE

BHC is a relatively simple chemical hexachlorocyclohexane, $C_6H_6Cl_6$. It exists as a number of isomers, of which the gamma is the most powerful insecticide. Gamma BHC is obtainable under the name 'lindane'. Technical BHC is a pale buff-coloured powder with a strong musty smell, insoluble in water, slightly soluble in kerosene (ranging from 3 per cent for the gamma isomer down to 0·05 per cent for the beta isomer) and more readily in acetone (12 per cent for gamma).

BHC has a slight fumigant action which makes it repellent to termites. It is reasonably persistent in action as a stomach poison or contact insecticide.

Formulations of BHC include dusts, wettable powders and emulsifiable concentrates.

BHC is a cumulative poison for mammals. It is not injurious to growing plants other than cucurbits, but causes tainting in food crops unless applied as lindane.

CHLORDANE

Technical chlordane is a yellow, viscous liquid consisting mainly of isomers of a complex organochlorine $C_{10}H_6Cl_8$. It is soluble in most organic solvents but not in water. It is only slightly volatile and has a marked residual toxicity to insects.

Formulations of chlordane include solutions in kerosene, emulsifiable concentrates and wettable powders.

Chlordane is not injurious to plants at normal concentrations. It has a low toxicity to mammals but may be cumulative, hence the need for care in its use.

DDT

Dichloro-diphenyl-trichloroethane was the first of the chlorinated hydrocarbons, as they were then known, to come into general use as an insecticide, particularly in the public health field. It is a white, waxy powder insoluble in water but soluble in organic solvents (e.g. 6 per cent in kerosene, 16 per cent in fuel oil and 25 per cent in acetone).

DDT is chemically stable and possesses valuable residual effects as an insecticide. It is obtainable in a variety of formulations, dusts, wettable powders, emulsifiable concentrates and dissolved in kerosene. It has a low toxicity to man and domestic animals but is cumulative. It is not injurious to growing crops other than cucurbits.

DIELDRIN

The main component of technical dieldrin is a complex organochlorine HEOD. It comes as a white crystalline powder insoluble in water but soluble in the usual organic solvents (e.g. 6 per cent in kerosene, 16 per cent in fuel oil and 25 per cent in acetone). It is not volatile so has little or no repellent action, but possesses a considerable residual life.

Dieldrin is available in the usual formulations. It is not harmful to growing crops. Dieldrin is not acutely toxic to man and domestic animals but its cumulative effects may give rise to some concern and care must be exercised in its use.

HEPTACHLOR

Heptachlor is an organochlorine closely allied to aldrin, and on exposure it converts to heptachlor epoxide which is analogous to dieldrin. It too is an active and persistant insecticide. It is mainly used as a seed dressing in agriculture, and in conjunction with pentachlorophenol in the external treatment of woodwork infested with drywood termites.

(b) Other Chemicals

COPPER-CHROME-ARSENIC

Some of the more widely used formulations for water-soluble preservatives used in vacuum-pressure systems of timber impregnation are based on copper sulphate, sodium dichromate and sodium arsenite. Variations include the substitution of fluorine and boron salts for the arsenic component in order to remove the potential hazards of contact with foodstuffs and the like. Commercially treated timber should comply with British Standard No. 144, or its equivalent in other countries. Resistance to termite attack depends on adequate retention of the preservative within the timber, reflecting the efficiency of the process of impregnation.

CREOSOTE

The type of creosote employed in wood preservation is obtained by the distillation of coal tar. It is a brown fluid of low volatility, not miscible with water, and comprising a large number of organic chemicals including phenol, cresol and naphthalene. For pressure treatment of timber to be used in contact with the ground British Standard No. 144 should be followed. Related coal tar distillates of a more refined nature and with greater penetrating power are used in the 'hot and cold treatment' of timber and for surface treatment by brushing, and these should conform to British Standard No. 3051.

METHYL BROMIDE

Methyl bromide, CH_3Br, is a stable, colourless, non-inflammable gas highly toxic to mammals and insects. It is obtainable under pressure as a liquid which evaporates rapidly under normal atmospheric conditions. Some chloropicrin is added as a general rule to provide a warning odour for methyl bromide employed in fumigation. Growing plants are damaged only through their leaves and may be fumigated when in a dormant, leafless state. Methyl bromide reacts with rubber, and all furnishings containing this material must be removed when buildings are to be fumigated. Fumigation with methyl bromide is probably the most effective treatment for buildings infested with drywood termites.

NAPHTHENATES

Metallic naphthenates are widely employed as preservatives for fabrics, ropes and timber, primarily as fungicidal agents. Indirectly they retard insect attack by preventing decay which attracts insect pests. In sufficient concentration they are toxic to wood borers, particularly if the treated timber is not exposed to weathering.

Copper naphthenate is an unpleasant-smelling, green, viscous fluid that does not mix with water but does so with the usual organic solvents. It is usually applied to timber as an emulsion with petroleum oils and water. It is phytotoxic and fungicidal but is not harmful to growing plants when treated timber has been given sufficient time to allow the solvent to evaporate.

Zinc naphthenate is colourless and non-staining, but generally not so effective as the copper salt in preventing insect attack.

SULFURYL FLUORIDE

Sulfuryl fluoride is a recent development in fumigants for termite control in buildings. It is more expensive than methyl bromide, but is effective at lower concentrations, it is quicker in action and because it does not react with rubber it is less liable to damage furnishing in dwellings.

Bibliography

AFFELTRANGER, C. E. (1968) 'Feeding by *Reticulitermes* spp. on radiation processed wood-plastic combinations', *J. econ. Ent.* **61**, 398–401.

AGARWALA, S. B. D. (1955) 'Control of sugarcane termites', *J. econ. Ent.*, **48**, 533–57.

AGARWALA, S. B. D. and SHARMA, C. (1954) 'Aldrin and dieldrin as outstanding agents in control of *Microtermes obesi* on maize in Bihar', *Indian. J. Ent.* **16**, 78–9.

AHMAD, M. (1958) 'Key to the Indomalayan termites', *Biologia* (Lahore) **4**, 33–198.

AHMAD, M. (1962) 'Termite fauna of West Pakistan', in *Termites in the Humid Tropics*, Paris, UNESCO.

AHMAD, M. (1965) 'Termites (Isoptera) of Thailand', *Bull. Amer. Mus. Nat. Hist.* **131**, 1–113.

AMANTE, E. (1962) (Field experiments for control of *Cornitermes cumulans*) *Arq. Inst. Biol. Sao Paulo* **29**, 133–8.

ARAUJO, R. L. (1958) 'Contribuicao a biogeografia dos Termitas de Sao Paulo, Brasil', *Arq. Inst. Biol. Sao Paulo*, **25**, 185–217.

ARAUJO, R. L. (1958) 'Contribuicao a biogeografia dos Termitas de Minas Gerais, Brasil', *Arq. Inst. Biol. Sao Paulo* **25**, 219–36.

AVASTHY, P. N. (1967) 'Sugarcane pests in India', *PANS* (A) **13**, 114.

AYOUB, M. A. (1959) 'Studies on the distribution . . . of *Microcerotermes diversus* attacking live plants in Saudi Arabia', *Bull. Soc. ent. Egypte* **43**, 429–32.

BATHELLIER, J. (1927) 'Contribution à l'étude systématique et biologique des termites de l'Indochine', *Faune Colon. franc.* **1**, 125–365.

BATHELLIER, J. (1933) 'Dégats causés par les termites d'Indochine . . .', *Trav. Congr. int. Ent. Paris* **5**, 747–50.

BAVENDAMM, W. (1955) 'Natürliche Dauerhaftigkeit der Hölzer gegen Termitenfrass', in Schmidt, H. *Die Termiten*, Leipzig, Geest & Portig, 1955.

BEELEY, F. (1934) 'Experiments in control of the termite pest of young rubber trees', *J. Rubber Res. Inst. Malaya* **5**, 160–75.

BEESON, C. F. C. (1941) *Ecology and Control of Forest Insects of India and Neighbouring Countries*, Dehra Dun.

BHATNAGAR, S. P. (1962) 'Insecticidal trials against termites infesting cotton plants in Rajasthan', in *Termites in the Humid Tropics*, Paris, UNESCO.

BIGGER, M. (1966) 'The biology and control of termites damaging field crops in Tanganyika', *Bull. ent. Res.* **56**, 417–44.

BODENHEIMER, F. S. (1951) *Citrus Entomology*, Den Haag, Junk.

BONDAR, G. (1939) 'Insetos daninhos do cacau na Bahia', *Bol. tech. Cacau Bahia*, no. 5.

BOUILLON, A. and MATHOT, G. (1965–6) *Quel est ce Termite Africain?* and supplement. Léopoldville, Université.

BUCHLI, H. H. R. (1958) 'L'origine des castes et les potentialités ontogéniques des termites Européens du genre *Reticulitermes* Holmgren', *Ann. Sci. Nat. Zool.* ser. 11, **20**, 249–263.

BUNTING, B., GEORGI, C. D. V. and MILSUM, J. N. (1934) *The Oil Palm in Malaya*, Kuala Lumpur, Dept. Agr.

BURTT, B. D. (1942) 'Some East African vegetation communities', *J. Ecol.* **30**, 67–146.

BUYCKX, E. J. E. (1962) 'Précis des maladies et des insectes nuisables rencontrés sur les plantes cultivées au Congo, au Rwanda et au Burundi', *Publ. Inst. natn. Etude agron. Congo.* hors sér.

CACHAN, P. (1949) 'Les termites de Madagascar', *Mem. Inst. Sci. Madagascar* (A) **3**, 177–275.

CARESCHE, L. (1937) 'Le termite destructeur de l'hévéa et du kapokier', *C. R. Inst. Réch. agron. for. Indochine* 1935–6, 195–212.

CASTEL-BRANCO, A. J. E. (1963) 'Entomofauna de S. Tomé (Insectos do cacaieiro),' *Est. Junta Invest. Ultramar Lisboa*, no. 107.

CHAMBERLAIN, W. F. and HOSKINS, W. M. (1949) 'The toxicity and repellance of organic chemicals towards termites, and their use in termite-proofing food packages', *Hilgardia* **19**, 285–307.

CHEO, C. C. (1948) 'Notes on fungus-growing termites in Yunnan', *Lloydia* **11**, 139–47.

CHILD, H. J. (1934) 'The internal anatomy of termites and the histology of the digestive tract', in Kofoid, C. A. and others, *Termites and Termite Control*, Berkeley, Cal. 1934.

CHILD, R. (1964) *Coconuts*, London, Longmans.

COATON, W. G. H. (1947) 'Toxic smoke generators for termite control', *Farm. S. Afr.* **22**, 713–27.

COATON, W. G. H. (1946) 'The Harvester Problem in South Africa', *Un. S. Afr. Dept. Agr. Bull.* **292**.

COATON, W. G. H. (1958) 'The Hodotermitid Harvester Termites of South Africa', *Un. S. Afr. Dept. Agri. Sci. Bull.* **375**.

COATON, W. G. H. (1962) 'Control of Harvester Termites', *J. ent. Soc. S. Afr.* **25**, 318–27.

COLWILL, D. J. (1958) 'Notes on the preservation of materials', *Pesticides Abstr.* **4**, 237–56.

CORBETT, G. H. (1932) 'Insects of coconut in Malaya', *Dept. Agr. FMS gen. ser.* **10**.

COURSEY, D. G. (1967) *Yams*, London, Longman.

CROWTHER, F. and BARLOW, H. W. B. (1943) 'Taproot damage to cotton ascribed to termites in the Sudan Gezira', *Emp. J. Expt. Agr.* **11**, 99–112.

CUFODONTIS, G. (1955) Kritisches Referat über die Bedeuting der Termiten für das Verständnis der afrikanischen Savannenvegetation, *Osterr. Bot. Zeitschr.* **102**, 501–19.

DAMMERMAN, K. W. (1913) 'De Hevea-termiet op Java', *Med. Afd. PlZiekt. Buitenzorg* **3**, 1. 12.

DAS, G. M. (1962) 'Termites in tea', in *Termites in the Humid Tropics*, Paris, UNESCO.

DEAN, H. A. (1954) 'Termites in citrus on newly-cleared brushland', *J. econ. Ent.* **47**, 365–6.

DE GEER, C. (1778) 'Des Termes', *Mem. Hist. Ins.* **7**, 40–62.

DAMANDT, K. (1914) 'Die Krankheiten und Schädlingen des Kakaos-Samoanische Kakaokultur', *Tropenpfl. Beih.* **15**, 273–4.

DEN DOOP, J. E. A. (1938) 'The utilisation of sisal waste in Java and Sumatra', *E. Afr. agric. J.* **4**, 93–8.

DESNEUX, J. (1904) 'Isoptera, Fam. Termitidae', *Gen. Insect.* **25**, 1–52.

DESNEUX, J. (1952) 'Les constructions hypogées des *Apicotermes*, termites de l'Afrique tropicale', *Ann. Mus. Roy. Congo Belge Sci. Zool.* **17**, 9–98.

EBELING, W. (1968) 'Termites; identification, biology and control of termites attacking buildings', *Calif. Expt. Stn. Extn. Serv. Manual* no. 38.

EGGELING, W. J. (1947) 'Observations on the ecology of the Budongo Forest, Uganda', *J. Ecol.* **34**, 20–87.

EDEN, T. (1958) *Tea*, London, Longman.

EMERSON, A. E. (1925) 'The termites of Kartabo, Bartica District, British Guiana', *Zoologica*, N.Y. **6**, 291–459.

EMERSON, A. E. (1928) 'Termites of the Belgian Congo and the Cameroon', *Bull. Amer. Mus. nat. Hist.* **57**, 401–574.

ERHART, H. (1951) 'Sur l'importance des phénomènes biologique dans la formation des cuirasses ferrugineuses en zone tropical', *C. R. Acad. Sci.* **233**, 804–6, 966–8.

FERNANDO, H. E. (1962) 'Termites of economic importance in Ceylon', in *Termites in the Humid Tropics*, Paris, UNESCO.

FERRERO, F. (1959) 'Les termites et leurs dégats sur vignes dans la region de Banyuls', *Phytoma* **11**, 30–1.

FINDLAY, W. P. K. (1962) *The Preservation of Timber*. London, Black.

FULLER, C. (1912) 'White ants in Natal', *Agr. J. Un. S. Afr.* **4**, 345–69.

GAMEEL, O. I. (1969) 'Summary of cotton pest control practices in the Sudan', *PANS* **15**, 168–70.

GAY, F. J. (1963) 'The synonomy, distribution and biology of *Coptotermes elisae*', *Pacif. Insects* **5**, 421–3.

GAY, F. J. and WETHERLY, A. H. (1958) 'Laboratory studies of termite resistance', *Melbourne CSIRO Div. Ent. Tech. Paper*, no. 2.

GAY, F. J. and WETHERLY, A. H. (1969) 'The termite resistance of plastics', *Melbourne CSIRO Div. Ent. Tech. Paper*, no. 10.

GAY, F. J., GREAVES, T., HOLDAWAY, F. G. and WETHERLY, A. H. (1955) 'Standard laboratory colonies of termites for evaluating the resistance of timber, timber preservatives and other materials to termite attack', *Melbourne CSIRO Bull.* no. 277.

GHILAROV, M. S. (1962) 'Termites in USSR', in *Termites in the Humid Tropics*, Paris, UNESCO.

GHOSE, S. K. (1964) 'Insecticidal control of termite *Microtermes* sp. damaging wheat crop', *Indian Agric.* **8**, 87–91.

GODWIN, A. J. H. (1958) 'Insects and human culture in Africa', *Scienta* **43**, 324–9.

GONÇALVES, C. R. and SILVA, A. G. A. (1962) 'Observacoes sobre Isopteros no Brasil', *Arq. Mus. nac. Rio de Janeiro* **52,** 193–208.

GÖSSWALD, K. (1956) 'Laboratory testing of termite resistance with the yellow-necked termite *Calotermes flavicollis* Fabr., *Composite Wood* 3, 65–70.

GRASSÉ, P. P. and NOIROT, C. (1951) 'La sociotomie', *Behaviour* 3, 146–66.

GRASSÉ, P. P. and NOIROT, C. (1958) 'La société de *Calotermes flavicollis* de sa fondation au premier essaimage', *C.R. Acad. Sci., Paris* **246,** 1789–95.

GRASSI, B. and SANDIAS, A. (1893–4) 'Constituzione e sviluppo della società dei termitidi', *Atti Accad. Gioenia* (4) **6** (13), 1–75, **7** (1), 1–76; translation *Quart. J. micro Sci.* (n.s.) **39,** 245–322; **40,** 1–82, 1897.

GREAVES, T. (1960) 'Termites as forest pests', *Austr. For.* **23,** 114–20.

GREAVES, T. (1962) 'Studies of foraging galleries and the invasion of living trees by *Coptotermes acinaciformis* and *C. brunneus*', *Austr. J. Zool.* **10,** 630–51.

GREEN, E. E. (1916) 'On some animal pests of the *Hevea* tree', *Trans. 3 Int. Congr. Trop. Agr.* 608–36.

GRIFFITH, G. (1953) 'Vesicular Laterite', *Nature* **171,** 530.

GUAGLIUMI, P. (1962) 'Las plagas de la cana de azúcar en Venezuela', *Monogr. Fondo nac. Invest. Agropec.* **1,** 405–9.

HAGEN, H. (1858) 'Specielle Monographie der Termiten', *Linn. Ent.* **12,** 4–419.

HAINSWORTH, E. (1952) *Tea Pests and Diseases and their control, with special reference to North-east India,* Cambridge, Heffer.

HARRIS, W. V. (1957) 'British Museum Expedition to South-west Arabia: Isoptera', *Brit. Mus. (N.H.) Rept. Exp. S.W. Arabia,* 412–33.

HARRIS, W. V. (1957) 'Introduction to Malayan Termites'. *Malay. nat. J.* **12,** 20–32.

HARRIS, W. V. (1967) 'Isoptera (Beitrage zur Kenntnis der Fauna Afghanis-tans)', *Act. Mus. Morav.* **52,** suppl., 211–16.

HARRIS, W. V. (1968a) 'Isoptera from Vietnam, Cambodia and Thailand', *Oposc. Ent.* **33,** 143–54.

HARRIS, W. V. (1968b) 'Termites of the Sudan', *Sudan nat. Hist. Mus. Bull.* no. 4.

HARTWIG, E. K. (1955) 'Control of Snouted Harvester Termites', *Farm. S. Afr.* **30,** 361–6.

HARVEY, P. A. (1934) 'Life history of *Kalotermes minor*', in Kofoid, C. A. and others, *Termites and Termite Control,* Berkeley, Cal.

HEDLEY, C. (1896) 'General account of the atoll of Funafuti', *Mem. Aust. Mus.* **3,** 100.

HESSE, P. R. (1955) 'A chemical and physical study of the soils of termite mounds in East Africa', *J. Ecol.* **43,** 449–61.

HETRICK, L. A. (1957) 'Ten years of testing organic insecticides as soil poisons against the Eastern Subterranean Termite', *J. econ. Ent.* **50,** 316–17.

HICKIN, N. E. (1969) 'The economic significance of termites', in *Termite Symposium,* 1969. London, Brit. Wood Preserv. Assoc.

HOLDAWAY, F. G. (1933) 'The composition of different regions of the mounds of *Eutermes exitiosus* Hill', *J. Counc. sci. indust. Res.* **6,** 160–5.

HOLMGREN, N. (1909) 'Termitenstudien I', *K. sv. Vet. Akad. Handl.* **44** (4), 1–215.

HOLMGREN, N. (1910) 'The Percy Sladen Trust Expedition to the Indian Ocean, 1905—Isoptera', *Trans. linn. Soc. Lond. (Zool.)* (2) **14**, 135–48.

IMMS, A. D. (1913) 'On the structure and biology of *Archotermopsis* . . .', *Phil. Trans. Roy. Soc.* (B) **209**, 75–180.

JACOBSON, G. (1904) 'Zur kenntnis der Termiten Russlands', *Ann. Mus. Zool. Acad. Imp. Sci. St. Petersburg* **9**, 57–107.

JEPSON, F. P. (1931) 'The termites which attack living plants in Ceylon', in *Rutherford's Planters Notebook* (9th edn.), Ceylon.

JONES, E. W. (1956) 'Ecological studies in the Rain Forest of South Nigeria, IV', *J. Ecol.* **44**, 83–117.

KALSHOVEN, L. G. E. (1930) 'De biologie van de Djatitermiet in verband met zijn bestrijding', *Medd. Inst. PlZiekt.* **76**, 1–154.

KALSHOVEN, L. G. E. (1952) 'Survival of Neotermes colonies in infested teak trunks after girdling or felling of the trees', *Tectona* **42**, 1–7.

KALSHOVEN, L. G. E. (1954) 'Survival of Neotermes colonies . . . (second communication)', *Tectona* **43**, 59–74.

KALSHOVEN, L. G. E. (1956) 'Observations on *Macrotermes gilvus* in Java', *Insectes Soc.* **3**, 455–61.

KALSHOVEN, L. G. E. (1962) 'Observations on *Coptotermes havilandi*', *Beaufortia* **9**, 121–37.

KALSHOVEN, L. G. E. (1963) '*Coptotermes curvignathus* causing death of trees in Indonesia and Malaya', *Ent. Ber.* **23**, 90–100.

KAPUR, A. P. (1962) 'Some observations on the nature of damage done by *Reticulitermes chinensis* at Shillong, Assam', in *Termites in the Humid Tropics*, Paris, UNESCO.

KAY, D. (1960) 'Termites attacking living tissues of *Theobroma cacao* in Nigeria', *Proc. R. ent. Soc. Lond.* (A) **35**, 90.

KEMNER, N. A. (1934) 'Systematische und biologische Studien über die Termiten Javas und Celebes', *K. sv. Vet. Akad. Handl.* (3) **13** (4), 1–241.

KING, C. B. R. (1938) 'Termites', *Tea Quarterly* **10**, 195–205.

KUMAR, R. (1965) 'Termites, a new pest of potato in India', *Ind. Potato J.* **7**, 49.

KRISHNA, K. (1961) 'A generic revision and phylogenetic study of the family Kalotermitidae', *Bull. Amer. Mus. Nat. Hist.* **122**, 303–408.

LUKE, W. J. and PLOEG, H. L. (1950) '*Heterotermes cardini*, a new pest of sugar cane', *Proc. 1950 Meet. B.W.I. Sugar Tech.*, 99–102.

LÜSCHER, M. (1951) 'Beobachtungen über die Koloniegründung bei verschiedenen afrikanischen Termitenarten', *Acta Tropica* **8**, 36–43.

LÜSCHER, M. (1952) 'Die Produktion und Elimination von Ersatzgeschlechstieren bei der Termite *Kalotermes flavicollis* Fabr.,' *Zeit vergleich. Phys.* **34**, 123–41.

MACGREGOR, W. D. (1950) 'The protection of buildings and timber against termites', *For. Prod. Res. Bull.* no. 24.

MACLEAN, J. D. (1952) 'Preservative treatment of wood by pressure methods', *U.S. Dept. Agr. Agr. Handbk.* no. 40.

MARTORELLI, L. F. (1945) 'A survey of forest insects of Puerto Rico', *J. Agr. Univ. Puerto Rico* **29**, 69–354; 355–608.

MUKERJI, D. and RAYCHAUDHURI, S. (1943) 'On the anatomy of the alimentary canal of the termite *Termes redemanni* Wasm.', *Ind. J. Ent.* **5**, 59–88.

MUTHUSWAMY, R. and ARAVAMUDHAN, P. (1958) 'Dual action seed treatment for sugarcane', *Ind. J. Sugcane. Res. Dev.* **2**, 61–70.

NAKAJIMA, S. and SHIMIZU, K. (1959) 'A note on the Formosan white ant injuring Japanese cedars', *Bull. Fac. Agr. Univ. Miyazaki* **4**, 261–6.

NARAYANAN, E. S. and LAL, R. (1952) 'A short review of recorded information on the control of termites damaging crops in India', *Ind. J. Ent.* **14**, 21–30.

NATIONAL BUILDING RESEARCH INSTITUTE, Pretoria (1950) Report of the Committee on the Protection of Building Timbers in South Africa.

NEL, J. J. C. (1968) 'Die Grasdraertermiet, *Hodotermes mossambicus*, as plaag van naturlike Werweld', *J. ent. Soc. S. Afr.* **31**, 309–21.

NEWSAM, A. and RAO, B. S. (1958) 'Control of *Coptotermes curvignathus* with chlorinated hydrocarbons', *J. Rubber Res. Inst. Malaya* **15**, 209–18.

NIRULA, K. K., ANTONY, J. and MENON, K. P. V. (1953)' Some investigations on the control of termites', *Ind. Coconut J.* **7**, 26–34.

NOIROT, C. and KOVOOR, J. (1958) 'Anatomie comparée du tube digestif des termites', *Insectes soc.* **5**, 439–71.

PARRY, M. S. (1956) *Tree Planting Practices in Tropical Africa*, Rome, F.A.O.

PATEL, R. M. (1962) 'Effect of BHC formulations in the control of field termites in Gujerat', in *Termites in the Humid Tropics*, Paris, UNESCO.

PEARSON, E. O. (1958) *The Insect Pests of Cotton in Tropical Africa*, London, Emp. Cotton Grow. Corp.

PENDLETON, R. L. (1941) 'Some results of termite activity in Thailand soils', *Thai Sci. Bull.* **3**, 29–53.

PICKENS, A. L. (1932) 'Observations on the genus *Reticulitermes* Holmgren', *Pan-Pac. Ent.* **8**, 178–80.

PROTA, R. (1962) 'L'infestiazione termitica in Sardegnia', *Boll. Inst. Patol. Libro.* **21**, 1–38.

PRUTHI, H. S. and NARAYANAN, E. S. (1939) 'Statistical study of the loss caused by borers and termites to mature sugarcane', *Ind. J. Agr. Sci.* **9**, 15–37.

RANAWEERA, D. J. W. (1962) 'Termites on Ceylon tea estates', *Tea Quart.* **33**, 88–103.

RATCLIFFE, F. N., GAY, F. J. and GREAVES, T. (1952) *Australian Termites*, Melbourne, CSIRO.

RAU, S. A. (1939) 'Report of the entomologist. Termites', *Adm. Rep. Tea scient. Dep. un. Plrs.' Ass. South India* 1938–39, 20–7.

REDDY, D. B. (1962) 'Termites in relation to agriculture', in *Termites in the Humid Tropics*, Paris, UNESCO.

ROBINSON, J. B. D. (1958) 'Some chemical characteristics of "Termite Soils" in Kenya coffee fields', *J. Soil Sci.* **9**, 58–65.

ROONWAL, M. L. and CHHOTANI, O. B. (1962) 'Termite fauna of Assam Region, Eastern India', *Proc. Nat. Inst. Sci. India* **28**, B, 281–406.

ROSE, D. J. W. (1962) 'Pests of maize and other cereal crops in Rhodesia', *Bull. Fedl. Minist. Agr. Rhod. Nyasa.* no. 2163.

ROUZAUD, H. (1962) 'La canne à sucre au Congo', *Agron. trop.* **17**, 541.

RUDMAN, P., DA COSTA, E. W. B., GAY, F. J. and WETHERLY, A. H. (1958) 'Relationship of tectoquinone to durability in *Tectona grandis*', *Nature* **181**, 721–2.

SANDS, W. A. (1956) 'Some factors affecting the survival of *Odontotermes badius*', *Insects Soc.* **3**, 531–6.

SANDS, W. A. (1960a) 'Observations on termites destructive to trees and crops', in Harris, W. V., *Termite Research in West Africa*, multigraph. London, Dep. tech. Co-op.

SANDS, W. A. (1960b) 'Termite control in West African afforestation', *Rep. 7 Commonw. ent. Conf.* (1960, 106–8.

SANDS, W. A. (1962) 'The evaluation of insecticides as soil and mound poisons against termites in agriculture and forestry', *Bull. ent. Res.* **53**, 179–92.

SANKARAN, T. (1962) 'Termites in relation to plant protection', in *Termites in the Humid Tropics*, Paris, UNESCO.

SCHMIDT, H. (1959) 'Beitrage zur Kenntnis der Ernahrungsorgane und Ernahrungs-biologie der Termiten II', *Zeit. angew. Ent.* **45**, 79–86.

SCHMUTTERER, H. (1961) 'Die Möglichkeiten zur Bekämpfung einiger wichtiger Schädlinge und Krankheiten in Sudan durch Saatgutbehandlung', *Z.PflKrankh.* **68**, 479–89.

SILLANS, R. (1959) *Les Savannes de l'Afrique centrale*, Paris, Lechevalier.

SILVESTRI, F. (1903) 'Contribuzione alla conoscenza dei Termitidi e Termophili dell' America meridionale', *Redia* **1**, 1–234.

SINGH, O. P. and SONEJA, P. C. (1966) 'Telodrin for control of sugarcane pests . . .', *J. Res. Punjab gar. Univ.* **3**, 41–9.

SKAIFE, S. H. (1955) *Dwellers in Darkness*, London, Longman.

SMEE, L. (1962) 'Control of the giant cacao termite', *Papua New Guinea agr. J.* **14**, 193–7.

SNYDER, T. E. (1948) *Our Enemy the Termite*, London, Constable.

SNYDER, T. E. (1949) 'Catalog of the Termites (Isoptera) of the World', *Smithson. misc. Coll.* **112**, 1–490.

SNYDER, T. E. (1956) 'Termites of the West Indies, the Bahamas and Bermuda', *J. Agr. Univ. Puerto Rico* **40**, 189–202.

SNYDER, T. E. and ZETEK, J. (1924) 'Damage by termites in the Canal Zone and Panama and how to prevent it', *U.S. Dept. Agr. Bull.* no. 1232.

THOMAS, A. S. (1941) 'The vegetation of the Sese Islands, Uganda', *J. Ecol.* **29**, 330–53.

TIHON, L. (1946) 'A propos des termites au point de vue alimentaire', *Bull. agr. Congo Belge* **37**, 865–8.

TROLL, C. (1936) 'Termiten Savannen', in *Festschr. Norbert Krebs*, Stuttgart, Englehorn.

TSAI, P. H. and CHEN, N. S. (1964) 'Problems in the classification of termites in China', *Acta Ent. Sinica* **13**, 25–37.

TUCKER, R. W. E. (1939) 'The termites of Barbados', *Agr. J. Barbados* **8**, 32–139.

VENTURI, F. (1965) 'Termiti e latifoglie arborea ornamentali nel Pisano', *Circ. Osserv. Mal. Piante, Pisa* no. 4.

WATERSTON, J. M. (1937) 'The termite menace', *Agr. Bull. Bermuda* **16**, 67–9.

WATERSTON, J. M. (1938) 'Diseases and pests of the Bermuda Cedar', *Rept. Dept. Agr. Bermuda* 1937, 30–2.

WEESNER, F. M. (1953) 'Biology of *Tenuirostritermes tenuirostris*', *Univ. California Publ. Zool.* **57**, 251–302.

WEESNER, F. M. (1965) *The Termites of the United States*, New Jersey, Nat. Pest Control Assoc.

WEIDNER, H. (1956 and 1961) 'Beiträge zur Kenntnis der Termiten Angolas . . .', *Publ. Cultur. Comp. Diam. Angola, Lisboa* **29**, 55–106 and **54**, 13–78.

WILLIAMS, R. M. C. (1959) 'Flight and colony formation in two *Cubitermes* species', *Insectes Soc.* **6**, 203–18.

WILLIAMS, R. M. C. (1965) 'Termite infestation of pines in British Honduras', *Overseas Res. Publ. Minist. Overseas Dev.* no. 11.

WILSON, G. (1969) 'Insecticides for the control of soil inhabiting pests of sugar cane', in Williams, J. R. and others, *Pests of Sugar Cane*, London, Elsevier.

WIMBUSH, S. H. (1962) 'A note on the Bukuru Forest Nursery, northern Nigeria', *Emp. For. Rev.* **41**, 153–8.

WOLCOTT, G. N. (1946) 'Factors in the natural resistance of woods to termite attack', *Carib. Forester* **7**, 121–34.

WOLCOTT, G. N. (1958) 'New termite repellent extractives', *Proc. X Int. Congr. Ent.* **4**, 417–21.

WU, C. F. (1935) *Catalogus Insectorum Sinensium*, vol. I, Peiping, Fan Mem. Inst. Biol.

WYNIGER, R. (1962) 'Pests of crops in warm climates and their control', *Acta trop.* suppl. 7.

INDEX

Abdomen, 5, fig. 3
Acacia, 107, 111; pl. 32
  longifolia, 107
Acanthotermes, 50
Achras sapota, 120
Achrestogonime, 20
Acorhinotermes, 48
Adina cordifolia, 120
Afzelia
  africans, 120; bipindensis, 120;
  pachyloba, 120; quanzensis, 120
Agathis, 109
Agriculture, 74, 78, 99
Alate, 2–6; fig. 1, 2, 3, 20, 21; pl.
  3
Albizzia, 105, 107, 108
  lebbek, 106
Aldrin, 76, 81, 84, 91, 95, 96, 97, 98,
  113, 168
Alimentary canal, 12–14; fig. 7, 8
Allodontermes, 33, 51, 96, pl. 20
  morogorensis, 87
Amitermes, 28, 32, 35, 48, 49, 66, 74;
  fig. 23
  atlanticus, 21; belli, 153; desertorum, 49; evuncifer, 90, 96, 101,
  103, 104, 114, 153; excellens, 154;
  hastatus, 54; herbertensis, 89, 101,
  154; latidens, 101; lonnbergianus,
  154; meridionalis, 49, 55, 66, 74; pl.
  14, 15; messinae, 49; neogermanus,
  98, 104; obeuntis, 154; obtusidens,
  101; schwarzi, 101; unidentatus,
  154; vilis, 49, 54, 154; wheeleri, 49,
  154
Amitermitinae, 38, 66, 153
Anacanthotermes, 6, 15, 27, 45, 97
  ahngerianus, 98, 104; macrocephalus, 93, 98, 102, 104, 107, 114;
  ochraceus, 45, 54, 92, 102, 151;
  vagans, 45, 54, 156
Analysis,
  of mounds, 73, 75; of termites,
  36
Anatomy, 2–7
Ancistrotermes, 51, 90, 93, 96, 106;
  fig. 1
  amphidon, 106; cavithorax, 114,
  154; crucifer, 96, 104, 106, 114;

equatorius, 103; guineensis, 99;
  latericius, 103; latinotus, 90, 94, 96,
  101, 104, 106, 114
Anoplotermes, 17, 24, 30, 32, 49, 56,
  66; pl. 11
Ant-guards, 140
Apicotermes, 33, 65; pl. 12, 13
Antennae, 2; fig. 2, 4
Araucaria, 107, 109
Architecture, 31–3
Archotermopsis, 12
  wroughtoni, 14, 42, 52, 55
Armitermes, 56
Artocarpus, 107, 108
Atta, 73
Avocado, see Persea

Baikiaea plurijuga, 120
Baiting, 98
Barriers,
  chemical, 145, 146; concrete, 140;
  mechanical, 140–3
Beetles, as termitophiles, 34
Benzene hexachloride, BHC, 76, 88,
  91, 94, 95, 96, 113, 145, 166, 168
Betula verrucosa, 127
Bifiditermes, 40
  beesoni, 107; madagascarensis, 83;
  mutubae, 151
Boats, 56, 57; pl. 51
Bombax, 108
Books, 164
Boron, 15, 123, 125, 139
Brachylaena hutchinsii, 120
Brachystegia, 106
Bridging, 144
British Standard CP 112.100, 123
Brood, 17–19
Brushing, 123
Buildings,
  construction, 139; damage, 133–62;
  fig. 24; design, 139; timbers, 119–22
Bulbitermes, 52

Cables, 167
Callitris, 106
Calobatinus grassei, 35
Calotermes, see Kalotermes
Camphor, 119

180

Campnosperma, 108
Canarium, 108
Capritermes, 12, 28, 50, 55
 nitobei, 90, 95
Carabid beetles, 34
Carapa guianensis, 120
Carbon bisulphide, 77
Cardboard, 164
Carpets, 164
Cassia, 105
 fistula, 108; siamea, 106
Cassava, 97
Caste determination, 24–6
Casuarina, 106, 111
Cedrella, 119
 mexicana, 120; toona, 120
Cedrus deodara, 127
Cedarwood oil, 119
Chamaecyparis lawsoniana, 127
Chemical barriers, 145
Chestnut, 111
Chilopsis, 111
Chlordane, 76, 81, 85, 91, 94, 95, 113,
 145, 146, 148, 168
Chlorophora
 excelsa, 118, 120, 127, 135; tinc-
 toria, 117, 120
Chloroxylon swietenia, 120
Cinnamomum camphora, 119
Citharexylum spinosum, 111
Citrus, 78, 92, 102
Cleveland, 15
Cocoa, 82, 83, 99
Coconut palm, 86–8, 100
Coffee, 72
Collembola, 16, 35
Colony foundation, 20–4
Compass termite, 49, 55, 66, 74; pl.
 14, 15
Concrete slab, 140
Copper-chrome-arsenic, 123, 169
Copper naphthenate, 145, 146
Coptotermes, 6, 17, 27, 33, 46, 55, 56,
 66, 74, 78, 105, 125, 148, 163,
 164; fig. 22, 24; pl. 51, 52, 56
 acinaciformis, 28, 47, 89, 92, 101,
 102, 109, 115, 132, 167; amanii, 23,
 94, 103, 107, 115; pl. 8, 43; brunneus, 110, 115; ceylonicus, 81, 85,
 86, 99, 100, 107, 115; curvignathus,
 79, 81, 87, 88, 92, 100, 102, 108,
 115; elisae, 109, 114, 115; formosanus, 47, 54, 55, 57, 90, 93, 95, 96,
 97, 101, 102, 103, 104, 109, 115, 167;
 frenchi, 92, 102, 109, 115; gestroi,
 80; grandiceps, fig. 22; havilandi,
 47, 57, 90, 101, 167; heimi, 47, 92,
 93, 101, 102, 107, 115; lacteus, 118,
 132; marabitanus, 81; niger, 87, 92,
 100, 102, 110, 115, 167; fig. 17;

 sinabangensis, 87, 100; sjoestedti,
 82, 94, 99, 103; testaceus, 81, 92,
 102; truncatus, 57, 86, 100, 107;
 vastator, 90
Coptotermitinae, 38, 46
Copulation, 22
Cordia alliodora, 120
Cornitermes, 51, 56, 90
 cumulans, 98; silvestri, fig. 23
Cotton,
 crop, 93–4; fabric, 164
Crawl space, 141
Crocodiles, 35
Creosote, 123, 145, 170
Cryptomeria, 109
Cryptotermes, 41, 55, 164; fig. 3, 22
 brevis, 41, 57, 117, 138, 151, 159,
 162; cavifrons, 151, 159; crassus,
 151, 159; cynocephalus, 138, 151;
 declivis, 93, 102; domesticus, 41, 57,
 138, 151, 159; fig. 22; dudleyi, 41,
 57, 135, 138, 151, 156, 159, 160; pl.
 45; havilandi, 57, 151, 159, 160;
 fig. 14; longicollis, 151, 159; pallidus, 151, 161; perforans, 151, 156;
 rospigliosi, 151, 160
Cubitermes, 12, 18, 28, 30, 33, 35, 50,
 65
 minitabundus, fig. 21, 23; testaceus,
 pl. 9; ugandensis, 11, 22
Cunninghamia, 109
Cupressus, 107; pl. 35
 lusitanica, 127; torulosa, 127
Cyclicodiscus gabunensis, 120
Cynometra alexandri, 120

Dalbergia, 107, 120
Dammara, 81
Daniella orgea, 121
Date palm, 92
De Geer, 37
D-D, 77
DDT, 145, 146, 169
Delonix regia, 106, 117
Desneux, 37
Development, 7–11
Dicorynia paraensis, 121
Dieldrin, 76, 81, 83, 84, 85, 88, 91, 93,
 94, 95, 97, 113, 145, 146, 148, 169
Diet, 12–16
Diffusion, 123, 125
Dinitriphenol, 122
Diospyros, 121
Dipping, 123. 124; pl. 41
Diptera, 34; fig. 12
Distemonanthus, 121
Documents, 164
Dolichorhinotermes, 48
Dorylus, 35
Drepanotermes, 98

External Anatomy

Winged termites vary in size according to their species, from the large African *Macrotermes* with a length of ¾ inch (19 mm) and a wing span of 3½ inches (90 mm), down to a *Microcerotermes* from the Middle East which is about ¼ inch (6 mm) long and has a wing span of ½ inch (12 mm). Their colour ranges from tan to dark brown; their wings vary between transparent and smoky brown (Plate 3).

The head is round or oval in shape, flattened above. Strong triangular mandibles project in front, after the manner of cockroaches and locusts, almost hidden below the labrum, and with maxillae, labium and hypopharynx making up the mouthparts (Fig. 2). The mandibles are of taxonomic importance as the teeth which they bear on the inner margins have undergone changes as the termites have evolved. Primitive *Mastotermes* and the Kalotermitidae have on the left mandible an apical tooth and two well-developed marginal teeth nearby, while on the right the two marginals are not so prominent. The Termopsidae resemble the Blattid type in having three marginal teeth on the left mandible, while on the right there is a small step-like subsidiary tooth at the base of the first marginal, which appears also in some of the higher families. This subsidiary tooth is absent in the closely related Hodotermitidae. In the large family of the Termitidae there are a number of trends towards reduction in the size and number of marginal teeth and the resulting prominence of the apical tooth (Fig. 21). A small pore, the fontanelle, is found in the frontal area in the Rhinotermitidae and Termitidae. It is the external opening of the frontal gland. Its purpose in the imago is not known, but in the soldiers of some species it has become a highly developed weapon.

On the underside of the head lies the gulamentum, formed by the fusion of the gula with the basal part of the labium, whose shape is of taxonomic value.

Large compound eyes are prominent on each side of the head. In all but the families Termopsidae and Hodotermitidae there are, in addition, two simple eyes, or ocelli, situated near the upper border of the compound eyes. A pair of long antennae arises from pits in front of the eyes. Each antenna is composed of a large basal segment and a number of smaller bead-like segments, the total number varying from about 15 in *Microtermes* to 32 in *Mastotermes*. Variations in the number of segments are sometimes the result of a variation in the number of moults in the nymphal stages, or to a failure in the second and third segments to divide at the proper time. The two antennae do not necessarily always have the same number of segments.

The thorax is formed of three distinct parts, the prothorax with a distinctive dorsal plate or pronotum, and the first pair of legs; the meso- and metathorax each with a pair of wings and the second and third pairs of legs respectively. The legs are long and slender, terminating in tarsi

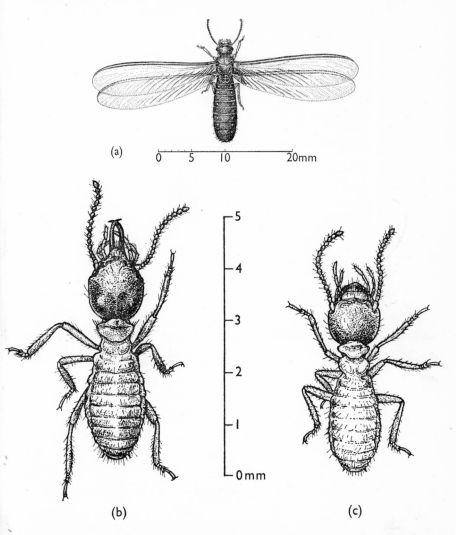

FIG. 1

Ancistrotermes latinotus

a, alate; b, soldier; c, worker

with five segments in the primitive families and four in the more advanced. A pulvillus is present in *Mastotermes*, and the more primitive genera in the Termopsidae and Kalotermitidae.

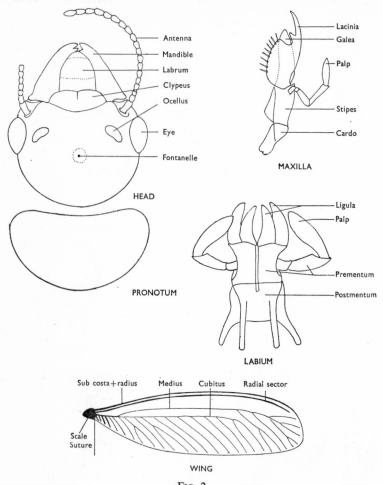

Fig. 2

The termite imago; details of the head and mouthparts, and the venation of the fore-wing

The four wings are elongate oval in shape, not differing greatly between the anterior and posterior pairs except in *Mastotermes*, where the hind wings have an enlarged anal lobe of the Blattid type. The venation is simple, only the subcostal and radius sector veins being